British Eco... and S... ...ry

The Manchester College

Please return/renew this item by the last date shown.
Books may also be renewed by phone or the internet.

St Johns Library
0161 920 2254

http://learning.themanchestercollege.ac.uk/lrc

A New Certificate Approach

First published in 1987 by:
Stanley Thornes (Publishers) Ltd
Old Station Drive
Leckhampton
CHELTENHAM GL53 0DN
England

British Library Cataloguing in Publication Data

Sauvain, Philip
    British economic and social history.
    From 1850 to the present day
    1. Great Britain—Social conditions
    I. Title
    941.07   HN385

    ISBN 0-85950-620-7

Cover illustration: *An Accident* by L. S. Lowry, reproduced by kind permission of Manchester City Art Gallery.

Typeset by Blackpool Typesetting Services Ltd, Blackpool
in 10½/12½ Times.
Printed and bound in Great Britain at The Bath Press, Avon.

Contents

Acknowledgements

The author and publishers are grateful to the following for supplying and giving permission to reproduce prints and artwork:

BBC Hulton Picture Library, pp 57, 60, 234, 262, 283, 298; Corporation of London, p 179; Farmers Weekly Picture Library, p 27; J. R. Freeman, p 321; The Illustrated London News Picture Library, pp 16, 18, 40, 52, 102, 112, 115, 130, 206, 207, 209, 232, 280, 285, 305, 309, 319, 326; Imperial War Museum, pp 20, 22; London Regional Transport, p 205; Macmillan London and Basingstoke for *European Historical Statistics, 1750–1975*, by B. R. Mitchell, pp 69, 138; Mary Evans Picture Library, p 308; National Coal Board, pp 68, 71; The National Motor Museum at Beaulieu, pp 63, 74; National Portrait Gallery, p 268; Nottinghamshire County Library, p 198; Picturepoint Ltd, p 240; *Punch*, pp 78, 105, 243, 262, 331; Topham Picture Library, pp 54, 155, 327; Trades Union Congress Library, p 216; Trustees of the Science Museum (London), p 79; University of Reading, Institute of Agricultural History and Museum of English Rural Life, p 9; Ward Lock Ltd, p 143; The Wellcome Institute, pp 294, 295; Welsh Folk Museum, p 1.

The author and publishers are also grateful to the following for permission to reproduce text extracts:

Cambridge University Press for *British Economic History 1870–1914: Commentary and Documents* by W. H. B. Court, pp 45, 142; W. & R. Chambers Ltd for *Chambers's Journal*, pp 5, 6, 33–4, 102, 103, 117, 128; *Daily Telegraph* for headline, p 241; *The Guardian* for headline, p 241; William Heinemann Ltd for *English Journey* by J. B. Priestley, pp 57, 60, 61; The Illustrated London News Picture Library for various editions of *The Illustrated London News*, pp 48–9, 52, 95, 102, 104, 130, 140, 141, 173, 175, 205, 258, 300; The *Lancet* for an extract by Dr Fawcett, p 106; Macmillan London and Basingstoke for tables from *European Historical Statistics 1750–1975* by B. R. Mitchell, pp 163, 172; Mail Newspapers plc for extract from the *Daily Sketch* and headline from the *Daily Mail*, pp 147, 241; Syndication International Ltd for headlines from the *Daily Mirror* and extracts from *Picture Post*, pp 96, 241, 265, 267; Times Newspapers Ltd for headline from *The Times*, p 241; J. Whitaker & Sons for material from *Whitaker's Almanack 1961*, p 160.

Every attempt has been made to contact copyright holders, but we apologise if any have been overlooked.

Notes for Students

In 1851, the Great Exhibition, held in the Crystal Palace, demonstrated clearly that Britain at that time was the world's leading industrial power and the envied 'Workshop of the World'. The greatest inventions of the age were British. Britain had the world's largest empire and the largest share of the world's riches. By 1870, roughly half the world's coal, cotton cloth and pig iron, and about three-quarters of its ships, came from the British Isles.

In the next eighty years, the position of Britain as the dominant industrial power in the world altered considerably. This was partly as the result of fighting two world wars but chiefly because the demand for the products of British industry underwent a fundamental change. By the time of the Festival of Britain in 1951, Britain could no longer claim to be the world's leading industrial nation. The textile, coal-mining, steel-making and shipbuilding industries had all declined relatively when compared with those of other countries.

It was true that the newer industries, such as chemicals, electronics and motor vehicles, offered some hope that manufacturing industry could continue to provide the people of Britain with a high standard of living. But by 1987, even these hopes had faded. British industry was then in serious decline, with over 3 million workers unemployed and once-prosperous towns blighted by recession.

Yet, despite unemployment, the majority of the people of Britain in the early 1980s still enjoyed a much higher standard of living than had been the case before the outbreak of the Second World War in 1939. This was partly because many non-industrial activities had prospered. Banking, insurance and other financial services continued to make the City of London a major force in the world's business affairs. A revolution in farming techniques and methods had transformed the countryside and made Britain self-sufficient in many foods. Developments on the railways, the coming of the motor ship, the invention of the motor vehicle and the aeroplane, the development of the telegraph and telephone systems, and the spread of broadcasting by radio and television, had all revolutionised communications and transformed living standards.

A vast new system of social welfare – 'the British Welfare State' – had become the envy of many parts of the world. State education from nursery to university and polytechnic, a comprehensive National Health Service with modern hospitals and clinics, and an all-embracing system of National Insurance, enabled politicians to claim, with justice, that the State looked after the individual 'from the cradle to the grave'.

These changes affected Britain in many ways. The population of Great Britain grew from 21 million in 1851 to 54 million in 1981. Public health and living conditions in the towns and in the major cities, such as London, Glasgow,

Birmingham, Liverpool, Manchester and Belfast, improved out of all recognition in the same period.

The appearance of the landscape, too, changed with the development of new forms of agriculture, urban growth, the rise of the leisure and holiday industries, and a new concern for the conservation of the environment and control of pollution.

Not surprisingly, these changes and the problems they created, met with mixed reactions from the people of Britain. The growing affluence of the ordinary worker meant that the old division into upper, middle and working classes was no longer an accurate or useful method of looking at society. The electoral system was completely reformed. The trade unions underwent remarkable changes. Women successfully challenged a male-dominated society to take their rightful place in the nation's affairs – a process which culminated in 1979 with the election of a woman Prime Minister.

These many and varied activities and developments are described in this book. At times the relationship between the different strands of development may not always be clear or obvious. This is why you should find the Time Chart, on pages 332–9, useful. It has been designed to show at a glance, how these various elements were all part of the same social and economic revolution.

Some of the extracts and quotations used in this book have been simplified – in rare cases with the substitution of a modern word or phrase for one that is obscure or obsolete, more commonly by inserting the meaning in brackets adjacent to the word or phrase in the quotation (rather than as a footnote which might be overlooked). In a very few instances, link words have been added to smooth the juncture between separate extracts from the same source.

Lack of space has inevitably prevented the inclusion of many long quotations and the usual technique of eliminating unnecessary sentences or phrases has been adopted in order to cut these extracts down to comprehensible proportions. However, the convention of indicating such exclusions with rows of dots has not normally been followed, to avoid confusing the reader with broken dotted text.

Notes for Teachers

Questions and exercises have been numbered in the text. As a general, but not invariable, rule the simpler, easier questions come first, followed by the more complicated, interpretative questions.

As far as possible these questions and exercises have been designed to provide students at all levels of ability with an opportunity to demonstrate what 'they know, understand and can do' as preparation for the differentiated questions in the GCSE examination.

Chapter One

Agriculture

INTRODUCTION

Harvesting in 1918

Harvesting in 1980

1 *What differences are there between the two photographs?*
2 *What effect would you expect the change in the method of harvesting corn to have had on the countryside and on the people who live and work there?*
3 *From your own experience write down five other ways in which farming methods have changed in the last hundred years.*

In the mid-nineteenth century, people talked in wonder of the changes that had taken place in farming during the previous hundred years. In 1750 a large part of England had been farmed in open fields, much of it by peasant farmers using techniques of cultivation which had changed little since the Middle Ages. By 1850 most of the open fields had been enclosed, the class of small peasant farmers had become one of farm labourers, new fertilisers were being used and machines were beginning to replace workers in the fields. Farmers were obtaining bigger and better yields of corn, rearing healthier livestock and benefiting considerably from the development of the railway.

Yet dramatic though these changes were, they were still relatively slight in effect compared with the startling transformation of agriculture in the period from 1850 to the present day. With only one-sixth the number of farm workers (about 350,000 in Great Britain in 1980 compared with two million in 1850), modern farms produce three times as much corn; rear well over twice as many cattle and four times as many pigs; employ machines as diverse as combine harvesters and microcomputers; and use scientific methods to control the growth of livestock.

THE GOLDEN AGE OF BRITISH AGRICULTURE

The period of twenty years from 1850 to 1870 is often called the Golden Age of British Agriculture – a time when harvests were bountiful and farmers were prosperous.

Yet in 1846, Sir Robert Peel had persuaded Parliament to repeal the Corn Laws. These had hitherto protected British farmers against foreign competition by prohibiting the import of foreign corn when British prices fell below the minimum prices set by the government. Now began a period of nearly a hundred years of Free Trade. Cheap foreign grain could be sold on the open market in competition with home-grown corn from Britain.

To the surprise of opponents of the bill, who were fearful that it would reduce farm profits, the repeal of the Corn Laws did not at first have anything like the disastrous effect on farming that had been feared. Instead, the price of wheat remained relatively steady at a time when farmers' costs began to go down because of increased efficiency. A succession of fine harvests produced bumper crops, but demand for corn remained high because Britain's population was still growing rapidly. Working people in the industrial towns were more prosperous and could afford better food and more of it. Britain's farmers found a ready market for their produce and could use the developing railway network to get it to their customers.

As yet, foreign exports of food to Britain were still relatively low. This was partly because the great wheat-growing lands of North America had yet to be cultivated on a massive scale. Until they were put to the plough there was little serious competition for the British cereal grower to meet. In fact, it was not until

1869 that the Union Pacific and Central Pacific Railroads completed the railway line linking the Atlantic to the Pacific, which helped to open up the American West to large-scale farming.

During the Golden Age, many British farmers took advantage of the latest improvements in machinery and farming methods to improve their farms. Landowners also prospered, since they were able to increase the rents paid by their tenant farmers.

But for farm workers the Golden Age of British Agriculture was anything but golden. They took little share of this increasing prosperity. Farm cottages were often rural slums. Farm wages were appreciably lower than those paid by industry and demand for farm labourers was falling. At the time of the 1871 Census, there were 10 per cent fewer farm workers than in 1851. Farmers had less need for labourers when reapers, steam threshing machines and steam traction engines were employed.

THE COTTAGE.

MR. PUNCH (TO LANDLORD). "YOUR STABLE ARRANGEMENTS ARE EXCELLENT! SUPPOSE YOU TRY SOMETHING OF THE SORT HERE! EH?"

Punch, 12 January 1861

In the same issue of *Punch*, a labourer described his cottage as:

'badly built, is not drained, has no ventilation, has a rotten floor, and is so cold that in winter the only way the family can keep bodies and souls together is by huddling together, adults, children, grown-up lads and girls, all together in one wretched bedroom.'

1 *What was the point of the cartoon?*

2 *What did farmers fear when the Corn Laws were repealed? Why were their fears unfounded in the years before 1870?*

THE GREAT DEPRESSION IN FARMING

Reasons for the Depression in British Agriculture

The repeal of the Corn Laws had its effect in the years after 1873, when the Golden Age of Agriculture was followed by the Great Depression. Corn prices began to fall at a time of poor harvests, yet prices usually rose when grain was scarce. The effect was catastrophic, as you can see see from these Sources.

Source A

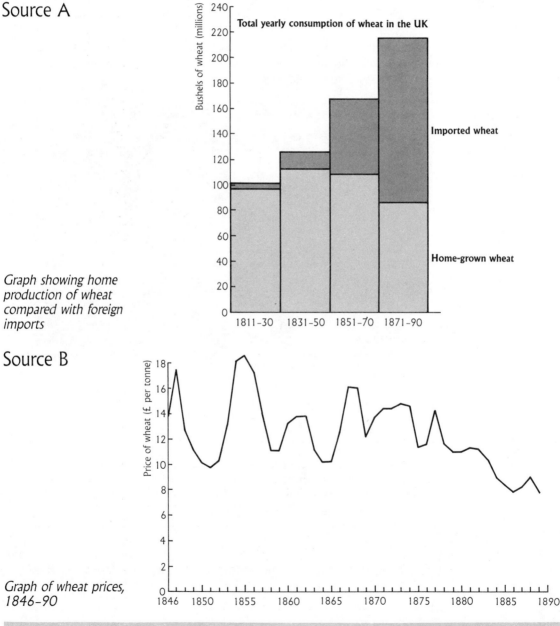

Graph showing home production of wheat compared with foreign imports

Source B

Graph of wheat prices, 1846–90

Source C

'Farming has recently been in a very depressed condition in many parts of England. Mr Thompson [a Sussex farmer] attributes this circumstance to increased wages, rise in expense of mechanical work, unfavourable weather for several years, and foreign competition.

Mr Ford [another Sussex farmer] gives me an idea of what they have suffered from wet in recent years. In such wet seasons sheep are affected by the rot. In 1879 such was the quantity of rain that acres and acres of cut grass were washed away, and the water lay up to the knees of the cattle, so that they could not pasture. She [Mrs Ford] tells me there is great depression now in farming, from bad seasons four years in succession; then she adds that you might say through high rents, bad seasons and high taxes. However, she admits that rents are being reduced.'

Harper's New Monthly Magazine, *April 1883*

Source D

'In Essex a great part of the land has been allowed to go out of cultivation because wheat was the principal crop cultivated, and it cannot be produced to pay under forty-five shillings per quarter, while the price of it at present is under twenty shillings per quarter; the farmers have lost all their capital, and are therefore unable to change their system of farming without outside aid. Scots farmers who have been following the dairy system, have been enabled to survive the ruin which has overtaken others.'

Report of the Royal Commission on Agriculture – *quoted in* Chambers's Journal, *February 1895*

Source E

'The British farmer has only too good reason to take to dairying. Milk is too bulky an article for carriage by sea, and too quickly perishes to make it a regular source of export from countries so near us as Holland and Sweden.'

Chambers's Journal, *October 1895*

Source F

	Area under Wheat (million acres)	Yield of Wheat (bushels per acre)
1856	4.2	27.5
1866	3.6	25.5
1876	3.1	25.4
1886	2.4	29.8
1894	2.0	30.6

Source G

'The universal spread of wheat lands and the capacity of transporting grain easily and cheaply to any given spot contains dangers as well as benefits. New lands, lightly-taxed lands, which need no fertilising, can compete so successfully as to destroy the industry in older countries. In England, in consequence, wheat growing has fallen into decay. In time of naval war where should we be without a home supply of breadstuffs?'

Ernest E. Williams, The London Magazine, *1903*

Source H

'From every quarter of the country comes the cry of despair – from wheat counties and sheep counties, cattle, hop-yards and orchards – the universal tale of woe. Bad harvests; ruinous prices; the foreigner with his wheat and his wool, and, above all, his frozen carcasses.'

Chambers's Journal, October 1896

Source I

'1870	Below average	1875	Very unsatisfactory
1871	Deficient	1876	Unsatisfactory
1872	Deficient	1877	Unsatisfactory
1873	Much below average	1878	Good
1874	Very good	1879	Worst harvest known'

'Good and Bad Harvests' in Whitaker's Almanack, *1881*

Source J

Selling up the old farm in about 1890

Source K

'The exportation of frozen meat from Australia has only attained large dimensions within the last few years; but it dates back to about 1880, prior to which year Australian beef and mutton reached us only in tins. New Zealand was the first of the colonies to go extensively into this business and by the year 1889 was already exporting frozen meat to the value of £780,000. There are now some twenty-two freezing-works in New Zealand alone, capable of freezing about four millions of sheep per annum; and in Australia some seventeen establishments, capable of freezing about three millions annually.'

Chambers's Journal, 1894

> 1   *What effect did foreign imports have on wheat prices in Britain in the 1870s? Why did the price of wheat vary sharply from one year to another between 1846 and 1877? Why was there less fluctuation in wheat prices after 1877?*

2 *How catastrophic was the Great Depression in British farming in the last quarter of the nineteenth century? Which sources would you use to show the decline in the importance of wheat farming in Britain?*

3 *What was the effect of bad weather on the farmer in the 1870s? How did it affect (a) the cereal-grower, (b) the livestock farmer? What other reasons were used to account for the slump in farming?*

4 *Why were American farmers able to compete so successfully with British wheat farmers? What other types of farming were threatened by foreign competition? Why?*

5 *Which source correctly identified a potential danger to Britain in allowing farming to deteriorate?*

6 *What possible solutions to the problems of the wheat farmer were suggested? What reasons were given?*

7 *Why was there relatively little foreign competition for the British livestock farmer before 1880? Why could fresh meat only be transported over relatively short distances? Why was foreign meat a serious threat to British agriculture in the 1880s and 1890s?*

8 *Write a short essay about the Great Depression, using these sources to explain what it was, what its effects were, and how and why it had such an effect on British agriculture.*

The losses due to the spread of agricultural diseases included those from mildew in wheat, rinderpest disease and foot and mouth disease affecting cattle, and an estimated three million sheep lost as a result of sheep rot. When some farmers began to go out of business in the 1870s, it was easy enough, at first, to assume that this was because of the combined effects of poor harvests and these livestock diseases, rather than because of foreign competition.

The Effects of Foreign Competition

Some countries reacted to foreign competition by putting up tariffs on foreign grain. In Denmark and Holland, farmers turned instead to intensive dairy farming and used cheap American grain to feed their livestock. Much of their produce – bacon, eggs, butter, cheese – was sold to Britain, causing further problems for the British farmer. By 1890, people in Britain were eating more Danish butter than British, and meat imports from Argentina, Australia, New Zealand, the United States and Canada were threatening to overtake home livestock production. Despite this, British farmers turned increasingly to dairying and livestock farming as an alternative to cereals.

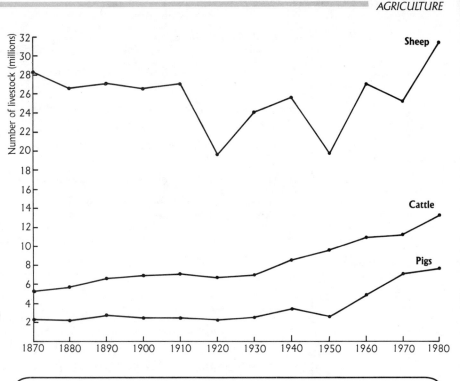

Graph of livestock numbers, 1870–1980 (statistics shown at ten-year intervals)

1 *What were the approximate percentage increases/decreases in cattle, sheep and pig production (a) between 1870 and 1920, (b) between 1920 and 1980?*

2 *Between which two sets of dates were there significant falls in the number of sheep kept in Britain? How do you explain this? What happened to cattle and pig production in the same periods?*

The problem for the farmer was that Britain was primarily a rapidly growing, highly industrialised country, reliant on exporting manufactures and no longer able to grow all the food she needed. Politicians thought it more sensible to import cheap food than to protect the farmer by imposing tariffs on foreign imports. Tariffs would have had two main effects:

● They would have put up the cost of food in Britain – putting pressure on industrialists to raise wages. This would have made British manufactured goods more expensive and therefore less competitive overseas.

● They might have prompted foreign governments to retaliate by putting higher tariffs on imported goods from Britain, making British manufactures even less competitive.

As a result, demands to introduce tariffs (see Chapter 4) were rejected and nothing was done. By the 1890s, the area of land sown with wheat had fallen by half in only twenty years.

THE EFFECTS OF AGRICULTURAL CHANGES ON SOCIETY

The Condition of the Farm Worker

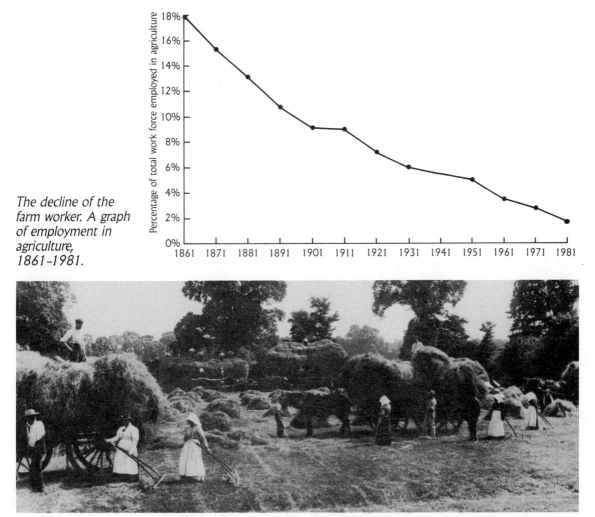

The decline of the farm worker. A graph of employment in agriculture, 1861–1981.

1 *How many people are at work in this hay field in 1905?*
2 *Write a brief note commenting on the facts you can deduce from the graph.*

Farm workers have always tended to be underpaid in relation to comparable skilled workers in industry. In the nineteenth century, wages on the land varied from one part of the country to another, since there was no national wage scale for farm workers at that time. In 1909, the average wage of 15s [75p] a week was regarded as being well below the poverty line for a man with a family to support – even though it was generally agreed that the lot of the farm worker had improved considerably since the 1850s. In 1895, H.G.Pearce in *The English Illustrated Magazine*, wrote that the oldest inhabitants of a Dorset village had told her:

> 'though there was much a-wanting to be done, yet things had wonderfully improved all round these last fifty years, and the man who had his regular place on a farm had not half as much to complain of as his father afore him had.'

Farm workers were in a difficult and unique position. They worked for employers who might employ only ten or a dozen men on a regular basis, supplemented by a much larger gang of workers at harvest time. Farm labourers lived in tied cottages owned by the estate and had a small plot of land on which to keep a pig and a few hens. If they were sacked they were evicted and lost their homes.

The National Agricultural Labourers' Union

The lot of the farm worker was taken up by Joseph Arch, a farm worker himself since the age of nine, a lay preacher and the founder of the National Agricultural Labourers' Union in 1872.

At first people laughed at the idea of the farm worker joining a trade union – the 'Revolt of Hodge', as it was called (Hodge was the disparaging nickname for a farm labourer). But when farm workers went on strike for more pay and better working conditions in 1872–4, many farmers replied with lock-outs. Initially, the union had great success, raising wages by as much as 50 per cent on some farms and attracting a membership of 86,000 workers by 1874.

The Great Depression in farming, however, put paid to hopes of a permanent improvement because, as you have seen, it was a time when some farmers were going bankrupt, changing to livestock farming or re-equipping their farms with labour-saving machinery. By 1880, the Union's membership had dropped to only 20,000 and to only 5,000 by 1889. You can see why the Union got support, and why it failed, in the following Sources.

Source A

Aims of the Warwickshire Agricultural Labourers' Union in 1872 (quoted in *The History of the TUC, 1868–1968)*:

- 'to elevate the social position of the farm labourers of the county by assisting them to increase their wages;
- to lessen the number of ordinary working hours;
- to improve their habitations;
- to provide them with gardens or allotments;
- to assist deserving and suitable labourers to migrate and emigrate.'

Source B

Account of a meeting between a Suffolk farmer and his men:

'all of whom had had notice that after the coming Friday evening they would be locked out. The labourers, sixteen in all, followed us into a large room in the bailiff's house. There was no defiance, or bitterness, or jeering on their side, but a manly self-respect which made itself felt, and their replies showed no little shrewdness and appreciation of the points just now at issue. The talk ended, as it began, with mutual good feeling.'

The Times, *April 1874*

Source C

'Hitherto the labourers in the locked-out districts of the Eastern Counties have, for the most part, stood out firmly against the arguments of the farmers, and have refused to accept the offer of higher wages if it was coupled with the condition of tearing the blue ribbon of the Farm Labourers' Guild, an organisation dreaded and detested by the masters, and regarded with an almost superstitious reverence by the men. Meanwhile the farmers are, in many cases, dependent on their own physical exertions. Our picture represents an actual incident. The master is doing his own work, his wife is bringing him his dinner, and the man who once did his ploughing and reaping looks idly on, being bound for the Land of Promise, Queensland.'

The Graphic, *16 May 1874*

Source D

The Graphic,
16 May 1874

Source E

'Determined and confident as the farmers appear to be at their association meetings when prompting each other to continued resistance to the Union, there can be little doubt but that in quieter moments they are often troubled with strong misgivings as to the issue of the struggle.'

The Graphic, *6 June 1874*

Source F

LAND AND LABOUR; OR, "HOW TO SETTLE IT."

LORD BROADACRES. "COME, FARMER, I THINK *WE* MAY MANAGE TO MEND MATTERS FOR OUR FRIEND HODGE, WITHOUT THE HELP OF THAT *PROFESSIONAL MEDDLER!*"

Punch, *20 April 1872*

1 *Why do you think Joseph Arch's union ultimately failed? Why were farm workers difficult to organise into a trade union?*

2 *Imagine you are a farm worker in 1872, living in a tied cottage without amenities in a small village in Eastern England, paid 10s [50p] a week, rarely eating a proper meal and working long, tedious hours in the fields. There are no other employers in the area apart from farmers. What would you have done in the years between 1872 and 1875?*

3 *What did* Punch *think about the new union? Was Joseph Arch a 'professional meddler'? How did* Punch *think the dispute should be settled? Do you agree or disagree with this view?*

4 *Compare the attitudes taken by* Punch *in the LAND AND LABOUR cartoon (1872) and THE COTTAGE (1861) on page 3. How do you account for the change?*

5 *What evidence quoted in this chapter can be used to show that:*

(a) *the farm labourers had a strong case for higher pay and better working conditions;*

(b) *there was some sympathy for their cause;*

(c) *many farm workers were at the end of their tether and genuinely determined to improve their living standards and working conditions;*

> (d) the farmers were not always united in their opposition to the union?
>
> **6** From the extracts printed here, would you say The Graphic sympathised with the farmers or the farm workers? Explain the reasons for your answer.
>
> **7** Which, if any, of the sources quoted here may be biased? Give an example and explain your choice. What value is such evidence to a historian?
>
> **8** Which of the aims of the Warwickshire Union would be regarded as unusual by a modern trade union? Why?

By 1914, the position of the farm worker had improved. More farm workers had left the land of their own free will than the pressure of mechanisation warranted. Good farm workers were less easy to find. The decrease in the number of available workers led to a rise in farm wages, even though farmers' incomes were falling. In northern England, where farm workers were most highly paid, farm wages rose from 15s 1d [75p] a week in about 1870 to 22s 3d [£1.11] a week in 1914. In the West Country, where farm labour was cheapest, wages rose from 10s 6d [53p] a week in about 1870 to 14s 3d [71p] a week in 1914. Even so the average farm worker still had a low standard of living compared with that of the average factory worker.

The Flight from the Land

One of the most important consequences of the Great Depression in farming was a change in land tenure. In the mid-nineteenth century, most of Britain's farmland was owned by a small number of large landowners. Indeed, it has been estimated that, in 1873, just 44 people owned 2 million hectares of farmland between them, with another 5 million hectares owned by a group of about 4,000 wealthy people. The tenant farmers who rented these farms rarely saw their landlords. They paid rents to an agent who made the necessary repairs to buildings and provided other maintenance services as well, such as laying pipes to drain a field.

But the Great Depression meant that landowners as well as tenant farmers faced financial problems. They were forced to reduce rents by about 33 per cent to keep pace with the deterioration in farm incomes, otherwise many more tenant farmers would have gone bankrupt. As a result average farm rents fell from 30s [£1.50] an acre in 1880 to 20s [£1] an acre by 1900.

This drop in estate income meant that the standard of maintenance deteriorated and the upkeep of many estates suffered. Neglected, broken-down cottages became a familiar sight in the countryside. Weeds and thistles grew in many fields. But tenant farmers were reluctant to make improvements themselves, since any benefit they added to their holdings could only enrich the landowner in the end.

If they failed to pay their rent they could be immediately evicted – a particular hazard at times of bad harvests and lower prices. This problem was something the government could try to alleviate and the Agricultural Holdings Act of 1875, and those of 1906 and 1908, gave the tenant farmer some protection against being evicted. As a result tenants were more willing to make improvements to their landholdings. Further help came with the Agricultural Rates Act of 1896, which cut rates on the land (but not on farm buildings) by 50 per cent.

An increasing proportion of landowners responded to these changes in economic circumstances and the law by breaking up their estates. Tenant farmers were given the opportunity to buy their holdings. In 1914, about 90 per cent of farmland was farmed by tenant farmers who paid a rent. By the early 1980s, this proportion had fallen to around 30 per cent with most farmers owning their land.

Scientific and Technological Change

This cartoon appeared in Punch *in 1884. What was the point of the cartoon? How could a modern cartoonist make a similar comment on the activities of farmers?*

DELIGHTS OF THE PEACEFUL COUNTRY. THRESHING TIME.

By the late nineteenth century, the steam threshing machine was becoming a familiar sight in the fields. Its dominance was not to be threatened until the arrival of the first combine harvesters in the 1930s. By 1907, potato-digging machines could be seen on some farms and the first tractors were already in use. But it is easy to exaggerate the pace of change. Despite the fact that a mechanical reaper had been invented in the 1820s, long lines of farm workers were still scything corn in the 1900s, whilst other farm workers tied it into sheaves and stacked it in a field to dry. On some farms corn was still threshed with a wooden flail, using a technique which had hardly changed since the Middle Ages. Tom Mullins, a Staffordshire farm worker in the 1870s, commented, 'How country folk laughed when the first machines appeared.'

---

1 *Was it inevitable that farm machinery would replace many of the jobs formerly done by hand?*

2 *Why do you think the new techniques and new machines were often slow to be accepted and adopted by farmers and farm workers? In what ways is this process of mechanisation continuing on modern farms?*

STATE INTERVENTION IN THE TWENTIETH CENTURY

The depression in farming lasted from the early 1870s until about 1907, when prosperity began slowly to return to Britain's farmers. This trend was heightened during the First World War when a high priority was placed on food production. It proved to be a short-lived prosperity, however, and farming plunged to new depths in the late 1920s.

Farming recovered again in the 1930s, partly as a result of government intervention to keep up prices for farm produce. Ever since 1931, however, farmers have been supported in one way or another by successive governments, whether National, Conservative or Labour – a far cry indeed from the *laissez-faire* (leave well alone) policy of the nineteenth century.

Farming during the First World War

During the 1914–18 War, German U-boats threatened to cut off Britain's food supplies from America by sinking merchant ships laden with wheat. Fears about how Britain would be supplied with food in wartime proved justified. The German aim was simple – by starving the United Kingdom of food they could bring the British war effort to an end. It was vital that Britain's food deficit be made up as far as possible from home-grown sources of supply. This is why the Government intervened to set up the Food Production Campaign, designed to increase the amount of land cultivated. Subsidies were paid to farmers to persuade them to plough up new fields in order to grow more corn. The Corn Production Act of 1917 guaranteed a minimum price for corn and minimum wages for farm workers. Many women land workers saw this as an opportunity to help the war effort and joined the Women's Land Army with its 16,000 members.

Land Girl in the
hayfield in May 1918

1 Look at the graph on page 29. What effect did the Food
   Production Campaign have on wheat production? What
   happened to wheat imports at this time?
2 Look at the graph on page 8. What effect did the Food
   Production Campaign have on livestock farming?

Farming between the Wars

Soon after the First World War ended, however, government subsidies were
withdrawn and farmers were left in the lurch once again. The worst affected
were the grain farmers of East Anglia who had been guaranteed steady wheat
prices during the war. Suddenly, in 1921, this price support was withdrawn and
the Corn Production Act was repealed. There were more votes for the politicians
in cheap food than in supporting the farming community.

Cheap foreign grain and meat flooded into Britain once again. The price of
wheat fell sharply bringing hard times to the arable farmers, who felt betrayed
after the demands made upon them during the war. Rents which had risen
during the war stayed high whilst farm income tumbled. Wheat production
slumped to an all-time low by 1931, and milk, too, was sold at an uneconomic
price.

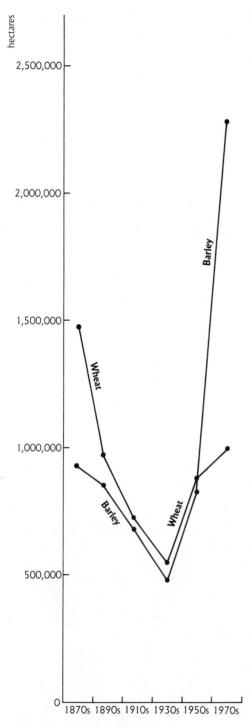

Graph showing the area sown with wheat and barley in Great Britain between the 1870s and the 1970s

Until this time, successive governments (Conservative and Liberal) had all stuck to the idea of Free Trade, even though many foreign governments imposed tariffs on British goods (see page 143). But, whilst the majority of people welcomed cheaper food bills, many farmers went out of business and others drastically cut the wages of their farm workers.

This provoked a strike of farm workers in the spring of 1923, with bitter consequences – some farmers lost livestock through neglect, and farm workers who went to work as blacklegs had to be protected by the police. In the end the farmers climbed down, guaranteeing their farm workers a minimum wage of 25s [£1.25] for a 50-hour week and a guaranteed weekly half holiday.

During the years of the Depression in the late 1920s and early 1930s, farming plunged to new depths. Many arable farmers gave up growing grain and tried livestock farming, dairying or poultry. It was often cheaper to leave the land uncultivated than try to grow crops. The countryside looked neglected, with weeds and thistles growing in fields that had formerly grown corn.

Some farmers gave up farming completely – especially the small farmers who had bought their holdings with mortgages and were now lumbered with heavy debts on properties which they could not sell and which were worth less than the money they had paid for them. 'For Sale' signs were a common sight in the 1920s and early 1930s – a problem not confined to Britain, since many of the farmers of the American prairies also saw their incomes plummet during the late 1920s and early 1930s. It was a good time to buy or take on the tenancy of a new farm if you had faith in the future. Some farmers did so – and prospered later on, when farming turned the corner of the Depression years.

One of the few attempts to help solve the crisis in farming came in 1924, with a government attempt to establish sugar beet farming in Britain. Subsidies were granted to farmers who grew sugar beet. This gave the arable farmers of eastern England a welcome alternative cash crop besides corn.

> Look at the graph on the previous page.
>
> **1** *When was production of wheat and barley (a) at its lowest, (b) at its highest?*
>
> **2** *Write a brief analysis of this graph, explaining the variations you can see here.*

New Methods

For the farm workers of the 1920s, conditions were hard. Even the introduction of the tractor was no blessing. One farm worker remembered that:

> 'they were really devils to start in the cold mornings; often you'd swing for an hour before you'd get 'em going. And they wouldn't pull until they were hot.'

The farm worker who used to guide the horses when ploughing had a skilled job with heavy physical activity to keep him warm. Not so the tractor-man in winter, sitting on a tractor going from one end of a field to the other. It was a chilly, boring job.

The first combine harvesters were only introduced into Britain from America in 1926 and there were still relatively few of them in use by 1939. Fewer than one farm in ten even had a tractor. But the telephone, radio, car and lorry reduced the isolation of farmers and made them more mobile.

A Ford farm tractor pulling a reaping machine in a Hertfordshire cornfield in 1918. What similarities and what differences are there between this harvest scene in 1918 and those to be seen on other farms in 1918 and 1980 (page 1)?

Government Intervention

The collapse of the New York Stock Market in 1929 marked the start of a worldwide depression and a rise in worldwide unemployment. World wheat prices fell sharply – dropping by 50 per cent in the space of two years. To arable farmers it was a nightmare.

In 1931 the new National Government took the first really constructive steps towards aiding the farmer. The old principle of Free Trade was abandoned and quotas were imposed on foreign imports, restricting the availability in Britain of cheap foreign food. In return for this protection, the Government took steps to make British farming more efficient, since they hoped this would lead to lower prices and therefore to a lower level of tariffs on foreign imports. This is why they brought in the Agricultural Marketing Acts of 1931 and 1933, which set up the Milk Marketing Boards. The main effects were as follows.

● Dairy farmers had to sell their milk to a Milk Marketing Board in return for a share of the profits made by the Board (based on the amount of milk they sold).

● The Milk Marketing Boards sold the milk at a fixed price to the consumer. As the Milk Marketing Boards held a monopoly of its sale, this meant that there was one price for milk throughout Britain. Fixed prices gave farmers a steady, regular income and stopped them trying to undercut one another.

● The Milk Marketing Boards also promoted the sale of milk with advertising campaigns. In the 1930s the slogan was 'Drink daily your protective pint of milk'. After the Second World War a similar impact was made with the slogan 'Drinka Pinta Milka Day'.

● The Milk Marketing Boards were able to insist on uniform standards of cleanliness and hygiene. The old hand-milking system with the farm worker sitting on a three-legged stool was eventually replaced by the white-coated dairy attendant and the electric milking machine. This cut down on the labour needed on a dairy farm and ensured a higher quality of milk for the consumer.

● It meant that dairy farmers sacrificed some control over their farms in return for a guaranteed income.

● It reduced competition, so in the long run the consumer paid more for food.

Other marketing boards were founded with similar powers to restrict and control production. They included the Meat Marketing Board, the Egg Marketing Board, the Potato Marketing Board and the Bacon Development Board. The Wheat Act of 1932 gave farmers a guaranteed price for their wheat, followed in 1937 by similar guarantees for barley and oats. Meat imports were controlled and reduced by as much as a third. Preference was given to food imports from the Empire. Free Trade was abandoned.

This reversal of policy was to affect agriculture for the rest of the century, since the government now acknowledged that it had a part to play in controlling the level of food prices in peacetime as well as at a time of war. As a result there was a small but significant swing away from dairying and livestock farming back to arable farming once more. By 1939, British farming had begun to recover. Farmers were guaranteed an income from their land. Farm values increased and wages were raised.

> **1** *What were the advantages and disadvantages of the marketing boards? How did the customer benefit?*
>
> **2** *What might have happened to the countryside if the government had allowed farming to deteriorate even further after 1931?*

The Impact of the Second World War

The outbreak of war in September 1939 threatened food supplies, especially since the early stages of the war were fought mainly at sea. Food convoys bringing North American grain to Britain were threatened by German U-boats. Once again, the Ministry of Agriculture and Fisheries took steps to increase food output from the land. That they were highly successful is seen from the statistics. In 1939, British farmers produced only 30 per cent of Britain's food requirements. By 1945, that proportion had increased to 80 per cent. Farm incomes grew fourfold, from £55 million in 1938–9 to £230 million in 1943–4, and twice as many tractors were being used at the end of the war as at the beginning.

GROW FOOD FOR THE NATION
FEEDING STUFFS FOR YOUR FARMS
KEEP OUR SHIPS AND MONEY FREE
FOR BUYING VITAL ARMS

A wartime poster encourages food production.

The government ran a big 'Dig for Victory' campaign. At the outset, in October 1939, the Minister of Agriculture, Sir Reginald Dorman-Smith, urged the nation to greater effort:

> 'Let "Dig for Victory" be the motto of everyone with a garden and of every able-bodied man and woman capable of digging an allotment in their spare time.'

There was even a popular song with the title 'Dig! Dig! Dig to Victory!' Allotments, potato fields and vegetable patches were everywhere. School playing fields were cultivated, leaving only small areas for football, hockey or cricket. Public parks were ploughed. Flowerbeds were turned into vegetable allotments. Some householders kept rabbits, hens and even cows and pigs.

But the biggest developments were on the farms. Farmers and Ministry experts formed War Agricultural Executive Committees in every county of England and Wales. These were further subdivided into smaller districts, run by local committees. They helped to set official ploughing targets to be met by the farmers in each area (usually by mutual agreement) – so much grassland to be ploughed up, so many acres of ploughland to be sown with cereals and potatoes.

The emphasis was on increasing productivity – particularly of foods which provided the maximum output of energy. More people could be kept alive on cereals and potatoes than on milk, butter, cheese and meat; so the emphasis was on growing crops rather than on rearing livestock.

The high priority given to this is shown by the fact that the Government allocated scarce resources to make the most of the land – fuel for tractors and combine harvesters, and grants to drain the low-lying fields and bring new land into cultivation. Government scientists devised and fostered the development of fertilisers, pesticides and weedkillers to help increase crop yields from the land. The high subsidies paid by the Government for these improvements made it economical to cultivate marginal land, which in pre-war days had been uneconomic to farm.

In some respects it was simply a reversion to the type of farming common enough in Britain in the Golden Age of High Farming in the 1850s.

The Land Army

One potential drawback to increased wartime output from the land was lack of labour, since the war had taken many men into the forces. The answer came partly from prisoners of war and volunteers. Schoolchildren, students and office workers helped at harvest time – encouraged sometimes by the likelihood of better food on a farm than in the ordinary home.

> 'Back to the land, we must all lend a hand.
> To the farms and the fields we must go.
> There's a job to be done
> Though we can't fire a gun
> We can still do our bit with the hoe.'

> *'The Land Army Song'*, c. 1939–45

The principal contribution, however, came with the formation of the Women's Land Army, founded initially in June 1939, in anticipation of the looming war. Women were recruited from the towns to work on the land and were treated as if they were soldiers. They were given a short course of training and wore uniforms (if these were available). In practice they often lacked the clothing (such as wellington boots) and farm equipment needed to do the job properly, because the fighting army was given priority over the Land Army. Eventually they formed a unit of about 100,000 workers, doing a vital job for the war effort, despite low pay and poor working conditions.

Unlike servicewomen in the armed forces they were free to leave the Land Army at any time and could also be sacked by a farmer. Many found it difficult to get accustomed to country life, particularly in the more remote rural areas where only one or two Land Girls would be needed on an isolated farm. They were often unprepared for the heavy physical labour that farming entailed and most were surprised to find just how primitive many country cottages still were in the mid-twentieth century, with outside earth toilets, no electricity and no hot-water taps.

But overall the enthusiasm and industry of the members of the Women's Land Army was high and they made a substantial contribution to the increased productivity of Britain's farms during the war. Most enjoyed the experience, although the Government gave them few of the rewards enjoyed by the members of the armed services.

'Victory Harvest' poster

> **1** *Why was it called the Women's Land Army? How did it differ from the army?*
>
> **2** *What was the aim of the 'Victory Harvest' poster? Write two or three sentences comparing the impression it gives of country life with the reality faced by many Land Girls.*

Agriculture since 1945

By the end of the war, arable land in Britain had increased by 50 per cent. Farmers in 1945 were growing twice the amount of cereals and potatoes produced in 1939.

After the First World War, farmers felt they had been betrayed by the Government, when their efforts to increase productivity were rewarded with the scrapping of the guaranteed prices policy in 1921. In 1945, they had no great expectation that the new Labour Government, with its electoral support coming mainly from the urban areas, would be any more sympathetic to the farming interest. Cheaper food could be produced in North America and, by 1947, 75 per cent of Britain's meat was being imported.

But there was a different type of price to be paid for food imports at this time. Every pound spent on foreign meat and cereals took money out of Britain and added to the country's growing financial crisis.

In 1947, the Labour Government took decisive action to persuade British farmers to increase the amount of home-produced food. In return for some government control of the industry, farmers were to be given guaranteed prices for their produce. Tom Williams, Minister of Agriculture, said:

> 'During the war the farmers and farm workers of Britain stood between us and starvation. Today they are still fighting the Battle for Bread. When that battle has been won they will be able to bring us more of the other foods we want – milk, meat, eggs, vegetables, fruit. But they must not be let down as they were after the 1914–18 War. This Agriculture Bill aims at giving farmers an assured market and guaranteed prices for their principal products, while at the same time ensuring a higher level of efficiency. These principles are endorsed not only by all sections of the industry itself but by all political parties.'

Through their representatives on the National Farmers' Union, farmers even had a say in determining the level of these prices at the annual price reviews. Encouragement came from other legislation as well. The Hill Farming Act of 1946 provided government grants to encourage hill farmers to stay on the land, helping them to build roads and new buildings, install drainage and reclaim open grazing land for pasture.

Critics said the farmers could not lose. They could get government money for digging new ditches, laying drainage pipes, and spreading fertilisers, as well as receiving guaranteed prices for the extra farm produce yielded by a land improved with government grants. Demand for food was still high and food rationing was still in force. One Labour Minister, Stanley Evans, even went so far as to say that the British farmer had been 'feather-bedded' – a phrase which stuck in the memory. Farmers were infuriated when he claimed that they were 'living on feather beds and carrying their money to the bank in pillow cases'. In 1956, he added:

> 'I think the housewife and the taxpayer have been baby-sitting the farmer all too long and it's time to call a halt.'

By then, subsidies to farmers were running at over £300 million a year. The consumer was paying twice for food – once in higher taxes to pay for these subsidies and then again in higher food prices in the shops (since cheaper food could have been imported from overseas). But to British governments, mindful of wartime food shortages and the outflow of currency to pay for foreign food, the price of these subsidies was more than justified. Dependence on foreign food would have reduced the value of the pound even further and affected the ability of the country to purchase other much-needed imports, such as oil and vital raw materials for manufacturing industry.

This is why the same policy was continued by the Conservative Government, which came to power in 1951. The only difference was that many of the controls on farming and food production were removed, including food rationing. Since farm produce could be freely sold, the Government substituted a new method of ensuring that the farmer got an adequate return for goods produced. Deficiency payments were made to farmers if the gap between the actual market price and the price guaranteed by the government widened. In this way cheap foreign food could also be imported without harming the British farmer. The main exception to this system of deficiency payments was milk, the price of which was still supported by the Milk Marketing Board.

---

1 *What did Tom Williams mean when he said that farmers 'must not be let down as they were after the 1914–18 War'?*

2 *Why was it unusual for a Labour Government to bring in a bill of this type, guaranteeing fair prices for the farmer? What made them do it?*

3 *Argue the case **either** for **or** against the idea that the farmers had been 'feather-bedded' by the Labour Government. Use facts and sources taken from the history of British farming since 1850 to support your argument.*

In time, government policy on guaranteed prices changed. As farming became more efficient and the cost of subsidising farming increased, the Ministry of Agriculture began to restrict its support on farm prices. There was to be a limit to the public funding of agriculture.

Mechanisation and Efficiency

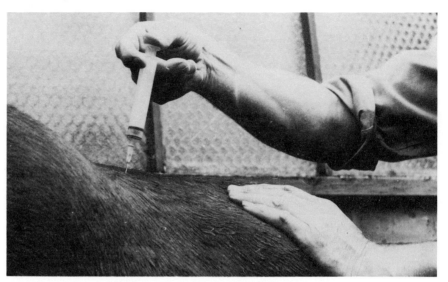

Injecting an animal on a farm

Government action helped to make farming more efficient. The Agriculture Act of 1957 gave government grants to help farmers erect new buildings and make similar improvements to their farms.

The increased prosperity of the farmers encouraged manufacturers to develop new products to increase productivity. New machines were devised, and new fertilisers and new strains of crop were introduced. British farming between 1945 and 1980 underwent a revolution every bit as drastic and as effective as the Agricultural Revolution between 1700 and 1850. Farm output shot up. Fields which had produced 2 or 3 tonnes of wheat per hectare in 1945 were producing 5 to 8 tonnes per hectare in the 1980s. Overall, wheat yields doubled between 1950 and 1980. Milk yields also rose from an average of 2,000 litres per cow to as much as 5,500 litres in some cases – double the output thirty years earlier.

Labour-saving dairies were erected and by 1973 over half of Britain's milk was collected by bulk tanker instead of in churns. Better breeds of cow produced better milk. New breeds of cattle – notably the French Limousin and Charollais – increased meat output. Farmers used far more artificial fertiliser in the early 1980s than they did in the 1950s – as much as ten times more according to one Suffolk farmer interviewed on television in 1984. At the same time the output of produce per farm worker increased five or sixfold after the war, whilst the number of farm workers fell by about 70 per cent between 1951 and 1981. Farmers were so successful that they made Britain self-sufficient in barley, eggs and pigs.

Farms were also better managed and run, partly because farmers now had access to a wealth of informed technical advice from the sales representatives of the big fertiliser and animal-feed manufacturers, from farming magazines, radio and television broadcasts, and by attending courses at farm institutes and agricultural colleges. Farming itself was more scientific. Microcomputers were increasingly applied to the study of farm problems – controlling the quantity and quality of feed to dairy herds, allocating fertilisers, controlling farm accounts and maintaining records. The government also played its part in the development of the new scientific agriculture. The Agricultural Development and Advisory Service (ADAS) tried different experiments, ran experimental farms and gave farmers invaluable economic help as well as scientific advice.

Among the many benefits of modern technology have been:

● the development of chemical sprays, weedkillers and pesticides to prevent disease and kill insect pests;

● the development of high-yielding strains of wheat, barley and other crops;

● the introduction of many new fertilisers – to the extent that many arable farmers no longer rotate their crops but continue to grow cereals year after year in the same fields;

● the development of new techniques in veterinary medicine – not only pro-longing the lives of animals, but also artificially stimulating the production of fatter animals;

● the development of more powerful tractors and of many new machines – capable of picking peas, potatoes and sugar beet, ploughing several furrows at a time, making huge round bales of hay or straw, making silage from green grass, spreading manure and fertilisers, and spraying chemicals;

● the bringing of mains water and electricity to outlying farms, so that farming communities no longer feel isolated from society.

Part of the price paid for increased efficiency has been the introduction of factory farming methods, such as the fattening of beef cattle in conditions which restrict the movement of the animals (to reduce weight loss) or the large-scale production of oven-ready chickens. Working conditions on the land have also changed. The modern farm worker is a highly skilled technician.

1 *What have been the advantages and disadvantages to Britain of the revolution in farming since 1945?*

2 *Why have environmentalists (people who are concerned about the problems of pollution and conservation) been worried by some of the developments which have taken place in farming in the last forty years or so?*

The Impact of the European Economic Community

British membership of the EEC or Common Market (see page 152) has also had a profound effect on British farming, with its Common Agricultural Policy (CAP), which aimed to:

● increase agricultural productivity;

● ensure a fair standard of living for people living off the land;

● keep market prices steady;

● ensure adequate food supplies at fair prices to the consumer.

The EEC has supported its farmers by controlling the prices they obtain for their foodstuffs. This has usually been achieved by giving each product a target price – such as those for cereals, sugar beet, milk and other dairy products. If the market price falls below this target price, then the EEC buys up part of the surplus produce from the farmers until scarcity of supply causes the market price to rise once more. Obviously the quality and quantity of the harvest, the efficiency of the farmers and the demand from the consumer all play a part in determining what the market price is and how it differs from product to product. Where there is substantial over-production large surpluses are accumulated by the EEC. These are called the beef, wheat and butter 'mountains' and the wine and milk 'lakes'. In theory, this food can be resold on the market in times of scarcity. In practice, some of it has been sold to the Soviet Union at rock bottom prices.

EEC grain mountain

Another aspect of the CAP has been the financial help it has given to farmers to encourage them to modernise the industry or even to leave farming altogether. Unfortunately, each of the member countries has tended to manipulate, or even ignore, the CAP to suit its own farmers, consumers and taxpayers. Since a large proportion of the EEC budget is spent on the CAP it has tended to dominate people's thinking about the Common Market. Overall its effect has been to raise the effective price of food to the consumer by:

- keeping food prices artificially above the market price – since cheaper world food can only be imported into the EEC after paying customs duties and import levies which raise it to EEC price levels;

- lowering the amount of money in the consumer's pocket – through the increased taxation needed to pay the EEC budget.

The CAP tends to favour the larger, more efficient farmers, and British cereal farmers, in particular, have done well. As a result, marginal lands have been brought under the plough – even though conditions in Britain are not always ideal for corn growing. Another consequence has been the elimination of hedges and fences to create huge prairie-like fields which make it more economical to run combine harvesters and powerful tractors.

The cost of the CAP to the consumer has been high. In 1980 it was estimated that British farmers were being paid nearly £2,000 million in EEC and British government subsidies or guaranteed high food prices.

FURTHER QUESTIONS AND EXERCISES

1 *What were the causes of the Great Depression in British farming in the years after 1873? What effect did it have on the countryside? How did some farmers recover from the effects of the Depression?*

A NEW ARCH-BISHOP.

2 *The Bishop of Manchester wrote to* The Times *in April 1874 in support of farm labourers in the Eastern Counties. Explain this cartoon from* Punch *which was published on 13 April 1874.*

3 *Explain what is meant by each of the following and describe its importance to the farmer:*

(a) protection,

(b) Free Trade,

(c) government subsidies,

(d) the Common Agricultural Policy,

(e) the marketing boards.

4 *Imagine you are an 80-year-old farmer or farm worker in 1920. You started work on a farm as a child of ten. Write an account of the changes you have seen in a lifetime of farming in East Anglia.*

5 *Why did successive British governments fail to protect the British farming industry against foreign competition between 1846 and 1931? What effect did this have on farming and on the countryside? Why was this policy changed?*

Graph comparing wheat production in Great Britain with imports of foreign corn, 1873–1973

6 *Write notes on this graph, describing and explaining the fluctuations in trend lines showing (a) wheat production, (b) the import of foreign corn into Great Britain, between the late nineteenth century and the present day.*

7 *In the late nineteenth century, the agricultural historian James Caird commented that 'in nine years there have been seven defective harvests'. To which nine years was he referring? What effect did this have on British farming? Why was its importance exaggerated at the time? What was the real cause of the Great Depression in farming?*

8 *What changes have taken place in British farming in the last twenty years and how have they affected (a) the farmer and farm worker, (b) the consumer?*

Chapter Two

Industry

INTRODUCTION

Panoramic view of industrial Leeds in The Graphic, *18 July 1885*

'Electricity is the secret of progress. It is not too much to say that as the last century saw the development of steam as the great motive force both on land and sea, so the new century will see steam supplanted to a very large extent by electricity, which will undoubtedly become the great mechanical power of the future.'

W. J. Wintle, The Harmsworth Magazine, 1901

1 Look at the picture showing the Leeds skyline in 1885. How do you think a modern picture of Leeds might differ from this? What changes have taken place since 1885?

2 How accurate was the forecast, in 1901, that electricity would be the 'secret of progress' in the twentieth century?

3 Can any other form of power claim to have been as important as electricity in the twentieth century?

On 1 May 1851, Queen Victoria opened the Great Exhibition in the Crystal Palace. It was probably the most successful exhibition ever held in Britain and millions of people went to see it, many of them from overseas. The Great Exhibition was a showcase for British industry. A gigantic display of machinery, marvellous inventions and sparkling new ideas proved to British and foreign visitors alike that Britain was the 'Workshop of the World'.

A hundred years later, the Festival of Britain was also held in London, to celebrate the centenary of the Great Exhibition. Britain, although by then no longer dominant in the world, was still the leading industrial nation in Europe. But by 1986, only the bravest optimist looked to the industrial future of Britain with any confidence. One expert even forecast that Britain would change from being an industrial nation to one providing services (such as banking, insurance and tourism).

Despite new sources of power, new raw materials, new inventions and new industries, Britain was no longer an industrial giant. In this chapter you will see what happened to change the bright industrial future that most Victorians, in 1850, would have forecast for Britain in the years ahead.

INDUSTRY IN THE LATE NINETEENTH AND EARLY TWENTIETH CENTURIES

The phenomenal growth of British industry in the middle years of the nineteenth century is well illustrated in these production statistics for the four most important industries at that time.

	1840 (tonnes)	1880 (tonnes)
Coal production	30,000,000	147,000,000
Iron production	1,400,000	7,700,000
Ships launched	120,000	660,000
Cotton imports	200,000	650,000

1 *Draw a graph from these statistics to show how British industry grew between 1840 and 1880.*

2 *By how many times did each of these industries grow in the space of forty years?*

Reasons for the Dominance of British Industry

Britain had become the 'Workshop of the World' for a number of reasons. Briefly these were as follows.

1. Power and Mineral Resources

Britain originally had rich seams of excellent coal near the surface. By 1851, most of the cheaply mined coal had gone, although the deeper reserves were still enormous. Most of the rich iron ore found near the coal had also gone, but there were still large deposits of a lower grade of iron ore.

2. Transport

The early development of canals, navigable rivers and railways gave Britain an unrivalled network of communications facilitating the cheap transport of fuel and raw materials to factories. But by 1851, other countries had also started to build railways, often employing British engineers and contractors to do the work and using iron rails made in Britain.

3. Inventors

Most of the great inventions before 1851 had been British, such as the steam engine, the railway train, the coke-burning blast furnace, the power loom, spinning jenny, and water frame. After 1851, many of the greatest inventions, such as the motor car and the aeroplane, were made by German, French and American inventors.

4. Population

The rapid growth in the British population, which occurred between 1750 and 1870, increased the domestic market for manufactures and provided the extra factory workers who were needed as industries grew. After 1870, population growth began to slow down – at a time when the population of the United States grew rapidly.

5. An Island of Peace

In contrast to other developed countries, Britain escaped invasion and revolution between 1700 and 1870. Unlike Germany (split up into different states before 1871) or the United States (split between North and South in the Civil War of the early 1860s), Britain had a strong central government. After 1871, however, there were no good political reasons why the United States and Germany should not also make full use of their abundant natural resources. Britain no longer had a political advantage over her rivals.

6. Finance

Britain was lucky in having people with capital (money) to invest in industry. Shares in many companies could be bought on the London Stock Exchange. The development of the Bank of England and the growth of hundreds of banks also helped to make it possible for companies to borrow money in order to buy machines and pay for new buildings. In the late nineteenth century, however, an increasing amount of British money also helped foreign companies to build factories and railways. It was a good investment, but it also assisted the development of industries abroad to rival those of Britain.

7. Empire

The growth of the British Empire provided industry with raw materials, such as wool from Australia, and the peoples of the Empire gave British factories a huge market for their exports. In return, some of the profits were invested in Empire enterprises. Increasingly, however, the peoples of the Empire began to develop their own industries.

The Coal-mining Industry

'Twenty-two trainloads of best steam coal waiting to charge the Mauretania *with energy for one voyage',* The Sphere, *30 April 1910. Which workers in Britain suffered when ocean liners and cargo ships changed from coal to oil?*

Coal was by far the most important industry in Britain in the late nineteenth and early twentieth centuries, if measured by the value of its annual output. In 1907 this was estimated to be £106 million (at least £4,000 million by modern standards). This was well over twice the value of the output from coal's principal rivals – the engineering and cotton industries. But all was not well with the coal industry, and slogans such as 'The Mines for the Nation' and 'Enterprise for the public and not for the profiteers' were already being heard in the 1890s.

> 'The modern cry for the nationalisation of our coal-mines, is evidence of the knowledge that coal is the first necessity of industrial existence under modern conditions.

What seems to us more probable than the early exhaustion of our coal-fields is our displacement from the position of first place among the coal-suppliers of the world. We may call our normal output 185 million tons. The average price is 6s 9d [34p] per ton at the pit's mouth. The number of persons employed in coal-mining is 640,660.

The American output in 1894 was over 165 million tons, and it has increased about sixty per cent within ten years. The American coal-mines give employment to about 365,000 persons, and the average price of the annual output is equal to only 5s 4d [27p] per ton at the pit-mouth.'

'The Coal of the World' in Chambers's Journal, 5 October 1895

---

1 What was the average annual output of coal per miner in 1895 (a) in Britain, (b) in the United States?
2 How much dearer was British coal than American coal?
3 The writer of this article warned that Britain could lose her position as the world's leading supplier of coal. Why did he think this might happen?

On the face of it, the coal-mining industry had little to worry about. In 1870 Britain's nearest rivals, the United States (36 million tonnes) and Germany (34 million tonnes), were easily outstripped by Britain's coal industry (112 million tonnes). In 1897, when British coal output exceeded 200 million tonnes for the first time, production was still accelerating, reaching an all-time production peak of 292 million tonnes in 1913. But by then German output of coal (including brown coal) was not far behind with 277 million tonnes, and the United States, with 517 million tonnes, was way ahead. Nonetheless, coal exports were still important, amounting to about a third of total output in 1913. In Britain in the 1880s, the main users of coal were: steam engines in factories 37 per cent; domestic fires 27 per cent; coal-gas manufacture 14 per cent; railway locomotives and steamships 14 per cent.

But relations between landowners (paid a royalty for every tonne of coal dug from their estates) and managers on the one side and workers on the other, were not happy. Neither side trusted the other and industrial disputes were frequent between 1890 and 1930 (see Chapter 7). Part of the problem lay in the fact that responsibility for the industry was shared by 1,000 separate mining companies running 3,000 collieries. Some were old family mines with thin, depleted coal seams. Few owners had the money to invest in new coal-cutting machinery. By 1914, only 8 per cent of Britain's coal was cut by machines, the rest was still extracted by pick and shovel. Working conditions were poor. Over 1,000 miners a year lost their lives and as many as 500 were injured on a typical working day – mostly from roof falls.

Pit disaster at the Llanerch Colliery in South Wales, The Illustrated London News, *15 February 1890. How does this Victorian colliery differ from the modern colliery shown on page 71?*

Lancashire 'pit-brow women', The Illustrated London News, *28 May 1887*

Even those who successfully avoided physical injury often had their health ruined through undue exposure to coal dust and damp. Wages were low and in no way an adequate reward for the dangers and hardships undergone by the men. In 1900, one in ten of all underground workers was still under sixteen years of age. A small number of women, too, worked in the collieries, but at the pit head, sorting coal according to its quality.

'The sympathy of sensible people, not unmixed with amusement, wonder and a trifle of admiration, has been recently expressed in favour of the sturdy Lancashire lasses, who came up to London and called upon the Home Secretary, asking him to resist the proposed clauses of the Mines Regulation Bill.

Women and girls never go down into the pit at a colliery, but they are employed at the pit-brow, the mound of earth and shale around the mouth of the shaft, in the work of screening or sifting the smaller coal.'

The Illustrated London News, *28 May 1887*

---

1 *What was a 'pit-brow woman'? What job did she do?*

2 *What proposal do you think the Government was considering? Why? What did the writer think about the proposal?*

3 *Imagine you are a reader of this magazine in 1887. Write a letter to the Editor expressing your point of view.*

The Growth and Development of the Iron and Steel Industry

Some of the most significant industrial changes of the nineteenth century affected the iron and steel industry. Their subsequent effect on steel production in Germany and the United States hastened the eclipse of Britain as the 'Workshop of the World'.

The first great breakthrough of the mid-nineteenth century came in 1856, with the development by Henry Bessemer of a method of making steel by forcing air through molten pig iron. For the first time, good quality steel was cheap and plentiful. This was of incalculable value in the development of the engineering industries.

The main advantage of the Bessemer Converter was that it made a substantial amount of steel in a relatively short time. Its main disadvantage was that it could not be used with iron made from ores containing phosphorus. As a result, only the ironworks of Cumbria, such as those at Barrow and Workington, were able to use the Bessemer Converter with iron made from local ores. Other British iron and steel plants had to use iron ores imported from Sweden and Spain. This had an important effect on the location of the iron and steel industry. The older iron and steelworks had been situated inland on the coalfield. The use of foreign iron ores made it more sensible to build new steelworks at the coast, either along the estuary of a river or at a port.

Within a few years, the Bessemer Converter had a rival, the open-hearth furnace, developed by a German-born scientist called William Siemens, who had come to work in Britain. The open-hearth process was easier to control than the Bessemer Converter, and eventually took its place. But, like Bessemer's process, the open-hearth furnace could not use iron derived from phosphoric iron ores.

Blast furnaces in South Wales in 1885, contemporary print by A. Morrow

In 1877, yet another new method of making steel was developed in Britain. This was the Gilchrist-Thomas basic steel-making process, invented by Sidney Gilchrist-Thomas, a police court clerk, and his cousin Percy Gilchrist. At last, phosphoric iron ores could be used to make steel. The 'basic' method meant lining the Bessemer Converter or the open-hearth furnace with dolomite (a limestone).

The development of all three steel-making processes played a major part in the growth of Middlesbrough as an iron and steel town in the nineteenth century, from marshland in 1829 to a thriving industrial town of 91,000 people in 1901 and the centre of an important industrial district (now called Teesside).

Middlesbrough was situated halfway between the phosphoric iron ores of the Cleveland Hills (to the south) and the excellent coking coal of the Durham Coalfield (to the north). In addition, there was Pennine limestone (to the west) and access to the sea and foreign ores (to the east).

The Bessemer process was first used on Teesside in 1875, with imported haematite iron ore from Spain. At that time, iron production was more important than steel, since railways still used iron rails and the rapidly growing shipbuilding industry had not yet changed to steel plates. Then in 1879, the Gilchrist-Thomas basic steel-making process was successfully demonstrated in Middlesbrough for the first time.

> 'The progress of Middlesbrough has been marvellous. It has quarried out of the hills and from the dales of Cleveland millions of tons of ore yearly; it has built in its own bounds about two-score huge smelting furnaces; whilst rolling-mills, steel works, plate-mills, engineering establishments, have arisen to use the raw iron made yearly.
>   The river is flanked by the furnaces, converters, foundries; the lines of railway are never weary of the rumble of the wagons of coal and coke, ore and limestone, iron and steel.'
>
> *'Ironopolis and its people' in* Cassell's Family Magazine, *1889*

---

1 Why did the author of the article call Middlesbrough 'Ironopolis' instead of 'Steelopolis'?

2 Why were some of the 'wagons' filled with limestone?

3 What were the advantages of Middlesbrough as a site for an iron and steelworks (a) before 1856, (b) between 1856 and 1877, (c) after 1877?

Unfortunately, it was the foreign steel producers who made the more effective use of the Gilchrist-Thomas process. Many British steel producers continued to use imported, rich, non-phosphoric ores from Spain and Sweden, rather than change over to the 'basic' process using the plentiful but low-grade phosphoric iron ores of the East Midlands. It was only in the twentieth century that Scunthorpe in Lincolnshire and Corby in Northamptonshire began to grow rapidly, using the phosphoric iron ores close by.

Foreign Competition

Meanwhile, the British iron and steel industry, once the world's main producer, was overtaken by both Germany and the United States. On the face of it, Britain was making more iron and steel than ever before and the people of Middlesbrough could note with pride, that foreigners came to Teesside to see the basic process for themselves. One of Middlesbrough's great ironmasters said that the town 'was besieged by the combined forces of Belgium, France, Prussia, Austria and America'.

But European countries (such as France) could now make effective use of the phosphoric iron ores of northern Europe and supply their own industries with steel. They could also compete with Britain in the export markets of the world.

The United States pulled ahead of Britain in 1890 and Germany did likewise in 1896. German steel production rose from 1 million tonnes in 1883 (UK production two million tonnes) to 18 million tonnes in 1913 (UK 8 million tonnes). The reasons were partly geographical, since they had richer and more accessible coalfields, extensive reserves of iron ore and a bigger home demand for iron and steel; partly technological, since they had newer and more up-to-date plant and some automatic machinery; and partly political, since both Germany and the United States imposed tariffs on foreign steel imports, unlike Britain where Free Trade was still the guiding principle.

CAUGHT NAPPING!

This cartoon was published in *Punch* in September 1896. The following rhyme accompanied the picture:

> 'There was an old lady as I've heard tell,
> She went to market her goods for to sell,
> She went to market on a market day
> And she fell asleep on the world's highway.
> By came a pedlar – German – and stout,
> And he cut her petticoats all round about.'

1 We can assume that Queen Victoria was not amused by this
   cartoon. Write an explanatory paragraph, telling her what the
   cartoonist was driving at.

2 Why was Germany's achievement in steel manufacture a matter
   of concern to people in Britain at that time? Were they justified
   in worrying?

3 Use the statistics already quoted in this chapter to disprove the
   idea that British industry declined in the period before 1914.
   Why, then, did Punch publish the cartoon CAUGHT
   NAPPING?

The Growth and Development of the Shipbuilding Industry

Shipbuilding yards on
the Clyde in 1878,
contemporary print by
W. A. Donnelly

1 Imagine you are standing next to the artist who drew this picture
   in 1878. Write a detailed description of this scene, highlighting
   the things it tells you about the Clyde shipbuilding industry and
   its effect on the environment.

2 How had the shipbuilding industry changed by 1910, when the
   photograph opposite was taken?

Shipbuilding yard on the Tyne in 1910

Until the accession of Queen Victoria in 1837, the British shipbuilding industry, with its shipyards on the Thames and other estuaries, concentrated mainly on building wooden sailing ships in competition with the United States, which had better and more plentiful timber and better ship designs. But with the launching of the wooden paddle steamer, the *Great Western*, in 1837, and of the iron steamship, the *Great Britain* (with its screw propeller), in 1843, the industry changed. By the 1890s Britain's shipyards were building 80 per cent of the world's ships.

The rise of the iron steamship gave shipyards on coalfields a big advantage, and those close to the ironworks which produced iron, and later steel, plates began to dominate – such as Birkenhead on the Mersey, Barrow-in-Furness, Tyneside and the shipbuilding yards on the River Clyde. British merchant ships were regarded as being the best in the world and the Royal Navy was by far the strongest fleet at sea. British shipyards even equipped other world powers with their warships, such as those of Russia and Japan which engaged in the naval battle of the Tsushima Straits in 1905. British naval ships were faster and cheaper than any in the world. British shipyard workers were said to be twice as productive as the Americans and five times as productive as the Japanese.

But this reputation for quality and productivity was not to last, and by 1914 Britain's share of the world market had dropped to 60 per cent. In 1983 it was about 3 per cent.

One of the reasons for this relative decline is the fact that the industry was dominated by a large number of small family firms. Shipbuilders were reluctant to change the methods which had served them well in the past, even though effective labour-saving methods had been developed. Nor were the trade unions prepared to co-operate with measures designed to cut jobs. Demarcation disputes were common, since the different trades involved in the building of a ship jealously preserved their skills. Each of the different trades had its own trade union. Disputes between unions, rather than with the employers, often led to delays in the completion of ships and to the cancellation of overseas orders for new ships.

By 1914, oil-fired engines were beginning to replace steam engines in ships. Oil was easier to carry, cleaner to use, easier to control and more efficient than coal. Soon oil rather than coal would be the universal fuel to power shipping. But Britain was not then an oil producer. She was beginning to lose the edge she once had over other shipbuilding nations.

The Textile Industry

Although working conditions had changed since the days of the early nineteenth century, when child labour was common, textile workers still had many grievances. In the 1890s, the woolcombers of Bradford complained about long hours (64 hours a week or more), low wages, insecurity of employment, insanitary working conditions and tyrannical actions on the part of their employers.

> 'A woolcombing room is usually about 100 ft [around 30 m] long, and in such a room sixty machines, running at full speed are at work. The noise is deafening – a grinding, screeching noise; the whole place vibrates. The heat is very great, and the air is full of a yellow, noisome [offensive] dust. And the smell – the horror of it when it comes to you through the woolsorting factories, from the heated rooms in which the wool is scoured of the grease.'
>
> *R. H. Sherard,* Pearson's Magazine, *1896*

By contrast, another writer said that the daily life of a Lancashire cotton worker was hardly 'irksome or even laborious':

> 'The machinery employed is so perfect now that the operatives have very little to do, except to "mind" the jenny or the loom. The work is likewise "clean work". There are more pale faces in a cotton-mill than one cares to see, but, except for the fine dust or "fluff" which flies about, the atmosphere cannot be considered unhealthy; there is plenty of ventilation in summer-time, and in winter the entire factory is heated by means of steam or hot-water pipes.'
>
> *'North-Countryman',* Cassell's Family Magazine, *1882*

At work in a woollen factory in 1883, contemporary print by A. E. Emslie

Half-timer attending a cotton-winding machine in a cotton mill in 1884, contemporary print by A. Morrow

1 What was a 'half-timer'? What do you think she did for the other half of her time?

2 How do these sources deal with the problem of noise in textile mills?

3 *How do the writers differ in the way they describe the working conditions to be found in textile mills in the 1880s and 1890s? Give examples.*

4 *Do these sources show any signs of being biased in any way? Do you think it likely that 'North-Countryman' would have described the woolcombing room in the same way that R. H. Sherard did? If not, why not?*

5 *Do the pictures support or cast doubt in any way on the evidence provided by the written descriptions?*

6 *Use these pictures and sources to write a general description of the working conditions to be found in a typical textile mill in the 1880s and 1890s.*

The Lancashire cotton industry had other problems to face in the next fifty years. Like coal, steel and ships, the industry met fierce competition – from foreign cotton industries and from the newly invented artificial fibres, such as rayon and nylon.

In the late nineteenth century, most of Lancashire's vast output of cotton cloth was exported, contributing about a quarter of Britain's earnings from the export trade. Much of the cotton cloth went to hotter lands than the British Isles – to India, southern China, South America and Africa. Towns like Blackburn specialised in producing cheaper cloths for the Indian market (which took half of Britain's cotton exports in 1914). But the industry was very vulnerable – as you can see in this extract:

'Shrewd observers have realised for years that nothing could avert eventual disaster from the Lancashire cotton trade. For India possesses the tremendous advantages of producing cotton on her own soil, and commanding an abundant supply of cheap labour. She only needed modern machinery to enable her to oust Lancashire from the huge Indian market, and probably from other Asian markets. Year by year the smoke curling from the chimneys of Indian cotton-mills increases in volume. It writes the doom of Lancashire.'

'The Peril of Lancashire' by S. N. Singh in The London Magazine, *1913*

In 1880, India had about 50 cotton mills with 1,400,000 spindles, 13,000 looms and about 50,000 workers. By 1910, this had increased to 220 mills with 5,800,000 spindles, 75,000 looms and 220,000 workers. Japan was also exporting cotton goods to India by this time, but Lancashire's mill owners tended to shrug off facts like these because the Lancashire cotton industry gave employment to about a million workers and the mills were equipped with over 50,000,000 spindles.

'My lad never again let anybody in Lancashire hear you talk this childish stuff about foreign competition. It's just twaddle. In the first place, we've got the only climate in the world where cotton piece goods in any quantity can ever be produced. In the second place, no foreign Johnnies can ever be bred that can spin and weave like Lancashire lasses and lads. In the third place, there are more spindles in Oldham than in all the rest of the world put together. Foreigners could never find the brains Lancashire cotton men have for the job. We've been making all the world's cotton cloth that matters for more years than I can tell, and we always shall.'

Lancashire cotton manufacturer, 1911

Other Lancashire cotton manufacturers took a more realistic, if unhelpful, view. An Indian who wanted to work in a cotton mill to learn the business was told by the owner:

'We in Lancashire do not want to encourage the building of mills in India; we want to supply India with manufactured cotton goods, it is against our interests to teach you or other young Indians our business in order that you may take it away from us.'

Letter quoted by The Times of India *in about 1912*

1 *What was the 'Peril of Lancashire'? Is there any indication of bias or distorted judgement in this extract? Which statements, if any, are (a) fact, (b) opinion?*

2 *How important was the Indian cotton industry in 1910, compared with the Lancashire cotton industry? Had S.N.Singh sufficient evidence to talk about the 'doom of Lancashire'?*

3 *What arguments were used by the cotton manufacturer in 1911, to dismiss the idea that foreign competition could ever be a threat to the cotton industry of Lancashire? Write a reply to counter his arguments.*

4 *Do you think the mill owner in the last extract was justified in refusing to let an Indian worker learn the cotton trade in his mill? What argument would you have used to try to change his mind?*

NEW INDUSTRIES, 1850–1914

After 1860, many new products were invented and new industries were begun – but in Europe and America, at first, rather than in Britain. A Belgian-born French engineer (Lenoir) built the first reliable internal-combustion engine; two Germans (Daimler and Benz) built the first motor car; and two Americans (Orville and Wilbur Wright) flew the first aircraft. The Americans established the world's first large-scale automobile industry and developed the idea of the production line. The Germans were quick to take the lead in the manufacture of chemicals and synthetic fibres, and in the production of electricity and electrical machinery.

Many of the new industries no longer needed large supplies of coal to operate steam-powered machinery. They used electricity, gas or oil as fuel instead. The cost of the raw materials in the new products was often small compared with the price of the finished article, so it was sometimes more important to build the factory near the consumer – such as close to the major centres of population, or in places with good access to railways, roads and water transport. Advantages which had once helped Britain to become the 'Workshop of the World' were becoming less important. Location on a coalfield was no longer essential for a new factory.

Other countries were often in a better position to develop the new inventions. Britain was not then an oil producer and the country still had its coal mines, so there was less incentive to develop the internal-combustion engine. Nor was there the same urge to use electricity, when coal was still available and cheap. Above all, it was hard to change old industries into new, to retrain workers skilled in the traditional industries to do new jobs, or to move workers and resources from the old sites of industry to the new.

The Chemical Industry

One of the most important of the new industries was the manufacture of chemicals. At first this was based mainly on salt as the raw material and coal as the fuel (later coal was also used as a raw material). This is why a chemical industry developed in the St Helens, Widnes and Warrington area, using coal from the Lancashire coalfield and salt from Cheshire.

Salt was also discovered on Teesside in 1863, when an ironworks, which was drilling for a supply of pure water, came across a bed of salt. In 1870, the Tees Salt Company was formed to exploit the deposits, and this later became the foundation of the great chemical industry which dominates Teesside today. A writer in 1883 correctly forecast that, 'With cheap fuel near, the brine that will be made from the salt may build up new and great industries in the county of coal.' The industry processed the raw materials which supplied other important industries with their chemicals – such as those needed for the manufacture of soap, glass, dyestuffs, bleaching powder, drugs and disinfectants.

In 1890, Messrs Lever Brothers' soap works at Port Sunlight, in Cheshire, was featured in an article in *The Illustrated London News*. Photographs showed the science laboratory, where the company's scientists did their research on new products, and the newly built houses for the workmen in Port Sunlight, a model town. They were built on semi-detached lines in blocks of two or three houses, along spacious, well-lit avenues, and had large front gardens. The chemical industry had a brand new image and was expanding fast. In 1841 there were fewer than 20,000 chemical workers in Britain, compared with 86,000 in 1901, 226,000 in 1931 and 518,000 by 1971.

But despite this, conditions in some chemical works were as bad as in any works in Britain. In 1896, Robert H. Sherard (see page 42) visited the alkali workers of Widnes and St Helens, near Liverpool.

'My time was passed almost entirely in the society of the workmen. I visited their cottages and conversed with their wives, comparing everywhere the statements of these and those, in an ardent quest of truth. I avoided contact with the masters as far as possible, and am in no way indebted to any of them for assistance in my enterprise.

The foul gases which belched forth night and day from the many factories, rot the clothes, the teeth, and, in the end, the bodies of the workers, have killed every tree and every blade of grass for miles around. One sees numerous and fine children, but never any old people. The certainty of a shortened life, the possibility of a sudden and terrible death, and constant risks of painful accidents are well known to all the chemical workers in these alkali factories. The men who pack the bleaching powder work with goggles on their eyes and twenty thicknesses of flannel over their mouths.'

R. H. Sherard, Pearson's Magazine, *1896*

Packing bleaching powder in an alkali works, from R. H. Sherard's article in Pearson's Magazine, *1896*

Sherard said that toothless, asthmatic, half-blind workers broke up the stones from which sulphur was extracted, whilst the salt-cake men could be recognised from the blackened stumps of their teeth – such that they could not eat the crusts on bread. The firm had introduced an eight-hour day but even this was not appreciated by one worker, 'They go swaggering about their eight hours but they put more on us than before.' A trade-union leader claimed, 'The men have to do twelve hours work in eight hours.'

1 What does the clothing worn by the workers tell you about the risks they ran in their jobs in the chemical industry?

2 Can we be certain that Robert H. Sherard was writing with first-hand knowledge? Is this a primary or a secondary source of information? Is there any sign of bias, distortion of facts, questionable opinion or exaggeration in his account? Was he right to avoid 'contact with the masters as far as possible'?

3 By how many times did the number of employees in the chemical industry increase between 1871 and 1971?

The Electrical Industry

In the 1880s and 1890s, electricity was the most-talked-about and exciting new development in technology. It was a period of fevered activity for inventors, applying the new source of power to a wide range of applications. In 1892, for instance, *Cassell's Magazine* reported a number of new inventions during the year, including an electric arc lamp, electro-magnetic photography, electric streetlamps, electric bells, an electric travelling crane, electric fans, an electric fire engine, the electro-photographic thief detector and, in Canada, an electric census machine, using punched cards.

The first two power stations in the world were both British. A small hydro-electric power station was opened at Godalming in Surrey in 1881, whilst the first to burn coal (to make steam power) produced electricity in London in 1882. Two years later a British engineer, Charles A. Parsons, invented the modern steam-turbine engine, which made it possible to make electricity effectively and economically on a large scale. Yet despite these British innovations, industry was slow to develop them in Britain, compared with Germany and the United States.

'American ingenuity has undoubtedly taken the lead in making motors of all kinds. A locomotive in which electricity instead of steam is the power was built for the elevated railroads in New York city, and is expected to possess considerable advantage – besides economy – over the present steam locomotives.

One of the most conspicuous applications of electric heating is the electric smelting furnace. The Cowles Electrical Furnace has been in practical manufacturing operation at Lockport, New York, for a year or more.'

S. S. Wheeler, The Illustrated London News, 7 April 1888

1 What 'considerable advantage' did the electric locomotive have compared with the steam locomotive?

2 Why do you think steam locomotives lasted until the 1960s in Britain? Why was Britain slow to electrify the railways?

3 What were the advantages of using electricity as the main source of power in factories? What were the disadvantages to Britain of such a change?

Electricity made relatively little immediate impact on British industry, partly because many streets, public buildings and houses were already lit by coal gas, so the demand for electric light was not pressing. Nor was there a great demand for electricity as a fuel, in a country where coal was abundant and relatively cheap. In any case, manufacturers saw no reason to convert existing steam-powered machines to run on electricity instead.

The Motor Industry

The motor car not only transformed the countryside (see Chapter 3), it also stimulated the growth of a remarkable new group of industries. There were many different motor car factories in the 1900s, most of them with unfamiliar names. In 1907, for instance, Argyll Motors made cars in a splendid new factory on a site near Loch Lomond (close to Glasgow), in which 'the factory system followed involves close inspection at every stage with rigorous tests'. The machines were turned by 'a maze of belts and shafting' and driven by thirteen powerful gas-powered engines. The company's 4,000 workers could make up to 3,000 cars a year and railway sidings linked the factory to the Dumbarton and Balloch Joint Railway. The employees were well looked after.

'The entire factory is warmed by hot air. Electric light, manufactured on the premises, is used everywhere, and there is an ample supply of hot water in every department. It is the first industrial concern in this country to establish a properly organised recreation department.'

The Illustrated London News, 1906

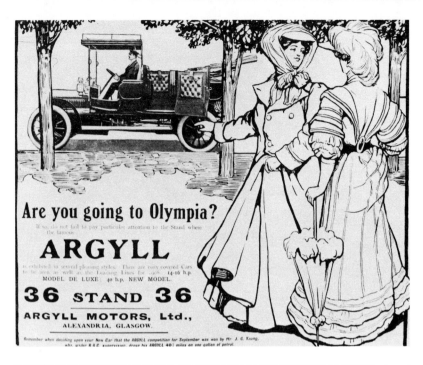

Advertisement for
Argyll Motors in 1907

1 *What sort of motor cars do you think the Argyll Company*
   produced? Were they for the rich or for the average person?
   Which modern cars are made in a similar way?

2 *What forms of power were used in this motor-car factory in*
   1906? Why was it built near the railway? Were there any
   compelling reasons why it should be sited near Loch Lomond?

3 *What was unusual about the amenities provided for the*
   employees of the company? What do you think R. H. Sherard
   (page 47) would have said?

The success of many of the new motor-car companies was not to last. In America, Henry Ford was already developing a range of cars, which led to the introduction of the moving assembly line. Instead of a worker doing a number of different jobs, he remained in one place and did one task over and over again as the assembly line (or production line) brought his work to him. On average a car which had previously taken twelve hours to assemble could now be made in less than two hours. By 1914, these methods were already being used in Manchester at the Ford works in Trafford Park, which was producing 10,000 cars a year.

The motor industry also created a large number of subsidiary industries making different car components, such as the Dunlop Tyres factories which were already making rubber tyres on a large scale by 1907.

Light Industries

Many light industries supplied consumers with everyday goods, processed foods, and other commodities. In *Living London*, 1905, George Sims wrote about London's new factories.

> 'There are factories for the preparation of almost everything that mortal man can desire – for tinned meats, jams, biscuits, pickles, cheap clothing, hats, babies' food, mineral waters, sweets, cakes, soaps, matches, tobacco, pipes, jewellery, upholstery, leather, pottery – indeed it is difficult to call to mind a single article in everyday use in the manufacture of which the Metropolis is not concerned.'

Most of these industries were market oriented. This means that they were situated near potential customers. Innovations and new machines which speeded up production had also been introduced in many industries by 1914, reducing costs and bringing down prices. For instance, in the 1880s, glass bottles were blown individually by skilled craftsmen – as many as 3,000 by one worker in a single day. But by 1907, an automatic glass-making machine in Manchester could take molten glass from a furnace and feed it automatically into a revolving mould to make 2,500 bottles an hour.

'Sweated' Industries

The 'sweating system' – matchbox making and shoemaking, The Illustrated London News, *26 May 1888*

Despite the advance of the factory system, many people were still employed at home or in small workshops – often working long hours in poor working conditions, for a pittance. These workers, most of them women, were being exploited. They were not protected by a trade union, nor were they protected by the Factory Acts which regulated hours of employment and working conditions in factories and workshops. This was called the 'sweating system'.

The pictures on page 51 were published in *The Illustrated London News* in 1888. The matchbox maker was paid 2d [less than 1p] for making 144 matchboxes. The reporter claimed that, 'Two people at the end of two days earn 1s 2d [6p]'. The shoemaker got 4s 6d [23p] for making twelve pairs of shoes.

> 'The "sweater" is the middleman, who contracts with the large manufacturer for quantities of work, and then gets it done by poor people at the lowest possible cost, making enormous profits without using any capital, skill or labour of his own. Women who work at their own homes are obliged to toil from early morning until midnight for a pittance hardly enough to keep them alive. Others have to do machine-work in the "sweating dens", which are horribly unwholesome, filthy and unventilated.'

1　*Why was it called the 'sweating system'? Who was the 'sweater'? What was a 'sweating den'?*

2　*How much money did a matchbox maker make in a week? What happened to her income when she was ill?*

THE IMPACT OF THE FIRST WORLD WAR

Fitting electrical wires on board a battleship in 1918

Britain was still a powerful industrial giant at the outbreak of war in 1914, but Germany had overtaken her in several important industries. Although German coal production was about the same, her steel output was over twice that of Britain. Germany produced three times as much electricity and her chemical industry was more advanced and more productive. Lord Haldane, a former Secretary of State for War, told the House of Lords in 1916 that, at the start of the war, he had been horrified to discover just how dependent Britain had become upon Germany for certain basic chemicals, such as synthetic dyes. He claimed the fault lay in not training people for the chemical industry. The matter was serious, since Britain's wartime needs – such as the supply of drugs to treat the wounded and the supply of nitrates for explosives – could not be met in full.

The war heightened the demand for many raw materials, such as those needed in the manufacture of armaments. This is why British steel output rose to just under 10 million tonnes in 1917 – a figure not exceeded again until 1935. Shipbuilding companies did particularly well, opening new yards and expanding production to build warships and merchant ships to replace those sunk as a result of enemy action. The Government even took over the running of the collieries and the railways, to ensure there were no hold-ups in the supply of fuel and raw materials.

Since many industrial workers had volunteered to join the armed forces in 1914, factories and works experienced a serious labour shortage. This gap was filled by women workers, many of them employed for the first time in what had hitherto been regarded as 'men's jobs', such as unskilled labourers in the shipyards (see page 42).

By 1918, some of the deficiencies of British industry had become clear, exposed by the pressures of wartime. There were too many small mills and factories, too many old and antiquated machines, too few modern industries. The First World War drove home the lesson that, in any future conflict, it was vital to have efficient motor, aeroplane, aluminium, chemical and electrical industries. The war also showed clearly that British industry was too dependent on imported raw materials, such as wool, cotton, timber and iron ore. When supply was curtailed, industry suffered.

Excessive dependence on the export trade was also brought home by the war. In 1918, Lancashire's cotton manufacturers found that some of their traditional overseas markets had been taken by Indian and Japanese cotton mills. Japan was too far away from the war zone to be affected by the conflict and was able to profit by (a) building new ships, guns and munitions for the Allies, (b) developing her cotton industry (Japanese exports of cotton goods rose by 600 per cent between 1910 and 1920), (c) doubling the size of her merchant fleet, and (d) doubling her production of iron and steel. By the end of the war, Japan's trade with the United States had multiplied sevenfold, much of it taken away from Britain.

In Britain, by contrast, the boom in industry during the war years had deluded many manufacturers into thinking that their profits were coming from efficient factories, instead of from the artificial demand created by the war and the lack of foreign competition in the home market. Prices and wages had risen, and after the war many British goods were no longer competitive in world markets.

---

1 *Why do you think the British Government took control of the coal mines during the First World War?*

2 *Was it inevitable that British industry would come out of the war a loser?*

3 *Write a paragraph describing and explaining the effects of the First World War on British industry.*

THE DECLINE OF THE TRADITIONAL INDUSTRIES, 1918–39

Coal Mining

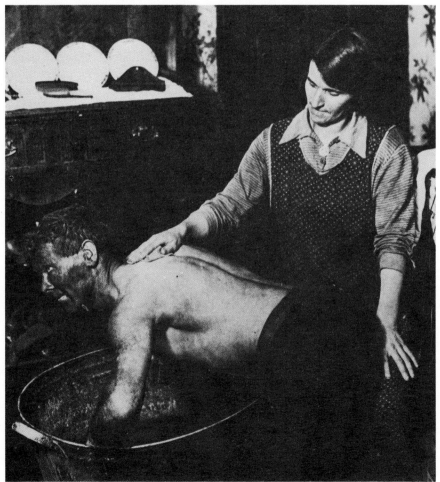

Coal miner's bath in the 1930s. What does this photograph tell you about conditions in the coal-mining industry before 1939?

At the end of the war in 1918, the coal-mining industry gradually returned to normal, but the annual output of about 230 million tonnes in 1918, 1919 and 1920 was substantially below the peak of 292 million tonnes reached in 1913. In this period of lowered output, pit owners tried to reduce their costs by cutting miners' wages and lengthening shifts of work. The alternative (apart from nationalisation or some form of government subsidy) was to make the mines more efficient, by installing automatic coal-cutting machinery and closing down inefficient pits, in order to concentrate production at the collieries with easily won coal.

The latter solution would not have been welcomed by the mining unions. As it was, the cuts in wages led to one damaging strike in 1921, when coal output fell to 166 million tonnes, and another in 1926 (see Chapter 8), when coal output dropped to 128 million tonnes. This only worsened the position of the coal-mining industry in world export markets. Although annual coal production otherwise always exceeded 210 million tonnes between the wars, the relative position of the United Kingdom suffered when compared with Germany, Russia and the United States.

Coal exports fell sharply to less than half their pre-war average. Poland and Germany, as well as the United States, were challenging Britain's supremacy in the export of coal. Their coal was easier to mine. They had lower labour costs and often lower transport costs as well.

In 1913, American coal exports were only 12 million tonnes a year compared with 77 million tonnes from Britain. But by 1920, the United States was exporting 34 million tonnes of coal, to 39 million tonnes from the United Kingdom. In April 1921, during the miners' strike, *The Graphic* warned of 'The Menace to our Mining Industry – the United States' and claimed:

> 'American coal is easy to obtain and can be mined cheaply because it is near the surface and in thick, easily worked seams in inexhaustible quantities.'

It said that American miners could cut 3.5 tonnes a day per shift, at a pithead cost of 13s [65p] a tonne. Britain's collieries, by contrast, were old and run down. Average output was only 0.8 tonnes a shift, at a pithead cost of 31s 3d [£1.56]. This was because:

> 'British coal is hard to obtain because it is very deep, often in thin seams, at a great distance from the pit-shaft and therefore expensive to mine.'

Coal-cutting machinery was standard in the United States and in Europe, but British pit owners were slow to follow suit. British mines were run by small and inefficient companies rather than by the large coal-mining organisations of Germany. Consequently, they did not have the financial resources to undertake the major improvements that were needed. This is why the trade unions pressed the Government to nationalise the industry – but their plea fell on deaf ears.

In 1930, however, the Labour Government passed the Coal Mines Act, designed to encourage the mining companies to merge. But even this had only a limited effect.

Mechanisation was increasingly brought in during the late 1930s – particularly with the introduction of underground conveyors – but it was neither a practical nor an economic proposition in the older mines with their faulted seams and lengthy wagonways. Overall, British productivity rose only slightly between 1918 and 1939, whereas that of Germany nearly doubled.

But no matter how efficient the industry, it could not fight the slackening of demand due to factors beyond the control of coal owner or miner. These included the following.

- Ships were changing from steam to oil whilst motor vehicles (using petrol) and aeroplanes (using aviation fuel) were challenging steam locomotives on the railways (later replaced by diesels in the 1960s).

- Foreign demand for coal fell during the Depression years, so there were fewer export sales. In any case, the decline in world trade reduced still further the demand for coal as a fuel for merchant ships.

- Home demand for coal also fell during the Depression years, since the industries which made heavy use of coal (such as iron and steelworks) were also affected by the general slump in industry.

But there was a brighter side as well. Coal was used to make coal gas and was the main source of fuel for the new power stations built by the Central Electricity Board after its formation in 1926. Electricity was fed to the National Grid and output trebled in the period between 1925 and 1939, when the CEGB made a strong effort to supply electric power to every home in the country. So the fact that the new light engineering and assembly industries used coal gas and electricity, rather than steam power, meant that the coal-mining industry ultimately benefited. After the Second World War, however, the industry was again faced with decline as natural gas replaced coal gas, and oil and nuclear power stations competed with those burning coal.

Textiles

The forecast, 'that nothing could avert eventual disaster from the Lancashire cotton trade' (see page 44), came true in the 1920s and 1930s. In 1933, Japan exported more cotton goods than did the United Kingdom and, by 1935, Japanese production of cotton goods had overtaken that from Britain's cotton mills.

When J. B. Priestley visited Blackburn in 1933, he was appalled at the misery and distress caused by unemployment in the Lancashire cotton industry. At one end of the social scale, former mill owners were reduced to serving drinks behind a bar or to 'picking up cigarette ends in the street'. Three weavers, a husband and wife and their daughter, living on the dole, had all 'been out of work three years'.

A familiar sight in Lancashire during the Great Depression of the 1930s

J. B. Priestley identified a number of reasons for the slump in trade. He claimed that Japanese students had acquired technical knowledge and know-how about weaving and spinning from courses at Lancashire's technical colleges. He also said:

> 'I met a most pleasant youngster who had a job in a firm that makes automatic looms. They sell these in Lancashire, and immediately put a few more weavers out of work. Every time one is loaded on to a ship at Liverpool a good piece is snipped off Lancashire's trade.'
>
> *J. B. Priestley,* English Journey, *1933*

1 *What causes of the decline of Lancashire's cotton industry did J. B. Priestley think were significant? Do you agree with him? In what respects are his arguments similar to those expressed in 1911 and 1912 (on page 45)?*

2 *Would the closure of a factory making automatic looms have solved the problem?*

Many of the reasons for the decline of the Lancashire cotton industry were similar to those which played a part in the decline of the coal-mining industry.

● Much of the machinery used in the mills was out of date. In particular, most British mills still used mule-spinning frames to produce cotton yarn rather than the rapid ring-spinning machines from America, which were quicker and cheaper to use. By 1930, about three-quarters of American looms were automatic in operation.

● Many of Lancashire's cotton mills were small family firms, competing with each other, instead of joining forces to promote their cotton goods throughout the world. Many lacked the financial resources needed to re-equip their mills with new machinery. As a result nearly a thousand cotton mills closed during the inter-war years, instead of merging to form stronger, more effective groupings.

● Foreign competition was strong – particularly from India and Japan – because Lancashire had higher labour costs. British cotton spinners were paid up to five times the wages received by Japanese workers. In Japan, weavers were more exploited by their employers, working longer shifts and in charge of ten looms, compared with the four permitted by the trade unions in Lancashire. In 1932, Lancashire's weavers went on strike against a proposal to make them mind eight looms instead of four. In the end they compromised with six.

● Synthetic fibres had been discovered, in 1883, by Sir Joseph Swan, when he produced thread from nitrocellulose. Some production of artificial fibres, mainly rayon, had begun in the years before 1914. But immediately after the war, the industry expanded rapidly, partly as a result of the demand for fine rayon stockings which came with the shorter skirt. Production of synthetic fibres rose tenfold between 1918 and 1928 and was seen as a direct competitor by the cotton industry. Textile mills had to adjust their production plans accordingly, and by 1934 it was estimated that three in every ten of Lancashire's cotton-weaving mills were using rayon in some form or other.

● Politics also played a part in the decline of the Lancashire cotton industry. Mahatma Gandhi's campaign against British rule in India included a virtual boycott of British cotton goods by his supporters.

The Government took some action to come to the aid of the industry when it re-introduced tariffs on foreign goods in 1931. But although this offered protection in the home market, it told against Britain in the export market. However, the Lancashire Cotton Corporation did manage to reduce the number of cotton spindles in the late 1930s to try to bring an ordered reduction in the output of the industry. By the late 1930s, the cotton industry (like many other industries) had begun to recover.

Iron and Steel

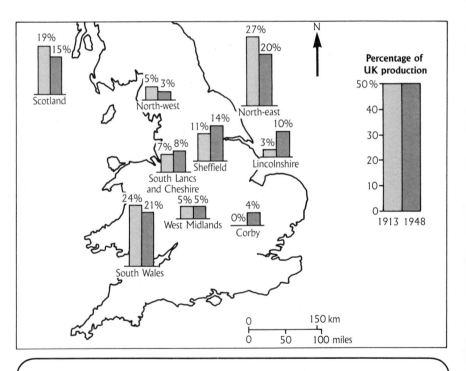

Steel production in Britain 1913–48

1 *Look at this map. Which were the three most important steel-producing areas (a) in 1913, (b) in 1948? Did any major changes take place in this period of 35 years?*

2 *Which areas showed the greatest growth in steel production? Why? Which areas showed the greatest fall?*

The factors which enabled Germany and the USA to overtake Britain in steel production in the 1900s, were brought home once again in the 1920s and 1930s, with the worldwide depression in trade and industry. British steel output fell from an annual average of 9.3 million tonnes in 1915–18 to only 6.3 million tonnes in 1921–6. It recovered, temporarily, to an annual average of 9.2 million tonnes in 1927–9, but fell back once more to 6.3 million tonnes in 1930–3. The industry picked up again to an annual average of 12.3 million tonnes in the period of rearmament from 1936 to 1939. The main reasons for the relative decline of the iron and steel industry were as follows.

- The original advantages of the industry – cheap, easily mined iron ore and coal – had gone, yet many small iron and steelworks were still situated on the old coalfield sites, many of them inland (such as in the valleys of South Wales). Large integrated iron and steelworks were needed, sited at the coast or on an estuary, and capable of handling the large ore carriers bringing iron ore from Sweden or Spain.

- The British steel industry still used small, out-dated, uneconomic furnaces, unlike the large efficient furnaces in the large steelworks of the United States or Germany, where two workers could make as much steel as three in Britain.

- There was a sharp decline in the demand for steel when the shipbuilding industry slumped, and other heavy users reduced their demand for steel.

- Many foreign steel manufacturers were protected by tariffs against foreign imports. Britain's continued policy of Free Trade in the 1920s meant that surplus foreign steel could be dumped (unloaded at low prices) on the British market, even though it undercut British steel.

In 1932, however, the British Government introduced the Import Duties Act, imposing a tariff of 33 per cent on all foreign steel imports into Britain. After 1932, imports of foreign steel fell by 65 per cent in the space of two years. In return for this protection, the Government expected the iron and steel industry to put its own house in order. The British Iron and Steel Federation was founded, and encouraged iron and steel companies to merge.

On the whole, the iron and steel industry survived the Depression better than most, because the thriving motor car and domestic appliance industries created a large new home demand for steel (see page 61), which helped to make up for the decline in other sales.

Shipbuilding

As you have seen, one of the reasons for the decline in demand for steel was the slump in the shipbuilding industry. Enemy action in the First World War led to a huge growth in shipbuilding capacity, followed in the first years of peace by an unexpected boom. Over 2 million tonnes of shipping were built in 1920.

But the declining need in peacetime for new warships and merchant ships soon led to a slump. In the depths of the Depression, in 1933, only one-fourteenth of the 1913 tonnage of ships was launched in Britain. When J.B.Priestley visited the Tyneside shipbuilding town of Jarrow in 1933, he wrote:

> 'Wherever we went there were men hanging about, not scores of them but hundreds and thousands of them. The whole town looked as if it had entered a perpetual penniless bleak Sabbath. The men wore the drawn masks of prisoners of war.'
>
> *J. B. Priestley,* English Journey, *1933*

---

1 *What was the effect on Jarrow of the slump in the shipbuilding industry?*

2 *What do you think J. B. Priestley meant by the last two sentences in this extract?*

In some shipbuilding areas the unemployment rate was over 60 per cent and in Jarrow it reached 68 per cent in 1934, when only three in ten of the working population had a job. In 1936, the unemployed shipyard workers of Jarrow, led by their local MP, Ellen Wilkinson, made a much publicised protest march – the Jarrow Crusade – to bring their plight to the attention of the Government. Ellen Wilkinson later highlighted the tragedy of Jarrow in a book called *The Town that was Murdered*.

The Jarrow Crusade

Some of the reasons for the slump in shipbuilding were as follows.

● There was a drastic decline in demand for new ships in line with the slump in world trade. When empty ships were idle in the docks (see page 96), there was little hope of new ones being launched.

- At the same time, shipyards in Sweden, Finland, Poland, Greece, Spain, Germany and Japan were able to undercut the prices quoted by British shipbuilders. German shipyards in the 1920s quoted faster delivery times and lower prices.

- British shipyards lost their technological superiority over other shipyards. The new ships used oil not coal. In 1914, only one ship in every 30 had been fuelled by oil. By 1939, the ratio had risen to one in every two.

- German shipyard workers were not hampered by demarcation issues. They put in more work in a day than the typical British shipyard worker, were better educated and better trained to do their jobs.

As with other industries, shipbuilding picked up again from 1935 onwards. By that time the Government was encouraging shipowners to close down unprofitable shipyards, to make the industry more competitive. Over one million tonnes of shipbuilding capacity were shut down, and the Government subsidised the building of the *Queen Mary* and placed new orders for warships in the period of rearmament after 1936.

THE NEW INDUSTRIES OF THE 1930s

Changes in the Location of Industry

As you have seen, serious unemployment was one of the products of the Depression of the 1920s and 1930s. But its effects were not felt equally throughout Britain. In the Midlands and the South-east unemployment levels were low. This was because the decline in world trade mainly affected the older traditional export industries (coal, steel, textiles and ships) much more than it did the newer industries which made products (such as radios and cars) primarily for the home market. These consumer durables, as they were called, included vacuum cleaners and many other electrical household goods. Demand rose sharply in the 1930s, factories became more efficient and prices fell. The cost of a car was halved between 1924 and 1935 and that of a vacuum cleaner fell by a similar proportion between 1930 and 1935.

> 'These picturesque remains of the old Coventry are besieged by an army of nuts, bolts, hammers, spanners, gauges, drills, and machine lathes, for in a thick ring round this ancient centre are the motor car and cycle factories, the machine tool makers, the magneto manufacturers, and the electrical companies. Beyond them again are whole new quarters, where the mechanics and fitters and turners and furnace men live in neat brick rows, and drink their beer in gigantic new public houses and take their wives to gigantic new picture theatres.
>
> Coventry seems to have acquired the trick of keeping up with the times, a trick that many of our industrial cities find hard to learn. It made bicycles when everybody was cycling, cars when everybody wanted a motor, and now it is also busy with aeroplanes, wireless sets, and various electrical contrivances, including the apparatus used by the Talkies.'
>
> *J. B. Priestley,* English Journey, *1933*

1 *What industries could you have seen in Coventry in 1933?*
   Which were the new industries, and which were the traditional
   industries dating back to the middle of the nineteenth century?

2 *What was the trick that the other industrial cities found 'hard to*
   learn'? Was this a fair criticism of other industrial towns?

3 *What effect did these new industries have on Coventry at the*
   height of the Depression?

Many of the new industries were attracted to London and the South-east rather than to the coalfields of the North for the following reasons.

● The northern industrial areas were further from London. They were often bleak and forbidding, and worn out after a century of heavy industry. Soot-blackened buildings and towering slag heaps scarred what was once a beautiful countryside, making it less attractive to the directors of the new light industries.

● The new manufacturers tended to prefer garden cities, where factories could be built in pleasant surroundings, often on industrial estates separated from the areas where people lived.

● These new light factories had little difficulty in attracting a competent work force, many of them women rather than men.

● Since the new light industries did not use steam engines there was no particular advantage in siting a factory on a coalfield – electricity was available at the turn of a switch.

● Nor was there any pressing need to build a factory close to the raw materials, such as steel, wire, glass or timber, used on the production line. The cost of the parts needed to make a radio or vacuum cleaner formed only a very small percentage of the final cost.

● Many of the new factories were assembly plants – assembling components produced in different works and factories over a wide area, such as the different parts which go to make a car (e.g. glass panes, steel panels, leather or plastic upholstery, floor carpets). Assembly industries needed access to the railway and to fast motor roads.

● Since these goods were aimed directly at the consumer (as opposed to products such as ships and steel which were bought by big companies), they needed to be close to the large centres of population – the market for these products. The London area was by far the largest centre of population in Britain and also the most prosperous.

However, the old industrial areas could still offer new industries a large, skilled work force, desperate for work, together with cheap building sites, existing warehouses and empty mill buildings, railway sidings and port facilities close by. As a result, some of the new industries were still attracted to the North, although most went to the South-east and the Midlands.

Car Manufacturing

One of the most important of the new industries was the motor industry. France and Germany took an early lead as pioneers in this industry in Europe before 1914, but after 1918 Britain soon built up the second most important motor industry in the world. At first, the British motor industry was slow to follow the example set by Henry Ford in using the assembly-line method of car production. Vehicles continued to be handmade by skilled craftsmen and were, therefore, very expensive. But when William Morris at Cowley (Oxford) and Herbert Austin at Longbridge (Birmingham) began to use the same mass-production methods in Britain, they brought motoring within the reach of ordinary people and changed the face of the industry.

Motor-car assembly line in the 1930s

The changes were well illustrated by the Ford Motor Company itself. In the early 1920s, Ford motor cars were assembled at Trafford Park in Manchester but, in 1924, Henry Ford decided to build a major new plant in Britain. The choice of a site for this new motor works tells us a lot about the rise of the South-east and the decline of the North in the inter-war years.

The Ford Motor Company chose a huge, low-lying marshland site by the banks of the Thames, about 20 km from London. There was space for an iron and steelworks, together with deep-water facilities capable of berthing large, ocean-going cargo ships. By moving to the London region, the Ford Motor Company ensured they were close to the factories making car components and near the most important markets for motor vehicles in the United Kingdom. London, of course, had excellent road and rail communications with every other major centre of population. Moreover, the new London County Council housing estate in the village of Dagenham could provide much of the extra labour needed, in addition to the 2,000 Ford workers who moved down to Dagenham from Manchester when the works opened in 1931.

> 1 Which do you think were the crucial reasons why the Ford Motor Company moved to Dagenham, instead of expanding their existing works in Manchester?

The Electronics Industry

The reasons why the Ford Motor Company moved to Dagenham in 1931 were not very different from those of the other firms which built factories in the South-east in the inter-war period. Firms making electrical appliances prospered as more and more people began to use electricity at home. Consumption of electricity doubled between 1920 and 1929, and again between 1929 and 1939.

> 'Seven huge factories – thousands of work people – thousands of planned and specialised operations. Long assembly lines – a huge transport fleet – branches all over the country – that, in outline, is the Cossor manufacturing organisation – the largest of its kind in the Empire.'
>
> *Cossor advertisement in* John Bull, *April 1938*

---

1 *How did Cossor send its products to the shops? What type of industry was this? Where would you have built a radio factory in the 1930s?*

2 *A portable radio featured in this advertisement cost £6 19s [£6.95]. In the same magazine a farm worker was said to earn 37s 6d [£1.88] per week. Were radios relatively cheap or expensive in 1938 compared with today?*

3 *How can an advertisement like this be a useful source of information for an historian? What are the drawbacks?*

Not all of the new electronics industries were sited in the South-east. An important factory making electronic valves for the radio industry was opened in the cotton-weaving town of Blackburn in the 1930s. Working conditions there were far superior to those in the nearby cotton mills. But this was the exception rather than the rule. Most of the new radio factories were situated in the London area and in the Midlands.

The radio industry mushroomed in the 1920s and 1930s. It owed its origin to the work of pioneers like Marconi (see page 124), the discovery of electrons by Joseph Thomson in 1897 and the invention of the valve by J. A. Fleming in 1904.

> 'Electrical engineering affords perhaps the most striking of all instances of the way new scientific discoveries may create new industries and give employment to great numbers of workers.'
>
> *Joseph Thomson, 1934*

---

1 *What other modern scientific discoveries have created new industries and given employment to thousands of workers?*

2 *How have modern scientific discoveries also caused the decline of existing industries and made thousands of workers redundant?*

The Chemical and Petrochemical Industries

Demand for chemicals boomed during the inter-war years and jobs in the industry doubled between 1918 and 1939. Nonetheless, the United Kingdom still lagged behind Germany in output. Between 1922 and 1939, UK production of synthetic fibres rose from 6,000 to 77,000 tonnes (in Germany from 5,000 to 273,000 tonnes). Output of sulphuric acid reached 1.1 million tonnes in Britain in 1939, but 2.7 million tonnes in Germany.

In 1923, the Brunner Mond Company built a plant at Billingham on the Tees to manufacture fertilisers from synthetic sulphate of ammonia. Brunner Mond were noted for their enlightened and advanced attitude to factory management and good working conditions on the shop floor.

Elsewhere in the chemical industry, working conditions were still poor and little different from those described earlier on pages 46–8. But in 1926, Brunner Mond merged with three other major British chemical firms to form a new and formidable company – Imperial Chemical Industries. ICI (as the new company was always known) continued the Brunner Mond policy of giving its workers paid holidays each year, fitting out their plants with sports and recreational facilities and paying above-average wages. Workers in other industries were

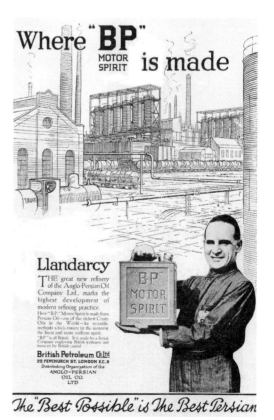

Advertisement for petrol in 1922

envious, particularly since disputes at ICI were resolved by the Works Council – a committee on which both the workers and the managers were represented. Instead of confrontation there was co-operation. A large number of scientists were attracted to the ICI laboratories to research new and better processes, and it was work like this which led to the discovery of polyethylene (polythene) in 1933 – an invaluable raw material during the Second World War – and terylene in 1941.

---

1 *Why were the new oil refineries, like Llandarcy in South Wales, built at the coast? From which country did BP get its crude oil?*

2 *What does the advertisement on page 65 tell you about the way many motorists bought petrol in the early days of motoring?*

BRITISH INDUSTRY SINCE 1939

The Impact of the Second World War

The declaration of war against Germany in September 1939 drastically reduced unemployment in British industry at a stroke. The thousands of hunger marchers, who had despaired of ever working again in the 1930s, now found themselves being coaxed back to work again. Industry was put on a wartime footing. Foreign competition for exports was irrelevant, so too was the idea of competing for home markets. The essential target was greater productivity. Workers were asked to work extra shifts, particularly on Sundays. Factory and works managements wanted to keep their plant running at full capacity seven days a week. Much of industry was converted to the manufacture of weapons and armaments. Textile firms turned out uniforms, electronics firms made radar, motor works made tanks and lorries.

At the end of the war, the coal mines were much the same as they had been in the 1930s – dilapidated, hopelessly out of date, overmanned and under-mechanised. Even during the war years, the coal-mining industry was still occasionally plagued by strikes and absenteeism. Output of coal actually declined from 235 million tonnes in 1939 to 186 million tonnes in 1945, despite the conscription of some young men as Bevin Boys to work in the pits instead of serving in the armed forces. As in the First World War, government interference in the running of the mines during the wartime years provided another precedent for the nationalisation of the industry in 1947.

The iron and steel industry, too, was inefficient and had a low productivity record. Steel output also fell, despite wartime needs, from 13.4 million tonnes in 1939 to 12 million tonnes in 1945. This was partly due to the disruption caused by enemy air raids, but plant and machinery in too many steelworks dated from the Victorian or Edwardian past rather than from the middle years of the twentieth century.

Nowhere was this dependence on outdated technology better illustrated than in the shipbuilding industry. There was a huge demand for ships during the war and all the British shipyards worked flat out to meet the demand. But they were grossly inefficient when compared to the shipyards of the United States. British shipyards still used riveting, instead of welding plates together. Revolutionary new techniques were being used in America – even to the extent of building some ships upside down.

The Aftermath of the War

The period since 1945 has been a traumatic one for British industry. Germany and Japan, defeated, ruined and demoralised at the end of the war, both achieved economic miracles in the post-war years – shooting past Britain, and rivalling one another for second place in the world economy after the United States.

At first, British industry expanded in the immediate post-war years. The destruction caused by enemy action and the deprivations of the war created a huge demand for new ships, buildings, fabrics and products of every kind. Making up for wartime shortages led to full employment in the textile industries and to a boom in shipbuilding and steel, and in factories making consumer goods, such as radios, television sets, washing machines and other household appliances. Growing affluence created a huge new demand for the motor car.

Prime Minister Harold Macmillan summed it up in 1957 with his famous speech at Bedford, in which he said:

> 'Let's be frank about it; most of our people have never had it so good. Go around the country, go to the industrial towns, go to the farms, and you will see a state of prosperity such as we have never had in my lifetime – nor indeed ever in the history of the country.'

1　What did he mean by the phrase, 'never had it so good'?
2　Ask your older relatives and friends what they can remember of 1957, the year when Harold Macmillan made this speech. Did they think they had 'never had it so good' then?

But Europe was catching up fast, the United States was already far ahead and Japanese industry was growing at a phenomenal rate. By 1960, Germany was the richest country in Europe. British production grew by about 2–3 per cent in the post-war years – a substantial improvement on the 1930s, but no match for countries like France and Italy with twice that rate of growth.

The fundamental causes of Britain's relative decline (as in the 1880s and the 1920s) could not be rectified by building on old industries. Britain was paying the penalty for being the world's first industrial nation.

In the 1970s and 1980s, a number of factors led to high rates of unemployment (well over three million in 1986) and the closure of many works and factories. These factors included the decline in the value of the pound and falling demand for coal, steel, ships and traditional textiles. British manufacturers also faced competition in some of the newer industries from cheaper or more reliable foreign imports (such as cars, radios and television sets).

The Coal-mining Industry

The Labour Government which came to power in 1945 had long had its sights on coal mining and iron and steel as industries which ought to be nationalised. This meant compulsorily purchasing shares in the nationalised companies on behalf of the people and putting them into public ownership. Accordingly, the Coal Act of 1946 came into effect on 1 January 1947.

Newly nationalised colliery, 1 January 1947

At first the miners were full of hope. At a time when industry was booming, in the immediate post-war years, the National Coal Board (NCB) had every reason to think that the industry would continue to expand. Accordingly, it produced a *Plan for Coal*, which laid down targets for the different coalfields and made plans to transform the coal-mining industry by improving working conditions, making widespread use of coal-cutting machinery, developing up-to-date lines of communication underground, building pithead baths and mechanising any job that could be done more effectively and more efficiently by machines.

Conditions in the newly renovated mines were an eye-opener to the older miners. 'It's an entirely different industry. It's more like a factory' was a typical comment. But there was a major snag. Coal as a fuel was increasingly being challenged by three important rivals in the post-war years – oil, natural gas and electricity from oil-fired or nuclear power stations.

It soon became clear that the NCB planners had overestimated the amount of coal that would be needed in the second half of the twentieth century. The massive investment in the coal-mining industry had been based on miscalculations. Calder Hall, the world's first large-scale nuclear power station, was opened in 1956. Oil was very cheap before 1973 and the Central Electricity Generating Board built a number of oil-fired power stations in preference to the traditional coal-fired stations of the past.

1 What changes in everyday life in the post-war years were likely to affect the coal-mining industry (e.g. diesel trains, central heating, the rise of the motor car)?

2 Was it in the interest of the general public to have oil-fired or coal-burning power stations?

3 Was there anything the miners and the National Coal Board could have done to reverse the trend away from coal?

4 Look at the graphs below. What do you notice about the rise in electricity and oil consumption in recent years compared with coal production? Write a paragraph commenting on the trends shown in these graphs.

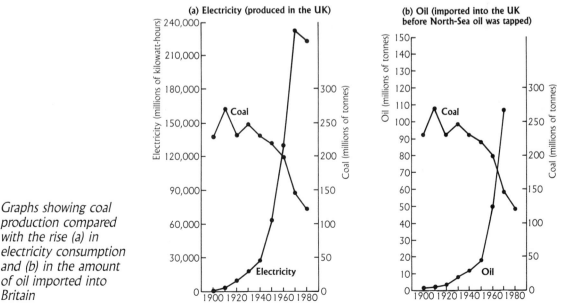

Graphs showing coal production compared with the rise (a) in electricity consumption and (b) in the amount of oil imported into Britain

In retrospect, the coal-mining industry was bound to contract in the face of competition from oil and the declining demand for coal. People who preferred central heating to coal fires, or package holidays by air to rail holidays by the sea, were as much to blame as the industrialists who scrapped steam engines. Even if Britain had reduced its consumption of oil, the overseas customers, who bought British coal before the war, could not have been expected to do likewise. Not surprisingly, the export trade in coal had dwindled to 4 million tonnes a year by 1958.

So, despite nationalisation, many pits were closed. The effects were dramatic. In 1947 there were well over 1,000 pits in Britain. In 1984 there were only 191. Of the 214 coal mines in South Wales in 1947, only 28 were still open in 1984 and fewer still in 1986. The number of miners employed in the pits fell from 700,000 in 1957 to 130,000 by 1986. Coal output fell from 231 million tonnes in 1938 to 124 million tonnes in 1982.

In the early 1980s, the Conservative Government told the Coal Board that in future it should be run like any other business, making a profit rather than a loss each year. Accordingly, the National Coal Board made plans to close down unprofitable pits. NCB spokesmen argued that it made more sense to invest money in collieries which did make money rather than spend money subsidising the older, loss-making pits which were approaching exhaustion – even though there were still millions of tonnes of coal left there.

The miners, on the other hand, insisted that coal mining was different from other industries and that when the world's oil ran out, more coal than ever before would be needed. In their view, it did not make sense to shut down collieries when there was still coal there to be mined. In the long term it would be needed. Re-opening the colliery in the future would be too expensive. In any case, closures would only condemn whole communities to a bleak and desperate future at a time of high unemployment, since new factories were unlikely to be attracted to the old coalfield areas.

In 1984, the National Union of Mineworkers, led by Arthur Scargill, decided to resist further pit closures and came out on strike. But, after a bitter year-long strike (see page 241) the miners gave up the struggle and returned to work. As a result further collieries were closed and about 30,000 miners left the industry. On 1 July 1986, *The Times* reported that the winding gear at the Maerdy Colliery in the Rhondda Valley was closing down – the last pit in a valley which had 'once boasted a workforce of 40,000 miners' and 54 collieries.

The National Coal Board (renamed British Coal in 1986) put its faith in the development of pits with profitable, easily won coal, such as the new coalfield at Selby (where the coal seam was up to 2–3 m thick and 20 km in length). The five pits on the Selby coalfield worked the coal using the very latest coal-cutting machinery, with underground conveyor belts controlled by computers, and non-stopping trains on the surface taking the coal direct to the massive Yorkshire power stations.

Modern colliery at Killoch, Scotland

Steel

The steel industry has also had a chequered life in the post-war period. It was nationalised by the Labour Government in 1949, the act coming into effect in February 1951 – just eight months before the return to power of the Conservatives. It was denationalised by the Conservative Government in March 1953, but when Labour returned to power in 1964, it was renationalised (taking effect once again in 1967). Not surprisingly, management and workers in the steel industry felt restricted by government policy, never knowing for certain whether the future of the industry lay in private or public hands.

These problems have been further aggravated by the general downturn in the steel industry in recent years – a problem not confined to the United Kingdom. Immediately after the war, output rose and continued to rise until 1970, stimulated by the demand for cars and household goods (such as refrigerators and washing machines). So long as steel was the principal raw material of British industry all was well.

Steel output grew from an average annual output of about 14 million tonnes in the late 1940s, to 20 million tonnes in the late 1950s, and then to about 27 million tonnes in the late 1960s. For a period it looked as if the future was rosy, and new works were built at Port Talbot and Llanwern in South Wales, Redcar on Teesside, Ravenscraig in Scotland and Shotton in Clwyd in 1953. Some of these works were built at the prompting of the governments in power – both Labour and Conservative – and their location was often dictated by the need to create new jobs, rather than for sound geographical reasons.

But increasing foreign competition (notably from Japan), the growing use of plastic as a constructional material, the drastic drop in car sales after the 1973 oil crisis, the decline in shipbuilding and other metal-using industries, and the general slump in trade in the late 1970s and early 1980s, caused a serious falling-off in demand. Output fell from 28 million tonnes in 1970 to only half that amount in 1982.

Drastic reorganisation in the early 1980s helped the industry to become profitable again by 1986. But there was a price to pay and the industry had, by then, been slimmed down from 170,000 to 63,000 workers. The Corby, Ebbw Vale, Shotton, Consett and Bilston steelworks had been closed, together with other steelworks and rolling mills. On the credit side, many of the restrictive working practices of the past had gone, and in the steelworks that remained, new and up-to-date plant had been installed, with productivity said to be the best in Europe.

Shipbuilding

In the late 1940s, Britain was still making half the world's ships. But this lead was steadily eroded as Japan, Germany, South Korea and other countries built up their own shipbuilding industries, often using more advanced technology, and unhampered by the antiquated working practices of British shipyards.

In the 1960s and 1970s a number of shipyards closed down, some merging with others to form larger groupings – such as the ill-fated Upper Clyde Shipbuilders (rescued by the Conservative Government in 1972). In 1977 the industry was nationalised, even though the omens were poor for the future, since by then there was a depression in world trade. Since nationalisation, the industry has been reorganised. New working practices, new technology and new management techniques have been introduced and the industry has been slimmed down. Even so, British share of world shipbuilding was little more than 3 per cent (500,000 tonnes) of the world total of 16,000,000 tonnes launched in 1983.

Cotton Textiles

There was a short boom in cotton production immediately after the war and in the 1950s many immigrant workers from India and Pakistan came over to work in the industry. But foreign competition and the challenge posed by synthetic fibres – nylon, rayon, terylene, and others – hit the traditional cotton textile industry hard. It is true that many firms took advantage of the new fibres to widen and vary the scope of their output and many installed modern machinery. But, in general, the improvements came too late. Whereas the industry used 500,000 tonnes of raw cotton in 1939, it used only 120,000 tonnes in 1974. By 1984, nearly a thousand British cotton mills had closed down and less than 40,000 workers were employed in the industry – compared with the million workers dependent on cotton in the nineteenth century.

The Motor Industry

The problems of British industry have not been confined exclusively to the old-established, traditional industries of the North. The motor industry has also suffered severely from the effects of foreign competition. On Britain's roads, in the 1960s, only one car in twenty was foreign-made. By the early 1980s this ratio had increased to one in two. In 1932, the British motor industry was second only in importance to the American industry. After the war it was overtaken by Germany in 1956, France in 1961 and Italy in 1970.

Initially there was a tremendous boom in the immediate post-war years. Growing affluence brought cars within the reach of many people. But then came decline, following the 1973 oil crisis, as you can see from this table of car production statistics for the British motor industry between 1937 and 1982.

1937	390,000	1957	861,000	1972	1,921,000
1947	287,000	1962	1,249,000	1977	1,328,000
1952	448,000	1967	1,552,000	1982	888,000

1 *Draw a graph to show these statistics.*

2 *Write two or three sentences to say what happened to the British motor industry between 1937 and 1982.*

3 *In which decade did the motor industry grow at the fastest rate? What happened to the industry between 1972 and 1982?*

The reasons for the decline of the industry cannot be reduced to any one single overriding cause, certainly not to a lack of innovation. The introduction of the transverse engine in the 1959 Austin Mini revolutionised the small-car industry. Some critics blamed the unofficial wildcat strikes of the 1960s – a serious problem in a motor-car assembly works, where the lack of a single component can hold up production.

Others blamed management for giving in too easily to wage demands; for poor design; for the lack of investment in new models, new plant and machinery; for lack of foresight in not developing petrol-saving models earlier; and for bad industrial relations. Like the steel industry, the motor industry has also suffered (and sometimes benefited) from well-meaning government interference. When Austin wanted to build another factory in Birmingham they were unable to do so, and were redirected instead to Scotland, which was short of new industries. Similarly, Ford were unable to expand their Dagenham plant and built their new works at Halewood on Merseyside instead. Although this was a positive move to alleviate distress in the Development Areas, it was not necessarily the best policy for a modern motor industry – especially one expected to earn money from foreign exports.

One of the most important reasons for the decline of the motor industry was the 1973 oil crisis. This drastically increased the cost of motoring, placing a premium on fuel-economy models rather than the larger, less economical family cars. Many foreign motor manufacturers were quicker to seize a share of this market than their British counterparts.

Robot assembly line at the British Leyland Motor Works at Cowley, Oxford

As the motor industry faced greater competition worldwide, so the disadvantages of the small motor company became apparent. Austin, Morris and Rover were merged to form the British Motor Corporation – later British Leyland and, later still, Austin Rover. The company streamlined its production line in the early 1980s, shutting 60 per cent of its factories, cutting its work force in half, developing new models and installing robots on a highly sophisticated production line.

> 1 *Find out how many of your older friends and relatives owned foreign cars in the 1960s. How many own foreign cars today?*
>
> 2 *Compare your results with those of your friends and draw a bar graph or pie chart to show your findings.*

The Electronics Industry

The British electronics industry employed more workers in 1984 than the steel, coal and shipbuilding industries put together. Electronics has been one of the great success stories of the post-war period, although its roots lie in the pre-war radio industry.

The great stimulus to development came during the war with the development of radar. The radio industry (using valves to amplify signals) continued to prosper after 1945 and the boom in television enabled it to expand at a rapid rate, manufacturing over two million television sets a year by the mid-1950s.

But the invention of the transistor in the United States, in 1948, enabled smaller, more reliable sets to be made. In this field foreign competition was extremely fierce – especially from Japan. Japanese transistor radios, in the 1960s, and colour television sets, in the 1970s, began to displace British-made sets from the shops. The British radio and television industry suffered a devastating blow.

However, many British firms have prospered, by working on the advanced electronics used in modern tanks, warships and aircraft, by developing large main-frame computers and, more recently, by making microcomputers in a rapidly expanding and highly competitive industry. In particular, they have helped to automate many industrial processes – making industry more efficient but creating unemployment as well.

The Chemical Industry

The chemical industry is another success story of the post-war period, deriving much of its growth from advances in petrochemicals, notably the development of plastics and synthetic fibres. Good labour relations, high pay and excellent working conditions have contributed to a fruitful period of growth and a reputation as a progressive industry. New oil refineries were opened after the war and new chemical plants built, such as the giant ICI works at Wilton on Teesside, based on petrochemicals and the manufacture of artificial fibres.

In the 1960s, the discovery and subsequent exploitation of North-Sea oil and natural gas, gave Britain a valuable new resource and made the United Kingdom

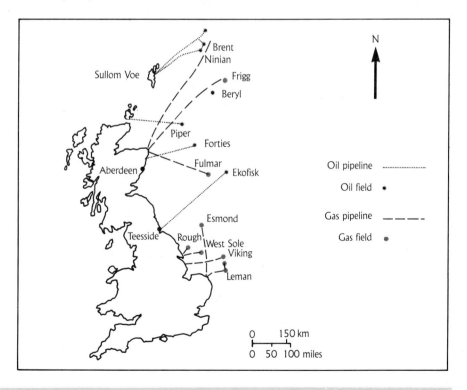

North-Sea oil and natural gas

one of the few developed industrial powers to be self-sufficient in the major fuels. But by 1986, North-Sea oil and natural gas had had little apparent effect on the creation of new industries, unlike the coal-based Industrial Revolution, 200 years earlier. Instead, the chemical industry had begun to feel the effect of the depression of the 1980s and, by 1986, many thousands of jobs had gone in the Teesside chemical industries.

1 *What reasons may help to explain why North-Sea oil and natural gas have failed to revitalise British industry?*

2 *Interview your older relatives and friends and see what reasons they give for the relative decline of British industry since 1945. Write a brief report summarising your findings.*

FURTHER QUESTIONS AND EXERCISES

"WHAT WILL HE GROW TO?"

1 *This cartoon appeared in Punch on 25 January 1881.*

 (a) *Name the two 'Kings' in the cartoon. Why are they depicted by the cartoonist as looking worried?*

 (b) *Who was 'he' and what did 'he grow to'?*

 (c) *What was the point of the cartoon?*

 (d) *Trace the history of this particular industry and explain its importance in the growth and development of British industry in the twentieth century.*

2 *When, and for what reasons, could you say that Britain ceased to be the 'Workshop of the World'?*

3   *Name three industries which declined and three industries which expanded between 1918 and 1939. For each industry state briefly the reasons for its decline or growth and say what effect this had on the life of people in Britain.*

4   *What processes were used to convert iron into steel in the nineteenth century? What effect did the development of these processes have on the location of new iron and steelworks in Britain?*

5   *Choose any two of the following industries and for each, trace its progress in the twentieth century, explaining the reasons for its successes and failures:*

   (a) coal mining
   (b) iron and steel
   (c) shipbuilding
   (d) cotton textiles
   (e) motor cars.

6   *What changes in the use of power have there been in Britain in the last 100 years? What effect have they had on the nature and distribution of British industry?*

7   *In a lecture in 1986, the Chairman of ICI, Sir John Harvey-Jones, said that:*

   'As each successive government has reversed the policies of its predecessor, British industry has been constantly marching up the hill and marching down again. The Grand Old Duke of York has been our constant companion.'

   What did he mean by this? Give examples to illustrate what he meant by 'marching up the hill and marching down again'.

8   *Why did south-eastern England survive the Depression years of the 1930s more effectively than the industrial North?*

9   *What social and economic problems have been caused by the decline of the traditional industries since 1918?*

10   *This chapter was written in 1986. What developments have taken place since that date, which have significantly affected the development or decline of British industry?*

11   *Look at the table overleaf.*
   (a) Which two industries employed fewer people in Britain in 1971 than in 1871? Why? Did they both decline at the same rate?
   (b) Which other industry grew rapidly at first but employed fewer workers in 1971 than in 1931? Why?
   (c) Which industries employed over ten times as many workers in Britain in 1971 compared with 1871? Why? Was their growth evenly spread throughout the whole of the period between 1871 and 1971?

(d) Which industry employed twice as many workers in 1971 compared with 1871, even though there was a decrease between 1901 and 1931? Why?

(e) Write a sentence to say what happened to the engineering industry between 1871 and 1971.

(f) Draw a graph to show these statistics.

(g) Write a detailed summary of the facts you can deduce from the graph you have drawn and from this table of statistics.

	1871	1901	1931	1971
		(thousands of workers)		
Mining and quarrying	510	890	1,080	390
Chemicals and oil	50	90	230	520
Metalworking	550	770	710	1,140
Engineering	200	470	510	1,270
Electrical engineering	0	50	250	840
Shipbuilding	60	120	200	180
Vehicles	60	130	410	790
Textiles	1,310	1,170	1,130	590

WANTED—A FAIRY GODMOTHER.

CINDERELLA (*sadly*). "AFTER ALL, I DO THE ROUGH WORK FOR BOTH OF THEM."

12 What was the point of this cartoon, published in Punch in December 1935?

Chapter Three

Transport and Communications

INTRODUCTION

Transport in 1908

1 *How many different types of transport can you see in this picture? How were they powered?*

2 *Which of these different types of transport could not have been seen in 1800?*

3 *How have these different types of transport changed in the period since 1908? What are the similarities and dissimilarities compared with today?*

4 *Which have changed most? Which have changed least? Which, if any, have disappeared or are rarely seen?*

The development of new methods of transport and communications in the last 150 years has had a startling effect on the everyday lives of people in Britain. The coming of the railway in the 1830s ruined the canals and also the stage and mailcoach services which had used the turnpike roads so effectively in the early years of the nineteenth century. But, about a hundred years later, the process was reversed as people began to desert the railways for the roads, travelling by car and bus, and sending their goods by van and lorry.

These changes have had a significant effect on the landscape and industries of Britain. Airports, motorways, garages, aerials, telegraph posts, railway stations and sidings have altered the countryside and shaped the way in which the towns have grown. New industries (such as factories making cars, radios and aeroplanes) have thrived on new types of transport and new means of communication. Old and new industries alike have benefited from the greater speed and ease of modern communications.

Faster transport and better communications have revolutionised other activities as well, such as entertainment, agriculture, education, politics, the armed forces and almost every other aspect of everyday life.

THE DEVELOPMENT OF THE RAILWAYS

The Railways at their Peak

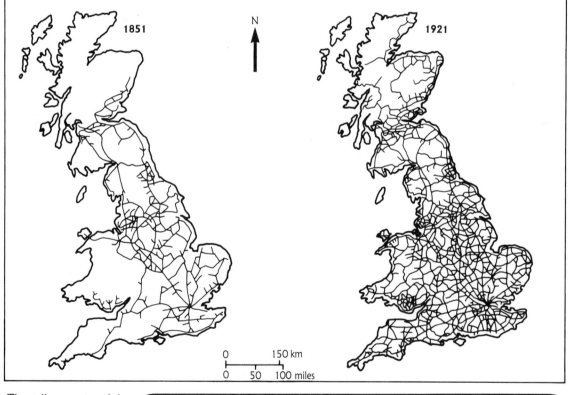

The railway network in
1851 and 1921

1 Look at these maps and at a recent map of the British Rail
network. Which areas of Britain had few railways (a) in 1851, (b)
in 1921, (c) today?

> **2** Write one or two sentences describing and explaining the maps of the railway system. How had the railway network changed by 1921? What lessons were learned between 1851 and the present day?

The early railways owed much to the great pioneers, such as George and Robert Stephenson who built the first effective steam locomotives; Isambard Kingdom Brunel, a brilliant railway engineer; George Hudson, 'the Railway King' of the 1840s; and Thomas Brassey, the biggest railway contractor of his day.

By 1850, the early stages of railway growth were over. The uncontrolled passion for building new railways, irrespective of whether they could pay their way or not (called 'railway mania' at the time), was over. Many railway companies were merging to form stronger, more effective companies.

Even so, where there were duplicate services between towns, the customer had a choice of route. This is why the railway companies fought tooth and nail to gain a monopoly over train travel in their regions. As bitter, often immensely wealthy, rivals, they continued to develop the railway network, criss-crossing and serving almost every part of Britain in competition with one another.

The rivalry gave the long-distance traveller faster services, better amenities, greater comfort, and cut-price fares. Among the many improvements were the first sleeping cars (on the North British Railway, 1873), the introduction of effective heating in carriages (on the Midland Railway, 1874), the first restaurant car (on the Great Northern Railway, 1879), the first train to be lit by electricity (on the London to Brighton Railway, 1881) and the first corridor trains with lavatories (on the Great Western Railway, 1892).

The railways reached their peak in the period between 1880 and 1914, at a time when the car, lorry, motor bus and aeroplane were still in their infancy.

Most of the technical problems had already been solved but there were still some spectacular engineering feats to be achieved, such as the opening of the 7 km Severn Tunnel in 1886 and the completion of a massive cantilever bridge across the Firth of Forth in 1890. Steel rails began to replace iron rails and locomotives became more powerful, benefiting from advances in the design of steam engines.

> **1** What were the advantages of having the railways run by different railway companies? What were the disadvantages?

Safety on the Railways

People who invested money in the railways were often critical of the railway companies. Greater rivalry, improved amenities and cut-throat price competition usually benefited the traveller not the investor. Inevitably, the railway companies became less profitable. But they were also accused of taking short cuts on safety so that railway accidents were frequent. The London, Chatham and Dover Railway was popularly, if unfairly, known as the 'London, Smashem and Turnover'!

RAILWAY UNDERTAKING.
TOUTER.—"GOING BY THIS TRAIN, SIR?"
PASSENGER.—"M? EH? YES."
TOUTER.—"ALLOW ME, THEN, TO GIVE YOU ONE OF MY CARDS, SIR."

Punch, *18 September 1852*

1　Look at the RAILWAY UNDER-TAKING cartoon. Who is the person on the right? Why does he offer his business card to the passenger with the words, 'Going by this train, Sir? Allow me, then, to give you one of my cards, Sir.'?

2　What other detail emphasises the grim point of the cartoon?

Human error caused many of the railway accidents. Engine drivers, firemen and guards on the long-distance trains often worked excessively long hours – as much as eighteen hours a shift in bad weather – without overtime pay. Signalmen sometimes had to work a double shift. Newspapers, magazines and Members of Parliament agitated for legislation to control the number of hours worked by railwaymen. In 1871, 1883 and 1884, legislation was passed to improve safety on the railways, whilst legislation in 1893 reduced the hours worked by engine drivers, firemen and other railway employees.

Government Control of the Railways

The period of railway mania in the 1840s showed only too clearly that unlimited freedom on the part of the railway companies was not in the public interest. This was recognised by successive governments. They regulated the railway companies and, almost from the start, imposed a tax on railway travel. In 1840, regulations were introduced providing for government inspection of new railway lines. The Broad Gauge Act of 1846 ensured that in future all railway lines in Britain would be built to the same (1.4 m) gauge, and Cardwell's Railway Act of 1854 made it compulsory for railways to make their facilities available to any rival company wishing to run through trains on railway tracks other than its own. Nonetheless, Brunel's Great Western Railway continued to operate broad-gauge (2.1 m) railways until 1892, by which time the company had converted all its railway track to standard gauge.

The 1844 Railway Act required all railway companies to run at least one train service a day in both directions on each of its lines, stopping at every station and charging a maximum rate of one penny a mile. Inevitably, these trains were slow and were called 'Parliamentary Trains' as a term of abuse. The 1844 Railway Act envisaged circumstances in which the government might intervene to reduce freight charges and even contemplated the purchase of a railway by the State.

High freight charges annoyed commercial customers, who resented the railway companies and their monopoly of goods transport. This agitation resulted in the passing of the Railway and Canal Traffic Act of 1888, through which the government proposed to regulate freight traffic by putting an upper limit on freight charges. Foolishly, the railway companies immediately raised their standard freight rates to the maximum charges permitted under the new law. Parliament responded with a new Railway and Canal Traffic Act in 1894, which had the effect of preventing the railway companies from raising their rates again until 1914, even though prices of many other goods were rising at the time.

Trade-union Problems

Since many of the costs of running the railways were fixed, the companies tried to economise by keeping the wages of their employees as low as possible. This time they faced pressure from the railway trade unions. There were frequent local railway strikes, culminating in the notorious Taff Vale Railway case. Its outcome in 1901 (see page 222), even threatened to cripple all trade unions. In 1907, a national railway strike was only averted at the last minute by the action of the President of the Board of Trade, David Lloyd George. Four years later, the national railway strike of 1911 brought widespread disruption to the social and economic life of Britain and showed how much the country depended on the railways at that time for the movement of vital supplies. Distribution of coal, food and many other essential commodities came to a standstill.

The Social and Economic Effects of the Railways

Steam locomotive at the Wheall Martyn Museum, Cornwall, used to pull wagons filled with china clay

The social and economic effects of the coming of the railways were massive and widespread.

- By 1850, the old turnpike roads had fallen into disuse and grass grew in the roadways. Some of the turnpike trusts and coaching inns had gone bankrupt. The canals had also declined in importance and many of the railway companies bought up the canal companies in order to monopolise local freight services. By 1870, the railway companies owned a third of the canal network.

- The railways provided industry with a huge market for coal, machine tools, iron rails, steel plate, steam engines, bricks and mortar. Britain, as the pioneer of the railways, also supplied many foreign railway companies as well as those at home, so the growth of the railways worldwide brought prosperity to Britain's industries.

- Proximity to a railway was an essential requirement for new factories. Steam-powered machinery could now be installed in factories well away from the coalfields, since coal could be taken there cheaply and quickly by rail.

- Passenger and cargo ports, such as Southampton and Liverpool, thrived on the railways. So too, did ferry ports like Dover, fishing ports like Grimsby, and seaside resorts like Brighton, Blackpool and Bournemouth.

- Manufacturers found it paid them to advertise branded goods, since their products could now be sold anywhere in Britain.

- Hundreds of thousands of new jobs were created by the railways – engine-drivers, railway guards, stationmasters, cleaners, porters and engineers.

- Farmers benefited in many ways. Railways helped them to keep in touch with new developments. They could buy coal cheaply for use in steam threshing engines. They could send farm produce all over Britain to fetch the best prices.

The Royal Agricultural Society's show yard at Plymouth, The Illustrated London News, *1889*

---

1 *Why did the organisers of the Royal Agricultural Show pick a site near a railway?*

2 *What advantages would the organisers of a modern agricultural show look for in a potential show ground?*

The railways also delivered the penny post, stimulated the growth of the electric telegraph and speeded up the distribution of daily newspapers. Theatre companies and sports teams could travel further afield, and politicians could attend distant meetings.

Without the railways, there would have been no popular seaside resorts. In 1856, *The Illustrated London News* described a typical Whit Monday at Brighton, a seaside town, which it said was 'ready to welcome the town-dried artisan and pent-up clerk'. The credit for this was said to be due entirely to the excursion train.

> 'The railway has done it all. The Road has become deserted and grass grown. Great credit is due to the managers of the South Coast Railway for their determination to supply to the labourers of mind and body the means of breathing for eight hours at least the invigorating sea-breeze, and to give change to the mind deadened by the association from week's end to week's end with brick walls, or whizzing wheels, or blazing furnaces, or other implements of labour.'

> **1** *Why did the author congratulate the South Coast Railway?*
>
> **2** *What do you think he meant by 'the town-dried artisan' and the 'pent-up clerk'?*
>
> **3** *Which form of transport had been hit hard by the coming of the railway to Brighton? How do you know this?*

Excursion trains took people to watch public hangings and to see exhibitions, military reviews and other spectacles. The Great Exhibition of 1851 was visited by over six million people, many travelling to London on cheap day excursions. The Great Exhibition made a profit – something it could not have done had it been held ten years earlier, when only a few railway services were in operation. Public schools began to thrive because pupils could travel there by rail from any part of the country. Many new public schools were founded in the 1840s and 1850s. Policemen and soldiers could be rushed by train to break up disturbances in distant parts of Britain.

The appearance of many towns was substantially altered, since the railway companies wanted to build their stations as close to the town centre as possible, although in many cases they had to build them on the edge of the existing town. Towns and cities grew even bigger, because people from outlying districts could now afford to shop there. This helped to stimulate the growth of chain and department stores in the towns.

Commuters could live at a distance from their work. Suburbs grew up around the railway stations outside London and the big cities. By 1900, many ordinary workers lived at a distance from the factories where they worked and the railway companies ran special workmen's trains for them.

'The Workman's Train',
The Illustrated London
News, *14 April 1883*

1 Write a sentence to describe the interior of this railway compartment. Does the engraving depict the ordinary worker in a fair, unfavourable or favourable light? Was 'The Workman's Train' an appropriate title?

2 What effect do you think trains like this had on the development of towns?

3 How did the railway affect your nearest town? Are there any Victorian buildings in the vicinity of the railway station? Is there a 'Station Hotel', or a Station Road, or a Victorian railway-station building?

4 Which of these economic and social effects do you think was the most important? Give reasons for your answer.

Before the First World War, the number of passengers and the amount of traffic carried by the railways increased with each decade. The railways handled an immense amount of merchandise in the 1890s and 1900s. Freight business was at its peak then, since motor transport offered little competition and goods for delivery were moved from the railway stations by horse-drawn railway vans.

The Decline of the Railways

During the First World War, the Government took control of the operation of the railways through the Railway Executive Committee, made up of representatives of the different railway companies. The heavy work of the war years, moving the armed forces, guns and munitions, could only be done by the railways. But, as a result, the railway companies suffered a serious deterioration in their tracks, locomotives and rolling stock, just at the time when road freight and passenger transport first became serious rivals. The Depression of the 1920s and 1930s (see Chapters 2 and 4) only made matters worse.

When railway workers went on strike for nine days in 1911, the widespread disruption to coal and food supplies gave the railway unions a swift victory. But in October 1919, *The Graphic* magazine claimed that the national railway strike of that year had been 'defeated by rival transport methods'.

'The railway strike has shown very clearly that the train has its rivals in other methods of transport. Motor road transport, which has already become very popular, proved of incalculable service in all parts of the country.'

In 1926, the General Strike (which also brought a halt to railway services) showed that the country, although greatly inconvenienced, could now struggle along, for a week or so, without the railways. Goods were being increasingly moved by lorries, and the growth of road haulage in the 1920s and 1930s, the rising popularity of the motor car and of the motor coach and motor bus, marked the beginning of a relative decline in the importance of the railways. You can see this in these statistics, shown at ten-yearly intervals, for the period from 1933 to 1983.

	1933	*1943*	*1953*	*1963*	*1973*	*1983*
Length (km)	32,580	32,028	31,022	27,330	18,227	16,964
Freight (millions of tonnes)	255	306	294	239	199	138
Passengers (millions)	799	1,037	711	647	428	386

1 *Use the statistics in this table to draw graphs for the fifty years between 1933 and 1983. Show (a) the length of railway route, (b) the number of passengers carried on the railways, (c) the volume of freight traffic.*

2 *Which decades saw the sharpest falls in (a) length of railway route, (b) passenger numbers, (c) amount of freight carried?*

3 *In what ways could the statistics for 1943 give a misleading picture of the importance of the railways?*

4 *From which date would you say the railways really started to decline? Give your reasons.*

5 *Write a paragraph comparing Britain's railways today with the inter-war period, using these statistics and the maps on page 80 as your main sources of information.*

Amalgamation between the Wars

In 1918, the Government seriously considered a proposal to nationalise the railways, but it was opposed by many influential Members of Parliament. Nonetheless, it was clear that something had to be done to restore the railways to their former importance. Some merging of the 120 main railway companies was essential.

In 1921, Parliament passed the Railways Act, giving the Ministry of Transport some degree of control over railway fares and freight charges, whilst at the same time amalgamating the 120 different railway companies into four new railway groupings – the LNER (London and North Eastern Railway), the LMS (London, Midland and Scottish), the GWR (Great Western Railway) and the SR (Southern Railway). The amalgamations came into effect on 1 January 1923.

The problems facing the Big Four railway groupings continued to mount during the Depression years, with the decline in heavy industry (a major user of the railways). As you saw in Chapter 2, less coal was mined, so fewer trains were needed to carry it away.

The 1920s and 1930s saw the first tentative moves away from steam-powered locomotives. In 1928, the LMS started a diesel service at Blackpool whilst the Southern Railway began an electric passenger service from London to Brighton in 1933.

Yet, despite these improvements, the railways were still in trouble. They could not offer an efficient public service on all their lines (as required by law) and still pay their way. The competition from cars, lorries and buses was far too fierce. Yet, in 1931, an LNER poster read:

'Pay one penny per mile by LNER Ordinary Special Trains. Greater choice of days. Wider choice of trains.'

Incredibly, passengers could still travel on the railways for the same fare paid by their great-grandparents in 1844!

Nationalisation

After the Second World War, the newly elected Labour Government, committed to the idea of State ownership, introduced the Transport Act of 1947, which nationalised the railway companies. But the rapid growth of motoring in the post-war years, meant a sharp decline in passenger traffic and an equivalent acceleration in the growth of road haulage. The volume of rail freight traffic was also strongly affected by the decline in the coal industry (see Chapter 2).

Nonetheless, British Railways (later British Rail) made very substantial improvements to the railway network in the post-war period, particularly in the introduction of faster, more comfortable trains, the changeover from steam to diesel and electric locomotives, and the introduction of freightliner services carrying containers (see page 98) to and from the ports.

The Beeching Plan

In 1961, Dr Beeching became Chairman of British Rail. In 1963, he published a sweeping report on the reshaping of Britain's railways. It was a damning indictment of the haphazard way in which the railway network had been allowed to mushroom, unplanned, from the middle years of the nineteenth century. In many parts of Britain, railway fares should have been increased by 300 per cent just to cover the cost of running the existing rail services. In 1963, British Rail began to implement Dr Beeching's recommendations with a major programme of line closures, cutting those train services which made a loss. As a result, hundreds of branch-line train services and over 8,000 km of railway track were shut down and 2,300 stations were closed. Even this was insufficient to bring British Rail into profit and the length of railway track continued to dwindle in the 1970s (see page 88).

Former track of the railway at Snettisham, Norfolk, linking the seaside resort of Hunstanton and a number of villages with the market town of King's Lynn

1 *Look at the photograph. How can you tell that this was probably once the course of a railway?*

2 *How would you have reacted if you had been living in the village of Snettisham when the station was closed? See if any of your friends or relatives have experienced similar closures on their nearest railway line in the last twenty years. Were they upset by, or indifferent to, the closure?*

THE DEVELOPMENT OF SHIPS AND SHIPPING

The Development of Steamships

For much of the first half of the nineteenth century, steamships and sailing ships were rivals. There was no sudden decline of the wooden sailing ship and no sudden rise of the iron steamship.

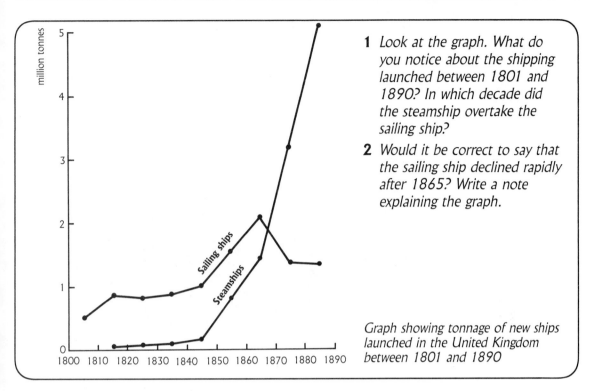

1 *Look at the graph. What do you notice about the shipping launched between 1801 and 1890? In which decade did the steamship overtake the sailing ship?*

2 *Would it be correct to say that the sailing ship declined rapidly after 1865? Write a note explaining the graph.*

Graph showing tonnage of new ships launched in the United Kingdom between 1801 and 1890

In the early days of the steamship, immense amounts of coal were needed to fire the boilers. Small steamships used so much coal that it was impossible to contemplate making a long ocean journey under steam, since such a ship would have had to carry more coal than cargo. This is why Brunel designed larger ships – the wooden paddle ship *Great Western* in 1837, and the iron screw-propeller ship *Great Britain* in 1843 – since they alone could carry enough coal to take a steamship across the Atlantic.

In 1854, John Elder invented the compound steam engine, which economised on the amount of coal required to produce a given amount of horsepower. The same basic principle resulted in the invention of the triple expansion engine in 1881 and the quadruple expansion engine in 1894. Boilers were constructed to re-use the steam three to four times over. On average, one tonne of coal produced as much power in 1899 as over three tonnes had done in 1840. If the top Cunard ocean liner of 1893, the *Campania*, had burned coal as inefficiently as the first Cunard ocean liner, the *Britannia*, had done in 1840, it would have had to carry 10,000 tonnes of coal instead of 3,000 tonnes.

The *Britannia* was a wooden paddle steamer, 63 m long, with engines of 740 horsepower burning 38 tonnes of coal a day. It was little bigger than a private yacht and carried 115 passengers, each paying £40 for the fifteen-day journey from Liverpool to Boston in the United States. By contrast, the *Campania* was built of steel, 190 m long, carried 1,440 passengers and a crew of 400, did the journey in just over five days and burned 500 tonnes of coal a day in the process.

The Campania *and the* Great Western – *a wooden paddle steamer which broke the record for the Atlantic crossing when it took fifteen days to steam from Britain to New York in 1838. Print by J. R. Wells, 1896.*

'Two other matters which have contributed to the development of steamships are the substitution of iron, and then of steel, for timber in the construction of the hull. The old wooden steamers were strained severely by their engines and paddles. Without steel, the construction of ships of the dimensions of those of the present times would be utterly impossible. The steel ship is, relatively speaking, light, yet immensely strong; rigid, though 600 feet [about 180 m] and more in length. It is cellular – a ship within a ship – and practically unsinkable.'

J. Horner, The Harmsworth Magazine, *1899*

1 *Imagine that you emigrated with your family to the United States on the* Britannia *or the* Great Western *in 1840, as a child of ten. In 1893, at the age of 63, you return for the first time to Britain on the* Campania. *Describe your reactions to the ship. How does the voyage on the* Campania *compare with the journey you made all those years ago on the* Britannia *or the* Great Western?

2 *What major improvements in the way in which an ocean liner was built and powered took place between 1840 and 1893?*

3 *What were the advantages of steel as a building material for ships? How did that pave the way for ships like the* Campania?

Britain's Progress as a Shipping Nation

Steel-plated steamships were a far cry from the wooden sailing boats of the early nineteenth century. But widespread adoption of the new methods took a long time to come. Shipowners had to be convinced and sailors had to learn new techniques.

In the 1890s, Sir Charles Parsons' revolutionary steam turbine engine made a big impression on the Admiralty, when his turbine-powered boat, the *Turbinia*, gave a remarkable but unofficial demonstration of its speed at the Spithead Review in 1897, evading the naval ships sent to intercept it! In the 1900s, it was the steam turbine which enabled British shipbuilders to build the fastest ocean liners afloat. The steam-turbine engine caused less vibration, was more economical, easier to use and more powerful.

Diesel engines were later used to power ships and changed the face of shipping once more, although this was primarily a development of the inter-war years. Nonetheless, oil was sometimes used instead of coal, to generate the heat to power steam engines. Oil was easier to store and cleaner to use. It was also quicker to refuel a ship with oil and, since it was fed automatically to the furnaces, fewer stokers were needed in the engine room.

Social and Economic Effects of the Changes in Sea Transport

Improved and swifter sea transport had an important effect on agriculture and industry in the nineteenth century. Ships brought guano (bird droppings rich in nutrients) from South America to fertilise British fields in the 1840s. In the 1870s and 1880s, refrigerated ships brought frozen meat from Argentina and New Zealand and grain from the prairies of North America (see Chapter 1). The cost of shipping wheat across the Atlantic dropped from £2 a tonne in the middle years of the century to 30p a tonne in 1900. So, indirectly, improvements in sea transport in the nineteenth century also hastened the decline of British farming (see Chapter 1).

But improvements in shipping also opened up new markets for British industry and made possible the export of heavy goods, such as coal and iron. The early development of the British coal and iron industries gave the British shipbuilding industry an overwhelming advantage during the changeover period from wooden sailing boats to iron steamships. Improvements in shipping also played a large part in ensuring the supremacy of the British Empire in the nineteenth century – ships took troops, guns, farmers, miners and settlers to the colonies. The number of people travelling overseas increased dramatically, partly because ships were now much bigger and much more comfortable, and partly because they were also much quicker and much safer. Large-scale emigration (see Chapter 5) would not have been possible otherwise.

Safety at sea improved when Samuel Plimsoll persuaded Parliament to pass the Merchant Shipping Act in 1876, limiting the amount of cargo a ship could take on board. A circular disc had to be painted on the hull of every ship to show the permitted level. This 'Plimsoll line', as it was called, had to be visible above the water-line when the ship was laden.

New lighthouses around the coast gave sailors greater protection against the hazards off Britain's rugged coastline, whilst lifeboats were stationed at most ports and harbours, as you can see in these two pictures from pictorial news magazines, depicting the launching of a new lifeboat at Blackpool in 1885.

The Illustrated London News, *10 October 1885*

The Graphic, *10 October 1885*

> **1** *What differences are there between these pictures? Are they significant enough to say that one of the artists, at least, must have exaggerated or omitted important detail?*

2 *How much value can be placed on artist-drawn pictures, like these, as historical evidence? Are they as valuable as eyewitness accounts? Are they as valuable as photographs?*

3 *Which do you think is the more informative picture? Which is the more interesting picture? Which picture would a modern tabloid newspaper be more likely to print?*

4 *Imagine you are at the launching ceremony in Blackpool in October 1885. Write a brief description of the ceremony, using only the information from these pictures that you think is probably **accurate** and **beyond dispute**.*

The growth in shipping had one other significant effect. It caused an equivalent expansion in the number and size of Britain's ports. New docks were built, closely linked to the expansion of the railway system. Many were constructed by the railway companies (such as those at Grimsby, Cleethorpes and Cardiff). By 1900, London, Liverpool, Hull, Glasgow, and Cardiff all ranked among the greatest ports in the world.

Ocean Liners in the Twentieth Century

'In view of the necessity of competing with German transatlantic liners, the White Star company has decided to remove its four crack Atlantic steamships, the *Oceania*, the *Majestic*, the *Teutonic* and the *Adriatic* from Liverpool to Southampton.'

The Illustrated London News, *12 January 1907*

Southampton had outstanding natural advantages as well. There were four high tides a day in the Solent and ocean-going ships could be berthed in deep water there at any time of the day.

1 *Why do you think the White Star Company (later merged with Cunard) decided to change the port of departure for its transatlantic liners from Liverpool to Southampton? What were Southampton's advantages for passengers to or from (a) the United Kingdom, (b) Europe?*

2 *How was it possible for Britain's White Star Company to be in competition with German liners? Why were transatlantic liners so important in 1907?*

3 *What do you think were the consequences for Southampton and Liverpool of this decision?*

In 1907, the White Star Company and Cunard were keen rivals. Later in 1907, Cunard took delivery of the 32,000-tonne *Lusitania* and her sister ship the *Mauretania*. In November, the *Mauretania* broke the previous North Atlantic speed record (known as the 'Blue Riband') by crossing in 4 days, 17 hours and 21 minutes to New York. The White Star Line responded with the launching of the ill-fated *Titanic* and the *Olympic*. With a length of 270 m, a displacement of 46,000 tonnes and sixteen watertight compartments, the *Titanic* was declared 'unsinkable'; but on 16 April 1912, *The Daily Mirror* carried the grim headline:

> 'DISASTER TO THE TITANIC: WORLD'S LARGEST LINER
> SINKS AFTER COLLIDING WITH AN ICEBERG
> DURING HER MAIDEN VOYAGE'

Despite this tragedy, the great ocean liners monopolised the transatlantic passenger trade in the years before the airliner. In 1930 Cunard ordered a new 80,000-tonne liner, *Number 535*, from the John Brown shipyard on Clydeside. But the Depression caused a hold-up and work ceased on the liner in December 1931. It was eventually launched in 1934 when the Government offered financial assistance if the White Star and Cunard lines merged. The ship made her maiden voyage in 1936 as the *Queen Mary* and crossed the Atlantic in 3 days, 23 hours and 57 minutes. Her sister ship, the 85,000-tonne *Queen Elizabeth*, followed suit in 1940.

Shipping During the Depression

'The Trade Slump's Effect on Shipping: A String of Large Ocean-going Liners Lying Idle in the East India Docks', The Graphic, *2 July 1921*

1 *Why did a slump in world trade hit Britain harder than any other nation?*

2 *What effect was this likely to have on other economic activities in Britain at that time?*

3 *Which types of worker would you have expected to see unemployed in July 1921?*

On 27 September 1919, *The Graphic* published an illustrated feature entitled 'The Coming Triumph of the Motor-Ship', in which it pointed out the overwhelming advantages of the oil-powered motor ship compared with the steamship. A complex diagram compared two 10,000-tonne cargo ships – one a steamship, the other a motor ship – both of the same carrying capacity and capable of travelling at the same speed. These were the main differences noted on the diagram:

- a '15 per cent gain in cargo space' in the motor ship, since oil 'takes up far less space than coal';
- 'a steamship uses 45 tonnes of coal daily at a cost of £110 a day in British waters and £250 a day in the Far East, whereas a motor-ship uses 12 tonnes of oil daily at a cost of about £39 to £54 a day; the same weight of oil can carry a ship four times as far as coal';
- filling coal bunkers is 'a long and dirty operation', whereas oil can be 'loaded quickly and cleanly through a pipe. Fuel tanks may be placed anywhere';
- 'machinery staff only one third that of steamer';
- 'boilers require one or two days to raise steam from cold' whereas 'motors can be started up from cold in a few minutes';
- ships using oil as a fuel for their steam engines (instead of coal) use 'three times as much oil as a motor-ship';
- 'working costs are less than 70 per cent of those of a steamer';
- 'motor-ships are selling at twice the figure given for steamers of like dimensions'.

1 *Write a short essay to summarise, in your own words, the advantages of the motor ship compared with the steamship. Were they worth the extra cost?*

2 *Why was coal more than twice as expensive in the Far East as in the waters off Britain? What effect might this have had on the development of shipping?*

3 *Why was Britain at a disadvantage, as a shipping and shipbuilding nation, after 1919?*

The Graphic was accurate in its forecast of 'The Coming Triumph of the Motor-Ship'. Increasingly, in the 1920s and 1930s, the more economical diesel motor engine supplanted the steam engine as the main power source for shipping. Before the First World War, well over nine ships in every ten used coal not oil. By 1939, the proportion had dropped to less than one ship in every two. Britain, not then an oil producer, had no special edge over any other nation. Gradually, the significance of her role as the greatest maritime nation in the world declined. Before the First World War, two in every five ships in the world were British. By 1939, the proportion had dropped to only one ship in every four. Even so, this was still substantial, and the British merchant fleet was twice as large as that of any other country.

Shipping since 1945

At the end of the Second World War, the transatlantic ocean liners began to flourish again. But this time their days were numbered. In 1958, for the first time, more people crossed the Atlantic by airliner than by ocean liner. People on business preferred speed to luxury. Gradually services were withdrawn from the Atlantic as the shipping companies began to use their liners for luxury cruises rather than for scheduled services.

The period since 1945 has seen a further deterioration in Britain's position as a maritime nation. Rotterdam, with its associated complex of facilities at Europoort, has replaced London as Europe's leading port. Many UK docking facilities have been closed down. Huge new supertankers carrying oil have had special berths built for them away from the main ports. For tax reasons, many of the cargo ships using British ports are registered in countries other than the United Kingdom.

The rapid growth in the number of container ships has caused a boom in special container ports, such as Tilbury on the Thames Estuary and Felixstowe in Suffolk. Containerisation, however, has caused a sharp decline in the number of dockers employed by the ports. Containers carried by lorries or freightliner trains, can be loaded and unloaded quickly by hoists, lifts and cranes. As a result, ships can be made ready for the next voyage in a fraction of the time taken in the past.

> **1** *Why are container ports able to handle more ships a year than ordinary cargo ports of the same size? Why do they need fewer dockers to handle the same volume of trade?*
>
> **2** *What other groups of workers have been put out of work by containerisation?*

THE DEVELOPMENT OF THE AUTOMOBILE

Horse-and-cart Britain

MIGHT IS RIGHT.

Van Driver. "I DON'T KNOW NUTHUN ABOUT NO RIGHT SIDES. YOU GET OUT OF THE WAY, IF YER DON'T WANT TO BE MADE A WAFER OF!"

This cartoon appeared in Punch *in 1853. What does it tell you about road travel at that time?*

The railways brought an end to the stagecoach and mailcoach services of the early nineteenth century. But in the towns, large horse-drawn wagons, carts, drays and vans (like the one shown in the cartoon), private horse-drawn traps and carriages, horse-buses and cabs for hire (the four-wheeled 'growler' and the two-wheeled hansom) continued to dominate door-to-door transport. Indeed, it was not until the end of the Second World War that the horse and cart became a rare sight in towns.

The dominance of horse-drawn transport for short distances provided great cities, like London, with huge problems. Vast cartloads of hay and straw had to be brought in every day to feed and bed the thousands of horses kept in London's stables. Every street had its horse trough filled with drinking water. Not surprisingly, the streets smelled of horse manure, and crossing sweepers armed with brooms earned a living by sweeping a path across the road for pedestrians. The house-proud installed footscrapers outside their front doors, so that visitors could clean their footwear before entering. Horse troughs, mews houses (formerly town stables) and footscrapers can be seen in London and other towns and cities to this day.

The Steam Traction Engine

The only competitor to the horse and cart, as a goods vehicle on the roads, was the steam traction engine. But its weight, size and shape made it unsuitable for city streets or for carrying passengers. It came into its own on farms and for moving heavy goods in areas where there were no railways. Inventors had long tried to build an effective steam-powered land vehicle, which could be used as a bus or private carriage, but without success.

Because of the great size of these steam engines (see picture on page 14), the Red Flag Act of 1865 sensibly required that all drivers of heavy road vehicles travel at no more than fast walking speed – 4 mph [6 kph]. In addition, they had to have a person walking in front, carrying a red flag as warning.

The Bicycle

Penny-farthing bicycle 1879. Why was it called a penny-farthing?

The invention of the bicycle enabled many more people to explore the countryside and gave young people a freedom they had not enjoyed earlier in the century. It made it possible for country people to make friends and take part in the activities of the towns.

A bicycle that could be moved by treadles was invented by Kirkpatrick MacMillan, in 1839, but the first pedal bicycles to become popular were the 'boneshakers' of the 1860s, forerunners of the 'penny-farthing' or 'ordinary' bicycle of the 1870s. A cyclist on a penny-farthing could travel faster than a horse and cart and there were cases of infuriated coachmen using their whips on cyclists who overtook them.

In 1885, the Rover safety bicycle was introduced, with its geared chain drive, wheels of equal size, diamond frame and lower seat. Pneumatic bicycle tyres (instead of solid rubber tyres) were invented soon afterwards – by a Belfast veterinary surgeon, called J.B. Dunlop, who made them for his son's tricycle in 1888.

The popularity of cycling was such that every town of any size had a cycle shop and there were a dozen cycling magazines for enthusiasts. Like many good inventions, it also started a new industry. Factories were built to make bicycles and tyres. They employed about 50,000 workers and brought prosperity to towns like Coventry (see page 61) and Nottingham.

The Internal-combustion Engine

Steam engines were too heavy for ordinary road vehicles; so when the lighter internal-combustion engine was developed in the 1860s by the Belgian-French engineer Lenoir, it was only a matter of time before an internal-combustion engine would be used to propel a motor car. This picture appeared in *Cassell's Family Magazine* in April 1881 under the heading, 'A Carriage Driven by Gas'.

'Several appliances have now been put before the public for driving vehicles by other than animal power. Most have proposed to utilise steam, but the carriage represented in our woodcut is driven by common gas, mixed with a certain proportion of air and exploded in the cylinder in the manner common to gas-engines. The box on which the passengers sit contains a weighted bellows full of gas.'

---

1 *What type of engine was this? Is the engine at the front or at the back of this vehicle?*

2 *What was its major disadvantage as a vehicle?*

The first genuine motorised vehicle, with a petrol-driven engine, was made by Karl Benz at Mannheim, in Germany, in 1885. His motor tricycle was similar in appearance to the gas-powered vehicle shown in the picture, and fitted with a battery and spark plugs. But a Mannheim newspaper queried, 'Who is interested in such a vehicle as long as there are horses for sale?'

In 1886, another German engineer, Gottlieb Daimler, converted a horse-drawn carriage (a phaeton) so that it could be driven by a petrol engine, and in 1889 he brought out a new model with gears. In 1891, two French motor engineers, Levassor and Panhard, put the engine in their motor vehicle at the front, to give the car greater stability.

Another significant advance came in 1895, with the development of the diesel engine, a particular type of internal-combustion engine, named after its inventor, Rudolf Diesel, a German engineer. By 1901, car design had advanced to the stage that a new model designed by Daimler had many of the features to be seen on a car today, such as a four-cylinder engine, modern gears and radiator grille. He called his new car 'Mercedes' after the daughter of an Austrian businessman who earned a living selling luxury cars to the very rich on the Riviera.

---

1 *Who developed the first horseless carriage? Why was it called a car?*

2 *What advantage had the internal-combustion engine over the steam engine?*

The Horseless Carriage in Britain

The Prince of Wales in a horseless carriage in 1900. Make a list of the differences between this vehicle and a modern car. In what ways was motoring more uncomfortable in 1900 than it is today?

Only five years before this photograph was taken, the Prince of Wales would have been breaking the law had he driven a horseless carriage on the highway – as you can see from the picture and the written extracts which follow.

Source A

'It is quite conceivable that but for this legislative hindrance, this country, as the pioneer of railways, steam-navigation, and cycles, would have now occupied a more prominent position as regards this movement, which bids fair to become soon a new industry, as well as a new force in civilisation.'

Source B

'A lighted match sets it off on its noiseless career. It will do all that horses can do, and something more; as, for instance, running backwards. Its speed is, if necessary, beyond that of a horse: twelve and a half miles an hour, and even more if wanted. The carriage has a supply of petroleum for four hours' running. Every thirty miles run, a small supply of cold water is required to be used for keeping the working parts cool.'

Source C

'The first journey made in this country in a petroleum motor carriage was on July 5th. This car is a neat, compact four-wheeled dogcart, with accommodation for four persons and two portmanteaus. The steering is simple, and the car could be brought to a standstill within little more than a yard.'

'Horseless Carriages', Chambers's Journal, 7 September 1895

Source D

'The first car in England was a Benz. It belonged to Mr Harry Hewetson who purchased it in Mannheim in 1894. It was a two-seated 3-hp car which cost £80. Mr Hewetson sent a bicycle scout ahead and had with him in the car a little boy, who when the scout reported a policeman got down and carried a flag. The flag was only a tiny scrap of red ribbon on a lead pencil, but it fulfilled the law.'

The Illustrated London News, 17 November 1906

Source E

'Exposing an Absurd Law: The First Motor Car in England Complying with the Unreasonable Regulation of the Red Flag, Abolished November 14, 1896', The Illustrated London News, 17 November 1906

1 What was the legislative hindrance? How did Harry Hewetson get round it? What reasons were given for urging the repeal of the law as soon as possible?

2 What did the writer of the 1895 article think were the main advantages of the petrol-driven motor vehicle compared with the horse and the horse-drawn vehicle? How did he see its future? Was he right?

3 How do these sources from 1895 and 1906 differ in what they tell you about the first motor car in Britain? Do these differences matter to a historian?

4 Are there any parts of these extracts which seem to you to be exaggerated or far-fetched in any way?

The Repeal of the Red Flag Act

'The bill which is now before Parliament will probably become law before many months have passed. It provides that the new vehicles shall be placed on exactly the same footing as horse-drawn carriages. The maximum weight of a horseless carriage is to be four tons; it must never be left without control, it must not whistle or make any other disagreeable noise, and its construction must be of an unobjectionable nature.'

Chambers's Journal, *8 August 1896*

The repeal of the Red Flag Act was greeted with great rejoicing by all potential motorists in Britain and they celebrated with a run from London to Brighton. But of the 60 vehicles, or so, taking part, few actually reached their destination.

In those early days of motoring, the motor car was very unreliable and designs were constantly changing. In 1898, a car was usually steered with a tiller, rather than a wheel. It looked like a horse-drawn carriage, with the rear wheels considerably larger than those at the front. But by 1903, motor engineers, in only five years, had produced cars with wheels the same size front and back, the use of a lever to change gears and a round steering wheel. They had even produced racing cars capable of doing 90 mph [145 kph], but not on the highway, where the speed limit was still only 12 mph [19 kph].

Problems in the Early Days of Motoring

As you can see from the illustrations on the previous pages, drivers and passengers were exposed to the weather in open-topped cars without glass windscreens. Roads were bumpy, unsurfaced, dusty and narrow. Solid rubber tyres gave an uncomfortable and bumpy ride, whilst pneumatic tyres were very unreliable and very expensive, rarely lasting more than 2,000 miles.

> 'I use my car in a reasonable sort of way, yet in six months for tyres alone I have spent £40.
>   People are becoming "fed up" with getting wet through day after day, and even a hood is more or less of another makeshift, growing extremely dirty and dusty when down, and admitting a great deal of wind and rain when up, so everybody who can afford it is going in for a covered body of some sort or other.'
>
> *Major C. G. Matson,* Badminton Magazine, *December 1905*

Other problems included slippery roads, potholes, cast-off horseshoes and nails likely to cause punctures, inexperienced drivers in cars with poor brakes, unreliable engines giving rise to frequent breakdowns, traffic jams on roads not intended for motor vehicles, damage to buildings from vibration, frequent accidents at busy and unregulated road junctions, and a pressing need for regular petrol filling stations (motorists had to carry their spare petrol with them in separate cans).

The motorist's biggest grumbles were about the roads. Since they were unsurfaced, dust was an appalling problem in summer, especially when there was a vehicle in front.

> 'The question of roads for motor-cars is being hotly canvassed just now. It has been estimated that to put the existing roads in England and Wales into perfect order for motors, so as to avoid the troubles of dust and too weak surface, would cost £287,000,000, and it has therefore been asked whether it would not be better at once to make new trunk roads for the traffic.'
>
> The Illustrated London News, *11 May 1907*

DEA EX MACHINA. THE GODDESS OUT OF THE CAR.

Cartoon in Punch, *1903*

---

1 *Why was Major Matson annoyed?*

2 *Why was dust regarded as such a problem? What was the solution? How did motorists protect themselves against it?*

3 *Describe the outfit worn by a female motorist in 1903. What clues does it provide about motoring conditions in the 1900s? Why did motoring have a very special appeal to women in the 1900s?*

4 *In view of the problems associated with it, why was motoring so popular amongst the rich? What were the compensations?*

Money to finance the building of new roads and to prepare hard-wearing, dust-free surfaces, was eventually derived from the sale of motor-vehicle licences and by imposing a tax of 3d [just over 1p] on the sale of each gallon of petrol. Lloyd George set up the Road Board in 1910 (later taken over by the Ministry of Transport in 1919) to make these funds available to the County Councils.

Road surfaces were improved, but relatively few new roads were built before the coming of the motorways in 1958. The most important were probably the bypasses, such as the Kingston Bypass (London) which was opened in 1930 and described at the time as 'one of the most famous of the great arterial roads that modern traffic has rendered necessary'. Even then there were complaints about traffic congestion. 'It is sometimes quicker to take the old road through the town it was intended to by-pass.'

It took time for the authorities to work out an effective method of controlling the flow of traffic. For instance, Piccadilly Circus in the centre of London was not a roundabout in 1919. A photograph shows traffic travelling in both directions instead of keeping to the left. It only became a 'one-way' roundabout in 1926.

In 1904, there were only 8,000 private cars and 4,000 vans or lorries in the United Kingdom. By 1914, there were 132,000 cars, 82,000 commercial vehicles and 124,000 motor bikes.

Lorries at the battle of the Somme in 1916

The motor vehicle came into its own during the First World War – as you can see from this photograph. Any lingering doubts about its utility disappeared when motor buses brought troop reinforcements up to the front and when the tank proved to be the most significant invention of the war.

The Social and Economic Effects of the Coming of the Automobile

'For the country medical man, the motor car has revolutionised work. The long monotonous journeys of the old days have become short and pleasant. The saving of time is enormous, and the exhilaration produced by this mode of transit, together with the mental relief which attention to the driving produces, acts as a very efficient tonic and mental stimulus to the very frequently tired and worried medical man.'

Letter from Dr Fawcett in the Lancet, *1903*

Motoring affected everyone. The many social and economic effects included the following.

- Factories built near main roads could easily assemble components and raw materials from any part of Britain. Finished products could be taken safely from the factory to the wholesaler or customer, without having to be loaded and unloaded from railway wagons. Lorries were usually quicker and easier to manipulate than goods trains. Ease of communications was of vital importance for the new industries of the 1920s and 1930s (see Chapter 2).

- Many hundreds of thousands of new jobs were created by the coming of the motor car, lorry and bus. They included jobs in oil refineries, car-assembly plants and in factories making components; ambulance, taxi, bus and lorry drivers; traffic police; chauffeurs; roadside-café and petrol-station attendants. Transport historians estimate that, by 1939, as many as 1.5 million people may have earned their living 'from the manufacture, operation and servicing of motor vehicles'. It was one of the few industries to escape the effects of the Depression in the 1930s.

- Equally, people dependent upon the horse for their jobs and livelihoods suffered badly – if they failed to take advantage of the changeover from horse to petrol engine. Their numbers included coachmen, ostlers, stable hands, cab drivers, grooms, stable owners, blacksmiths and cartwrights. In practice, many blacksmiths and cycle-repair shops were converted into motor garages, and coachmen became chauffeurs. Adverse effects were also felt by the other forms of inland transport affected by the coming of the motor vehicle, such as the railways and the trams.

- Although only the relatively well-to-do could afford to run a car between the wars, its influence on the growth of towns was such that houses were built along the main roads leading away from town centres. This is known as 'ribbon development'. Public services dependent on rapid communications (such as the ambulance, police and fire services), and professions and trades which travelled to serve the public (such as doctors, nurses, delivery vans), also benefited. Equally, criminals were able to leave the scene of a crime quickly – giving rise to the phrase 'get-away car'.

- The coming of the motor car inevitably created a new landscape of petrol stations, ring roads, roundabouts, road signs, town centres planned round the bus and the car, motels, roadside cafés, motorways and huge car parks.

- The horse virtually disappeared from the streets. There were nearly half a million horse-drawn carriages in 1903, and only 25,000 or so, thirty years later, in 1933.

- Road accidents became the leading cause of death for young people and a serious problem for police and medical services. In 1930, there were 1.5 million motor vehicles on the roads and 7,000 deaths. Despite new traffic laws, road deaths reached an all-time peak of nearly 9,000 in 1940, when there were 2 million motor vehicles. This was due partly to the wartime blackout. By the end of the war, although there were 2.3 million motor vehicles, the number of road deaths fell to 4,000 a year. The number rose again in the post-war boom years to 8,000 in 1966 (11 million vehicles), but had dropped to 7,000 by 1974 (15 million vehicles) and further still, to 5,200, by 1985 (when there were over 20 million vehicles on the roads).

● Improvements in public transport benefited all sections of the community – from people living in isolated villages to those commuting to work from the suburbs of a large city. Buses appealed to many of the travellers who would otherwise have gone by train. Only three years after the end of the First World War, Donald Maxwell forecast what would happen, when he wrote an article entitled 'The Return of the Coaching Days' in *The Graphic*. He began by talking about the old stagecoach services.

> 'Gradually the coach-owners went to the wall, and many unfortunate little towns and innumerable roadside inns, served neither by the stage-coach which had gone nor by the railway that had never come, were left stranded and forgotten.
>
> It has remained for the stage-coach to return after a long chrysalis-like sleep, bringing with it the possibilities of easy intercommunication between village and village. Time has at last brought a dramatic revenge. The railway which killed the stage-coach, is in turn seriously threatened by the renaissance [rebirth] of the King's highway, made possible by the development of the new-time stage-coach of today. The heavy cost of train travelling and the still more outrageous expense of sending parcels by rail, is helping fast to foster the rivalry of the road.'

Donald Maxwell, The Graphic, *21 May 1921*

Tourists from Sussex on a charabanc tour of the Lake District. How did the charabanc differ from a modern luxury coach?

1 What was the 'new-time stage-coach'? How did it differ from the old-time stagecoach?

2 What was the 'dramatic revenge'? When, by what type of vehicle and why did it eventually take place?

3 What effect did (a) the railway, (b) the motor coach, have on country villages? Are modern villages well served by bus or coach?

Development of Motor Transport in the Inter-war Period

The number of motor cars on the roads multiplied as the British motor industry began to expand rapidly to meet the demand (see Chapter 2). In particular, the use of mass-production methods by Herbert Austin (Austin Seven) and William Morris (Morris Eight), brought motoring within reach of hundreds of thousands of people.

After 1918, many old army lorries were bought up and converted to civilian use. As a result many small road-haulage enterprises sprang up, and for the first time the railways faced a serious new challenge for the carriage of freight. In addition, hundreds of private bus companies fought for customers on the roads. The drivers were often untrained, accidents were frequent and rivalry between competing bus companies vicious.

As traffic increased on the roads, deaths from accidents rose to frighteningly high levels, even though the number of vehicles was still small compared with those on the roads of today (see statistics on page 107). Something had to be done to control the way in which traffic used the highways.

Parliament recognised the need to regulate the motor industry and started what was to become a mountain of motoring legislation, dominating the working of the law courts ever since. These are just a few of the road-traffic controls introduced in the inter-war years:

1924 First white line painted in a London street.

1926 First traffic lights – not in general use until 1931.

1930 Road Traffic Act introduced licensing system for bus companies, compulsory driving tests for bus drivers and also mechanical inspection of buses; compulsory car insurance.

1934 Cat's-eyes in roads to indicate middle of road at night; special pedestrian crossings erected with yellow globes on black and white posts (known as Belisha beacons after Hore-Belisha, the Minister of Transport).

1935 Driving tests made compulsory for new motorists; 30 mph [48 kph] speed limit introduced on roads in towns.

1 *Oral history (recorded conversations, broadcasts, tape recordings of people talking about the past) is an important source of evidence used by modern historians. See if you can record on paper (or with a cassette recorder), the reminiscences of older friends or relatives, who can remember some of the landmarks in motoring history this century and their effects on everyday life.*

2 *Write a short essay using this evidence to describe a topic in motoring history since 1900.*

Motor Transport since 1939

The Second World War caused a halt in motor-car production, and the shortage of petrol seriously curtailed motoring for the duration of the war. But it soon picked up again after 1945 and, as you have seen in Chapter 2, the production of motor vehicles began to grow rapidly. The number of vehicles on the roads shot up at an alarming rate, putting great pressure on main roads and blocking up the streets of urban areas. Fast, modern motor roads were needed, like the autobahns of Germany and the *autostrade* of Italy which had been built before the war.

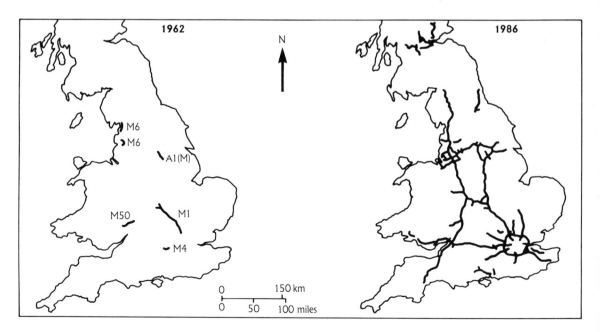

Motorways in Britain 1962–86. Write a sentence to say what changes took place between 1962 and 1986.

In 1958, the first British motorway (the Preston Bypass – later part of the M6) was opened, followed by a section of the M1 in 1959. Gradually a new network of super roads was developed, leading to and round, but rarely into, the major cities. The motorways speeded up cross-country travel and further helped to hasten the decline of the railways. New bridges were built – notably across the Severn (1966), Forth (1964), Tay (1966) and Humber (1981). By 1983, there were 2,700 km of motorways in Britain. But road accidents continued to give cause for worry. In 1965, a maximum 70 mph [112 kph] speed limit on motorways was introduced and, in 1983, seat belts were made compulsory for drivers and front-seat passengers.

> **1** *Do the statistics on page 107 provide any evidence to suggest that the traffic controls outlined above had any effect?*

THE DEVELOPMENT OF AVIATION

Pioneers of Flight

'At last M. Santos Dumont's triumphant flight of 235 yards in his aeroplane'

This picture, based on a photograph, appeared in *The Illustrated London News* in November 1906. When the photograph first appeared in the magazine, it was captioned:

> 'The First Flight of a Machine Heavier than Air: Santos Dumont Winning the Archdeacon Prize'

Yet three years earlier, on 17 December 1903, the American pioneer aviators, Orville and Wilbur Wright, had already made the first sustained flights in a 'heavier-than-air' machine at Kitty Hawk in North Carolina. One of these epic flights, in 'Flyer I', covered a distance of 284 yards [260 metres].

Europeans seemed unaware of the activities of the Wright brothers. On 13 April 1907, *The Illustrated London News* printed a picture of Orville Wright flying a glider and asked, 'Is he the first man to fly? – Mysterious Orville Wright.' The article went on to say about the Wright brothers, 'They have maintained so much secrecy, however, that it is impossible to give details of their methods.'

Even in the United States, little interest was shown at first in the new discovery. This was one of the reasons why Wilbur Wright came to Europe in 1908, to demonstrate his machine to a more interested public.

'Wilbur Wright flying at dusk on the occasion of his great flight last week', The Sphere, *October 1908*

'On the evening of September 22 Mr Wilbur Wright surpassed all previous achievements in aeroplane flight both for time and distance. The effect was marvellously impressive as this huge mechanical bird slipped through the evening air over the dim landscape. Mr Wright flew for 1 hr 31 min. 25.8 sec., and had covered an official distance of 66.6 kilometres before he alighted.'

The Sphere, *3 October 1908*

---

1 *What evidence in these extracts suggests that the early flights of the Wright brothers were shrouded in secrecy. Why? What had the Wright brothers to lose by making their methods known to the general public?*

2 *Why did Santos Dumont get credit for something he did not do? For what record should he have got credit in 1906?*

3 *What was Wilbur Wright's average speed in 1908? What did his plane have in common with the one piloted by Santos Dumont? How did their machines differ from later aeroplanes?*

After these early beginnings, interest soon mounted in the possibilities of flight. In 1909, Louis Blériot became the first pilot to fly an aeroplane across the English Channel – flying the 37 km from Calais to Dover. The *Daily Graphic* printed a large, front-page photograph on Monday, 26 July 1909, and added:

'BRAVO BLERIOT!

M. BLERIOT AND HIS MONOPLANE, IN WHICH HE YESTERDAY ACCOMPLISHED THE FIRST CROSS CHANNEL FLIGHT BY A "HEAVIER-THAN-AIR" MACHINE – THE FLIGHT FROM BARAQUES, NEAR CALAIS, TO DOVER OCCUPIED TWENTY-THREE MINUTES'

Another newspaper said it was 'an event which marks the dawn of a new age for man' and the *Daily Graphic* made this prediction:

'The lesson is for all to read. What M. Blériot can do in 1909, a hundred, nay a thousand aeroplanes may be able to do in five years' time. A machine which can fly from Calais to Dover is not a toy, but an instrument of warfare of which soldiers and statesmen must take account.'

But Lady Monkswell, wife of a former Under-Secretary for War, was not worried. In her diary, she wrote on 30 July 1909:

'we need hardly fear, while there is a man left who can hit a rocketing pheasant (like dear Papa) that our privacy will be trespassed upon or our little island invaded'.

R. D. Blumenfeld, Editor of the *Daily Express*, wrote in his diary:

'I agree with Shackleton that these things represent a foolish waste of money. Besides, flying across the Channel means nothing after you have done it. You can't carry goods or passengers.'

---

1 What did Lady Monkswell mean? Was she right to take this attitude? Why were people slow to see the real significance of these early flights? What was particularly significant about the prediction in the Daily Graphic?

2 Imagine you were standing on the cliffs at Dover on Sunday, 25 July 1909. How would you have reacted? Write an entry for your diary.

3 What was Blériot's average speed in kph? How long does it take today to cross from Calais to Dover by hovercraft?

4 Why did Blériot's flight arouse more public interest than the earlier pioneer flights, such as those by the Wright brothers?

Aviation during the First World War

It took the war years, between 1914 and 1918, to convince many doubting sceptics that the aeroplane was the vehicle of the future. But its utility as a reconnaissance plane, as a fighter and as a bomber, showed clearly its potential as a war machine. The development of large bombers paved the way for the development of airliners after the war. By the end of the war, the Royal Air Force had the world's biggest air force with over 20,000 aeroplanes and 700 aerodromes.

In less than twenty years, aeroplane design had made huge strides. The flimsy, kite-like machine flown by Santos Dumont (sitting in 'a willow basket') only twelve years earlier, had been replaced by sleek new aeroplanes.

Air Transport in the Inter-war Years

'A regular passenger air service to Paris and Brussels starts on Monday, thanks to the enterprise of the Handley–Page Transport Company. Comfortable accommodation will be provided for ten passengers, and provision will also be made for carrying from 500lb to 600lb [about 225–75kg] of freight. The flights starting in the meantime from Hounslow, will be made on Mondays, Wednesdays and Fridays to Brussels, and on Tuesdays, Thursdays and Saturdays to Paris. The single fare for the three hour trip to the French capital is 15 guineas [£15.75], and goods will be carried at the rate of 2s 6d per lb [about 28p per kg].'

The Graphic, *30 August 1919*

A traveller on the first flight said he had more difficulty getting to the airport by Underground railway and tram than the plane had in flying to Paris. Unfortunately, the service failed to pay its way and closed down just over a year later.

In October 1922, the Government introduced a new scheme to help subsidise airline services from London to Paris, Brussels and Cologne, and also from Manchester to London and Amsterdam. But these early airways also had difficulty in paying their way and were merged on 1 April 1924 to form Imperial Airways – an airline partially financed by the government but under strict instructions to 'use its best endeavours to make its services self-supporting at the earliest possible moment'.

1 *Write a short description of the 1920 airliner in the picture opposite. How did it differ from a modern airliner?*

2 *In 1922, you could travel to Paris by train and boat from London, in just under seven hours, for a return fare (via Dover) of 49s 9d [£2.49]. How much more expensive was the air fare in 1919?*

3 How much quicker was it to travel to Paris from central London, flying from Hounslow aerodrome (about 20 km from Trafalgar Square), than it was to go by train and boat from Charing Cross Station (less than five minutes walk from Trafalgar Square)? How much quicker is it today?

4 What reasons may help to explain why the airlines found it difficult to pay their way in the inter-war years?

Bristol Pullman airliner, The Graphic, 1920

Later in 1924, daily air services to Paris, Cologne, Basle and Zurich began. In 1927 Imperial Airways started a regular service every fortnight to the Middle East. Other services were introduced to Karachi (1929), Accra (1931), Cape Town (1932), Calcutta and Singapore (1933) and eventually Brisbane in Australia in 1935. This last journey took over ten days! Surprisingly, it was not until 1946 that the first regular British airline service from London to New York began – a journey of twenty hours.

In 1935, a new company, British Airways, was formed by the merger of five smaller airlines. The intention was to fly regular services to Europe, and the airline began flights from Heston Airport, London, to Sweden in 1936 and to Berlin in 1937. The years immediately before the Second World War saw some expansion of air services, and by 1939 there were over 40 municipal airports in the United Kingdom, such as Ringway (Manchester) and Speke (Liverpool).

The inter-war period also saw the establishment of many air records, such as Alcock and Brown in 1919 (first to cross the Atlantic), Charles Lindbergh in

1927 (first solo flight across the Atlantic) and Amy Johnson in 1930 (first solo flight by a woman to Australia – see page 328).

The economic and social consequences of the development of air transport were eventually to become almost as far-reaching in scope as the military uses, already demonstrated during the First World War. By 1939, people could travel from one corner of the globe to another in a matter of days. Politicians and statesmen could be summoned at a moment's notice to discuss a crisis, as in September 1938, when Neville Chamberlain made his first flight in an aeroplane by British Airways to Munich, in order to talk Hitler out of invading Czechoslovakia. But as yet, air travel had very little effect on the ordinary person, because of the high cost.

Air Transport since 1939

Since 1939, there has been a massive expansion in the scope and nature of air travel. During the Second World War, many remarkable developments took place – in radar, for instance, and in the development of the jet engine by Sir Frank Whittle in Britain and by Hans von Ohain in Germany. This later led to the introduction of the world's first jet airliner, the De Havilland Comet, in 1949. Other British post-war aviation successes included the hovercraft, designed by Sir Christopher Cockerell in 1955, the Harrier Vertical Take Off Jet, and the joint Anglo-British Concorde which came into service in 1976.

In 1940 British Airways and Imperial Airways were amalgamated to form the British Overseas Airways Corporation (BOAC) and, in 1946, British European Airways (BEA) was formed to operate services in Europe. In 1972 the two companies were amalgamated to form British Airways.

The post-war years saw a remarkable growth in air travel, with the development of package holidays abroad, particularly to Spain. Cheap flights by special charter aircraft made continental holidays as cheap as many holidays in Britain. However, domestic airline services in Britain were still relatively unimportant, unlike in the United States or Canada, for instance. Distances between major cities in Britain are relatively short and airlines find it difficult to compete with fast InterCity train journeys or the motorways.

But because Great Britain is an island, the volume of overseas traffic multiplied in the post-war period. London's Heathrow Airport became the busiest international airport in the world, used by 27 million passengers a year and employing a staff of over 50,000, in connection with more than 250,000 flights a year to over 90 countries. As well as airliners, many cargo planes use Heathrow, making it also one of the most important centres in Britain for handling foreign trade.

THE DEVELOPMENT OF COMMUNICATIONS
The Postal Services

In 1837, a person sending a two-page letter from London paid nothing to the Post Office. But the person who received it in Edinburgh had to pay 2s 3d [11p], whilst a person in London paid only 4d [less than 2p]. Many people were dissatisfied with the system and in 1837 Rowland Hill (1795–1879), a Worcestershire teacher, wrote a booklet called *Post-office Reform*, in which he persuaded the Government to change the postal system. He worked out that the cost of actually carrying a letter from London to Edinburgh was one-ninth part of one farthing [about 0.01p]. Hill argued that a large part of the cost of posting a letter lay in the time it took the Post Office clerks to calculate the charge (based on distance, weight and the number of enclosures) and for postmen to collect the money from the recipients at the other end. Since many people had discovered ingenious ways of avoiding payment, Hill said it made more sense to make every one pay a fixed sum in advance, irrespective of the destination of the letter.

He was appointed to the Treasury to oversee the introduction of the new postal scheme, which came into force on 10 January 1840, with a uniform rate of one penny for all letters not exceeding half an ounce [14 g] in weight. On 6 May 1840, the Penny Black stamp was introduced. It carried a portrait of Queen Victoria on one side and was gummed on the other. The new postal system was so well received by the public that, in 1844, *Punch* said it was:

> 'an event much greater in its ultimate results on the happiness of England, than the Battle of Waterloo. Much more beautiful is the red coat of the Postman with his bundle of penny missives, than the scarlet coat of the Life Guardsman! For the Postman is the soldier of peace – who will bring the remotest part of the United Kingdom close to his own door-step for a couple of halfpence.'

Yet a writer in the 20 May 1837 issue of *Chambers's Journal*, had argued the case against the penny post.

> 'Reader, imagine for a moment the idea of every one having to buy stamped covers beforehand for his letters, or having to pay a penny with every letter he submitted to the inspection of an office-keeper! You here see that nothing like delicacy of feeling, or the preservation of secrecy, is taken into account. As small a sum as a penny is, we believe that it would be grudged severely by many. We are sorry for this; but looking at human society as at present constituted, we are assured it would never work.'

> 1 *On what grounds did the writer of the article in* Chambers's Journal *object to the new postal system? Why was he wrong? Imagine you are Rowland Hill. Write a letter to* Chambers's Journal *pointing out the mistakes in this argument.*

2 *How important was the 'penny letter' as a means of communication before the invention of the telephone? Write a paragraph to say whether you think the writer in* Punch *was exaggerating the importance of the penny post, or not.*

3 *How did the coming of the railway make it possible for the new postal system to work effectively?*

4 *The cartoons below were published in* Punch *on 4 May 1844 as designs for the front and back of a 'Penny Post Medal'. St Martins-le-Grand was the site of the Post Office Headquarters in London. What inspired the cartoonist to design the front and back of a 'Penny Post Medal'? Identify (a) Rowland Hill, (b) the Prime Minister, Sir Robert Peel, (c) a Penny Black stamp.*

5 *Use the cartoons to say what you think happened to Rowland Hill after he had helped to supervise the introduction of the penny post between 1840 and 1843.*

ROWLAND HILL'S TRIUMPHAL ENTRY INTO ST. MARTIN'S-LE-GRAND.

BRITANNIA PRESENTING ROWLAND HILL WITH THE SACK.

Cartoons showing Sir Rowland Hill (a) in 1840, (b) in 1843

At first the profits of the Post Office fell sharply but business boomed, as you can see from these statistics, which show the number of letters posted in the UK in selected years between 1839 and 1913.

1839	82,000,000	1870	863,000,000
1840	169,000,000	1889	1,558,000,000
1851	670,000,000	1913	3,478,000,000

In succeeding years, the Post Office greatly extended the facilities it offered. The Post Office Savings Bank was founded in 1861, the inland telegraph system was taken over in 1866 and the parcel post was introduced in 1883, whilst most of the British telephone system came under the control of the Post Office in 1912. Further improvements have been made in the twentieth century, although the telephone service became a separate public corporation in 1981 and was later privatised (turned into a public limited company owned by shareholders not the government) under the title British Telecom, in 1984.

Development of the Telegraph

The earliest telegraphic messages were passed on by visually signalling from one receiving post to the next. But in 1837, the inventor William Cooke teamed up with Charles Wheatstone to develop the electric telegraph system, using electric batteries. An electric current moved the needles on two discs. At first different combinations of the positions of these needles provided the code which was read by the operator. This system was soon improved when, in 1838, Samuel Morse invented the Morse code.

In 1839, the first public electric telegraph service was opened between Slough and Paddington Station and later used, spectacularly, to capture criminals. One entry in the Telegraph Logbook at Paddington in the 1840s read as follows.

> '*Paddington, 10.50 a.m.* Special train just left. It contains two thieves: one named Oliver Martin, who is dressed in black, crape on his hat; the other named Fiddler Dick, in black trousers and light blouse. Both in the third compartment of the first second-class carriage.'

Fiddler Dick, a notorious pickpocket, was arrested when he got off the train at Slough half an hour later, caught red-handed with the contents of a fellow passenger's handbag!

The electric telegraph also linked the Admiralty in London with the Royal Navy in Portsmouth and it enabled the railway companies to send messages rapidly from one station to the next. In 1851, a telegraph cable on the bed of the English Channel linked Britain and France, and in 1858 the first transatlantic cable message was sent from North America to England. Unhappily, the signal faded in a matter of weeks and a new cable had to be laid. The new transatlantic service opened in 1866 and was followed, four years later, by a cable linking Britain with India. By 1900, telegraph cables stretched across the world, linking the major cities. But by then the telegraph was already losing ground to yet another invention – the telephone.

Receiving telegraph messages in the instrument room of the Submarine Telegraph Company, The Illustrated London News, 13 November 1852

1 *Look at the picture. Identify the two operators and say what jobs you think they were doing.*

2 *What is the Morse code? Why was it a more effective way of using the telegraph than the system originally devised by Cooke and Wheatstone?*

3 *How was the electric telegraph likely to benefit (a) the railways, (b) the shipping companies, (c) the armed forces, (d) the newspapers, (e) banks, factories and other businesses? Who else stood to gain from the invention of the electric telegraph?*

4 *Why are telegraph posts often found along railway lines?*

The Growth of the Press

A reader wanting to find out what *The Times* said about the Charge of the Light Brigade in 1854 had to pay 5d [2p] (including newspaper tax). This was as much as many workers earned in an hour. There were no photographs, maps or pictures in the newspaper and no large headlines. Not surprisingly, most people did not bother to buy a newspaper. Indeed, the newspaper tax had originally been imposed to dissuade the working classes from reading newspapers, especially those containing the dangerous views of radicals. It was not until 1855 that the tax was finally abolished. Newspaper circulation gradually increased, particularly since the development of the submarine telegraph cable, and later of the telephone, made it possible to gather news on a worldwide scale and print it within a matter of hours. News agencies employed correspondents in different countries to telegraph their stories back to London for sale to the press.

By 1900, most people had been to school (see Chapter 9) and many towns had free public libraries with reading rooms, where newspapers were available to the general public. There was obviously a demand for cheap newspapers, and a new breed of newspaper proprietor provided them. In 1900, the reader of the *Daily Express* paid one halfpenny (a tenth of the cost of the *The Times* in 1854) for

A newsboy, The Illustrated London News, *4 January 1862*

a brightly presented newspaper, with large banner headlines and short, readable news items. When Alfred Harmsworth started the *Daily Mail* in 1896, he deliberately aimed it at people who had not previously taken a daily newspaper.

The first illustrated tabloid newspapers were also published at this time, with the *Daily Graphic* in 1889, using pictures drawn by artists, and Alfred Harmsworth's halfpenny *Daily Mirror*, in January 1904, with photographs. Within a month he was selling 143,000 copies a day, and by 1914 a staggering 1,200,000 copies a day.

In the twentieth century, the press barons, such as Lord Northcliffe (Alfred Harmsworth 1865–1922), Lord Rothermere (Harold Sydney Harmsworth 1868–1940) and Lord Beaverbrook (1879–1964), acquired enormous power through their control of the press. In the inter-war years, ferocious competition between the daily papers resulted in a circulation war, with free offers and fantastic prizes. Much of the same sort of competition has been seen since 1945 – especially in the years when television rivalled the press as an up-to-date source of information.

---

1 *How many minutes would an ordinary worker have to work today to earn the price of a copy of* The Times?

2 *What changes have taken place in the way in which people hear news of a major event today, compared with 1854?*

The Telephone

New Year's greetings by telephone, The Illustrated London News, *1882*

'When Professor Graham Bell in 1877 introduced his remarkable invention, the first speaking telephone, to English-speaking audiences, he was in the habit of telling them that the day was not far distant when the instrument would be in general use amongst all classes of the people. The great cities would be linked by a network of wires into one gigantic system, so that a person at Land's End could have a chat with a friend in John O'Groats with as much ease as if he were conversing across a dinner table. So much for the inventor's dream.'

J. Munro, Cassell's Family Magazine, *1880*

Munro claimed that interest in the telephone had fallen off since 1877 and that little effort had been put into the realisation of Bell's dream. But many people soon saw the advantages that the telephone could offer them and telephone exchanges were opened in London and other major cities. Nine years later, Munro again described the latest developments in Britain – call offices open to the general public and telephone exchanges where:

'The young lady operators belong to a very good class of society. They are mostly the daughters of professional men, or the higher members of the middle class; and a number of them have entered the service from the desire of having an occupation, in preference to being idle. They are as a rule intelligent and well-bred young ladies, and they perform this work, with a deftness and skill which is highly pleasing.'

J. Munro, Cassell's Family Magazine, *1889*

Telephone operators in London, Cassell's Magazine, *1889*

1 *Was Alexander Graham Bell correct in his forecast for the future of the telephone in 1877? Which development of the twentieth century do you think might have surprised him?*

2 *Why do you think that Munro, in 1880, referred to Bell's forecast with the words 'so much for the inventor's dream'?*

3 *What does the second extract tell you about the position of women in Britain in the 1880s?*

In fact, the telephone operator's job was already under threat, for, in 1889, A. B. Strowger invented an automatic exchange. He wanted a 'cuss-less, out-of-order-less, wait-less telephone', but although the world's first automatic telephone exchange was put into operation, in 1892, in Indiana (USA), it was many years before a similar exchange was installed in Britain (at Epsom in 1912). By 1891, a telephone cable had been laid on the bed of the English Channel, linking Paris with London. Surprisingly, the first transatlantic cable was not laid until as late as 1956 – taking the place of the radio telephone.

The telephone made an immense impact on the economic and social life of the people of Britain. It made communication between businesses instantaneous, speeding up important decisions. It enabled the fire brigade, the police and ambulance services to be called immediately. For people who could afford it, the telephone lessened the loneliness of living on their own or in remote communities. It helped relatives and friends to keep in touch, transforming relationships and widening social contacts.

The Post Office took over the running of the main trunk lines in 1892, and of every telephone exchange (except Hull's) in 1912, when it acquired the National Telegraph Company. In 1914, there were approximately 750,000 telephones in the United Kingdom. This had increased to 1 million by 1921, 3 million by 1939, 11 million by 1968 and 23 million by 1978. The telephone was no longer a luxury.

In 1926, a radio telephone linked the United States with Britain and, in the following year, an automatic telephone exchange was installed at Holborn in London – although not without critics, who claimed that the telephone operators had been quicker! Subscriber Trunk Dialling (STD) was first introduced in Bristol in 1958. By 1986, calls could be dialled direct from Britain to many parts of the world.

Wireless Telegraphy

'In September of last year I made a discovery. I was sending waves through the air and getting signals at a distance of a mile or thereabouts, when I discovered that the wave which went to my receiver through the air was also affecting another receiver which I had set up on the other side of a hill.'

Guglielmo Marconi interviewed for The Strand Magazine *in 1897*

Guglielmo Marconi was then only 21 years of age yet his experimental work on wireless was already being developed in collaboration with the British Post Office. Marconi had left Italy because he was not getting 'satisfactory recognition of his discoveries in his own country'. His work was based on the earlier discovery by a German scientist, Hertz, that electric waves could be made to penetrate wood and brick.

At that time Marconi thought the furthest he would be able to transmit a message – at least with his present equipment – would be twenty miles, although he did not rule out transmitting messages to New York. He was already experimenting with ship-to-shore transmissions and said there was:

> 'no reason why the commander of an army should not be able to easily communicate telegraphically with his subordinate officers *without wires* over any distance up to twenty miles [32 km].'

In fact, that same year – 1897 – he succeeded in transmitting a radio signal over a distance of about 20 km. Two years later – in 1899 – he broadcast a signal to France and then, in 1901, across the Atlantic – a truly remarkable achievement. Six years later a regular wireless telegraphy service was opened between Britain and Canada.

The possibilities which broadcasting could provide were dramatically brought home to the public in 1910, when Captain Kendall of the SS *Montrose*, bound for Canada from Britain, sent a wireless message to Scotland Yard warning them that the wanted murderer, Dr Crippen, and his companion, Ethel Clara Le Neve (disguised as a boy), were on board his ship. Crippen was arrested as soon as he arrived in Canada. The *News of the World* for 31 July 1910, said:

> 'CRIPPEN AND WIRELESS ROMANCE. A Scientific interest attaches to the arrests. The long arm of the law has been lengthened by the Marconigram, and the captures now effected will long be remembered in connection with the development of wireless telegraphy.'

---

1 *What was a 'Marconigram'? Why was the 'wireless' so called?*
2 *What did the capture of Dr Crippen prove?*
3 *What possibilities did wireless telegraphy open up for the future?*
4 *Why do you think the use of the wireless for entertainment purposes was a much later development?*

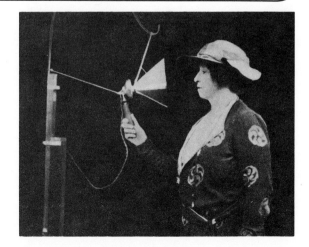

Dame Nellie Melba
broadcasting in 1920

By 1920, experiments at broadcasting were already well under way in Britain. *The Graphic* reported in May 1920, that at a demonstration by the Marconi Company in London:

> 'Words spoken and music played at Chelmsford were heard as distinctly as if they had been produced by a gramophone at one's elbow, the tune "Way down upon the Swanee River" being particularly striking.'

At that time the news-reader read the news bulletin directly from the evening newspaper! Broadcasting began in earnest, in 1922, from a transmitting station (known as 2LO) on the top of Marconi House in London. The British Broadcasting Company (which became the British Broadcasting Corporation in 1926) broadcast to the 8,000 owners who held wireless licences in 1922.

The later development of broadcasting, under the guidance of Sir John Reith, Director-General of the BBC from 1927 to 1938, brought entertainment and information to the remotest corners of the British Isles. By the outbreak of the Second World War, there were nearly 10 million radio sets in Britain.

The Development of Television

One of the early pioneers of television was John Logie Baird. He demonstrated the world's first television picture as early as 1926 and transmitted a colour picture in 1928. But the first public television service by the BBC did not begin until 1936.

John Logie Baird watching television in 1930

There were other pioneers as well as Baird, such as Vladimir Zworykin and Herbert Ives in the United States and Isaac Shoenberg in Britain, who helped to develop an electronic camera for Marconi and EMI in the 1930s. It was this which was eventually adopted by the BBC in the pioneering television service transmitted in the years immediately before 1939.

Since 1945, television has developed at a furious pace, catering for massive audiences (such as the regular audiences of over 20 million viewers watching the serial 'Eastenders' in the mid-1980s). The introduction of commercial television in 1955, BBC2 in 1962 and colour television in 1966, further tightened the grip of television as an entertainment medium, hastening the closure of thousands of cinemas and theatres in the process. In 1962, the Telstar satellite relayed live programmes across the Atlantic for the first time.

The Economic and Social Effects of the Development of Broadcasting

The social and economic effects of wireless broadcasting have been widespread and profound. Not only did it enable warnings and messages to be passed to ships at sea and to aircraft, it also revolutionised communications on the battle-field and enabled governments to carry messages instantaneously to their peoples. News of the outbreak of the First World War was carried by word of mouth or read about in the newspapers. Not so in the Second World War. Millions gathered round their radio sets at 11.15 a.m. on 3 September 1939, to hear the Prime Minister say 'this country is at war with Germany'.

The effects of television have been just as dramatic as those of radio. Not only has television brought a range of entertainments to millions of viewers, it has also helped many people to gain university degrees (through the Open University), brought help and entertainment to the handicapped, and given people instant access to the latest news.

1 *Collect oral evidence from your older friends and relatives, to illustrate the history of communications in the twentieth century. Make a list of suitable topics and find out people's recollections about the telephone, the early days of wireless and television, and their impact on everyday life.*

2 *Which do you think have been the most outstanding developments in the history of communications since the days of the telegraph and penny post?*

FURTHER QUESTIONS AND EXERCISES

1 *Write one or two sentences to explain the significance of each of the following in the history of transport and communications:*
- (a) John Logie Baird
- (b) Louis Blériot
- (c) Alfred Harmsworth
- (d) Imperial Airways
- (e) British Rail
- (f) the Red Flag Act
- (g) the First World War
- (h) the penny post.

2 *What does the picture show? What occasion does it commemorate? Who was SIR ROWLAND LE GRAND?*

SIR ROWLAND LE GRAND.   *Cartoon from* Punch, *19 March 1864*

3 *Account briefly for the decline of (a) the railways since 1930, (b) the telegraph since 1900.*

4 *In August 1896, a writer in* Chambers's Journal *said:*

'As matters at present stand, we are looking on, while other nations are doing a vast amount of pioneer work, from which we presently shall reap much advantage without paying the premium of costly experiments.'

(a) *What do you think the 'pioneer work' was? Use the information given to hazard a guess.*

(b) Why was Britain 'looking on' at that time?

(c) From which date did Britain begin to participate in this work?

(d) Was the author correct when he claimed that Britain would reap 'much advantage' from the trials then being undertaken?

(e) How important did Britain later become in the development of this particular form of communications?

5 Imagine you are placed in **one** of the following predicaments.

(a) You are a shipowner in 1870 and are torn between **either** ordering a new wooden sailing ship (like the others in your fleet of cargo ships) **or** buying a new steam cargo vessel built of iron plates (which will cost at least twice as much money).

(b) You are a shipowner from South Wales in 1920 and your shipbuilder on the Clyde suggests a motor engine rather than a steam engine for your new cargo ship. Many of your employees were brought up in the mining valleys and, as you know, a motor ship will require oil not coal.

Explain and justify the choice you make to your employees.

6 Write an explanatory account of the growth and development of motor transport in the twentieth century. Indicate the problems which have had to be overcome and estimate the success with which motor manufacturers and successive governments have attempted to resolve these problems.

7 What have been the major developments in the development of the steamship since 1850?

8 When, how and why have the following developments had an effect on social and economic life in Britain:

(a) the telephone

(b) sound broadcasting

(c) television

(d) the motor car

(e) the development of air transport?

9 Outline the main developments in the history of the railways in Britain since 1850. Show how government policy on the railways has changed and how the railways have been affected by other transport developments during this period.

Chapter Four

Trade and Economy

INTRODUCTION

'Ruin from Bank Failure'. The notice on the door of the bank reads, 'THIS BANK HAS SUSPENDED PAYMENT'. The Illustrated London News, 2 November 1907.

'During the past week the terrors of a financial panic have been threatening New York, and all ranks of society have felt the imminence of this grievous disaster, which means ruin alike for the man of wealth and for those of humble means, who may wake up to find themselves on the same dire level of poverty.'

The Illustrated London News, *2 November 1907*

This particular crisis was saved by the action of the American financier J. P. Morgan, when he obtained financial support from John D. Rockefeller and also from the Bank of England, which sent $10 million in gold in the *Lusitania* (see page 96) to help restore confidence in the banks affected by the crisis.

---

1 *What was the nature of the 'panic'? How is it illustrated in the picture? How could British gold in the* Lusitania *help to restore confidence in the banks of New York?*

2 *What would happen today, if investors lost confidence in a bank or building society?*

3 *Why do people invest money in a bank or business?*

Lack of confidence can affect governments as well as banks. Outside Britain, the pound is only worth what foreigners think it is worth. An economic crisis, a drop in North-Sea oil prices, or a change of government can frighten bankers, investors and foreign governments into selling some of their holdings of sterling (British currency) in exchange for American dollars or Japanese yen. If many do this, the value of the pound falls. This is called devaluation.

Without financial investment, industries and businesses would not survive. In this chapter you will see how banks and other financial activities have developed in Britain since 1840. You will also see how problems, such as inflation (rising prices), high tariffs (customs duties), devaluation and lack of confidence (such as a run on a bank), have affected the trade and economy of the country, and how their consequences – bank failures, decline in trade, and unemployment – have had a significant effect on the everyday lives of people.

BANKING AND FINANCE BEFORE 1914

This cartoon was published in Punch *on 23 February 1861, shortly after the first post office savings bank was opened.*

SEASONABLE ADVICE—"PUT BY FOR A FROSTY DAY."

1 *What was the point of the cartoon?*

2 *Why do you think post office savings banks were started in Britain in 1861? What was wrong with the existing banks?*

Bank Expansion

Banking in Britain today is dominated by the 'Big Four' – Midland, Barclays, National Westminster and Lloyds – huge banking groups with branches in almost every town and banking interests extending into every corner of the globe. The chances of a large general bank failing today are remote.

But banking was not like this a hundred years ago. Every town had its own local banks then, many of them issuing their own banknotes. At first there were very few large banks. It was not until the speeding up of communications, with the coming of the railway and the telegraph in the 1830s, that it became feasible for the larger banks to establish branches at a distance from head office.

Government regulations were introduced to make it easier for large banking groups to be formed. There was safety in size. Too many people had lost their money when small banks were unable to meet their commitments, and there had been notable bank failures in 1814 and 1816, and again in 1825, when 60 banks failed.

In 1844, the Government clamped down on the freedom of the banks to issue banknotes. The Bank Charter Act was designed to reassure customers that a five-pound note was worth the same as five gold sovereigns. In future the Bank of England would only issue new banknotes if there was an equivalent sum in gold in the Bank's vaults. Banks would not be allowed to issue their own banknotes if they merged with other banks. This was bound to affect every bank in England and Wales, since big banks were safer than small banks and mergers were almost inevitable.

As a result Bank of England banknotes came to be regarded as the standard paper currency. In Scotland the banking system was different, which is why some Scottish banks still issue their own banknotes to this day. In any case, many bank customers were already able to use cheques – a well-established, safe and simple way of making and receiving payments; so the chequebook system was expanded. It was already common in London by 1844 and its use gradually spread to the country banks as well. In the 1840s, the major London Clearing Banks dealt with transactions worth £3 million a day. Fifty years later, their daily turnover had risen to over £25 million.

By then, many mergers had taken place. A typical pattern of growth is demonstrated by the Midland Bank. In 1836, the small Birmingham and Midland Bank was founded by Charles Geach. Fifty years later the bank had acquired nine branches. In the 1880s and 1890s it embarked on a programme of rapid expansion and, in 1891, merged with another bank to form the London City and Midland Bank. This banking group had over 300 branches in 1900 and by 1918 had become the largest bank in the world. In 1980, there were over 200 branches of the Midland Bank in London alone. Bank mergers have continued to the present day. In 1968 the National Provincial and Westminster Banks combined to form National Westminster, and Barclays Bank absorbed Martins Bank, although it was refused Government permission to merge with Lloyds.

Size gave investors confidence that their money was safe, since the collapse of a business owing a large sum of money to a large bank obviously had less effect than it did when the large debt was owing to a small bank. Even after the passing of the Bank Charter Act in 1844, notable bank failures still occurred – as in 1857 (when the Northumberland and Durham District Bank failed) and in 1878 (when the City of Glasgow Bank collapsed).

In 1910, *The Sphere* printed an account of 'The Foolish Run on the Birkbeck Bank', with a photograph of the huge queue of 3,000 investors who had waited 'all night in the rain to be first at the doors in the morning'. The queue snaked its way round the extensive buildings of the bank, blocking several of the neighbouring streets. Many of the anxious investors were old and infirm and 'appeared far too fragile to stand for so long in the chill November air'.

> 'The run seems to have originated in the circulation by anonymous letters of an unfounded rumour that the Birkbeck Bank was in some way connected with the Charing Cross Bank which failed. The rumour, however, was absolutely false, and the Birkbeck Bank immediately issued an official intimation to this effect, and the Bank of England promptly came to the rescue with a guarantee of assistance.'
>
> The Sphere, *1910*

---

1 *Why was there a run on the Birkbeck Bank? Why was it 'foolish'? What effect did it have? Which evidence shows how worried the investors were?*

2 *How did the Bank of England come to the rescue?*

The City of London

Outside the London Stock Exchange, The Graphic, *1871*

As London grew rapidly in the eighteenth and nineteenth centuries, to become the largest and richest city in the world and the centre of the world's largest empire, so it developed other financial institutions as well as banks. These included the Stock Exchange, the great finance houses and the commodity markets, which specialised in handling and selling commodities, such as tea and tin.

London became the centre of world finance, holding huge sums of money belonging to countries all over the world. The effect of this financial growth was immense, since expanding companies could always find loans, banking facilities and insurance in the City of London. The insurance brokers, meeting at Lloyd's, accepted all types of insurance risks, from ships to steelworks. Stockbrokers dealt in company shares from all over the world.

Great merchant banks, such as Hambros and Rothschilds, prospered. They offered safe investments for the public and used the money deposited to grant loans to foreign governments to finance major projects, and also to British companies wishing to expand. These investments earned interest which went back to Britain. As an added bonus to the British economy, the money invested was usually spent on British machinery and equipment. By 1914, about £4 thousand million of British capital (money) had been invested overseas. Of this huge sum (worth at least £140 thousand million in 1986), about 10 per cent had been invested in Canada and Newfoundland, 20 per cent in the United States, 20 per cent in South America, and 10 per cent each in India and in Australia and New Zealand. Substantial sums had also been invested in Europe and Russia.

Although much of this capital was used to build railways and bridges, some of it went into the development of large-scale agriculture, factories, mines and other industrial projects abroad, which increasingly threatened the prosperity of British farms and factories. The reason for this huge investment was not that British investors wanted to help the developing world of the late nineteenth century to prosper. It was simply that they thought bigger profits could be made from these investments abroad than from investing their money at home.

The immense value of these overseas investments later helped Britain to finance the First and Second World Wars (see pages 144 and 149). They also helped to conceal the fact that the value of Britain's imports far exceeded the value of her exports as long ago as the late nineteenth century. In other words, we bought more goods from other countries than they bought from us – and we were doing this in the 1880s as well as in the 1980s. In ordinary circumstances this might have led to a financial crisis, but the earnings from overseas insurance, financial dealings and foreign investments (called 'invisible' exports) more than made up the deficit.

Taxation before 1914

The increasing intervention of the government in the affairs of the country, through social legislation (see Chapter 8) and state support for education (see Chapter 9), meant that taxation had to be increased to pay for it. The Victorians, who in general were very lightly taxed, made it seem a huge burden.

> 'Gradually but continuously the burden has been shifted from the indirect taxpayer to the direct taxpayer, that is to say, from the community at large to the propertied classes.'
>
> *Windsor Magazine, 1897*

This article, entitled 'John Bull's Balance Sheet: How the money comes and goes', was written by J. Holt Schooling for a popular magazine of the 1890s. Indirect taxes were taxes levied on goods or services, such as the customs and excise duties on tobacco or wine. Direct taxes were taxes actually paid by the individual on whom they were imposed, such as income tax or the estate duties charged on money and property left when a person died.

Taxes	*Annual Average 1837–51*	*1899*
Customs and excise duties	£36 million	£55 million
Income tax	£4 million	£18 million
Other direct taxes	£7 million	£24 million
Total	£47 million	£97 million

> 1 Who were the 'propertied classes'?
> 2 What was 'the burden' referred to in the article?
> 3 Why do you think direct taxes affected the 'propertied classes' rather than the working classes? Was this fair?
> 4 Do the taxation statistics agree with the opinion expressed in the article?

Income tax had first been introduced into Britain as a temporary tax in 1799, during the Napoleonic Wars. It was reintroduced by Peel in 1842, at 7d [3p] in the pound, to replace the money lost when many tariffs were removed as Britain began to adopt a policy of Free Trade.

In 1852, Gladstone promised to get rid of income tax in stages, by knocking a penny a year off the rate, but it was not until 1872 that it fell to a mere 2d in the pound. In 1894, Parliament gave its approval to another direct tax – Death Duties – and this was later given as one of the reasons for the break up of the great landed estates (see page 13).

Income tax was generally regarded by liberals as the fairest method of raising taxes, since it exempted the poor, the underpaid and the underprivileged from taxation. After 1906, an increase in taxes was needed to pay for the cost of the social reforms introduced by the Liberal Government (see Chapter 8).

In 1909, the Liberal Chancellor of the Exchequer, David Lloyd George, introduced his 'People's Budget'. Instead of spreading the 'burden', he taxed the well-to-do, increasing income tax from 1s [5p] in the pound to 1s 2d [6p], raising money from a new super tax on incomes over £3,000 a year (at least £100,000 a year by today's values) and increasing death duties. In the picture you can see how the news was received by London's newspapers, whilst *Punch* printed a cartoon of 'The Giant Lloyd-Gorgibuster', with a club in his hand labelled 'Budget' looking for a rich businessman hiding under a table. The caption read:

'Fee, Fi, Fo, Fat, I smell the blood of a Plutocrat;
Be he alive or be he dead I'll grind his bones to make my bread.'

Daily newspaper posters, Friday, 30 April 1909

1 Look at the morning newspaper posters after the Budget. Which newspapers supported Lloyd George? What did they think of the Budget?

2 Which newspapers were definitely against the Budget? How did they try to turn people against Lloyd George?

3 Which newspaper posters appear to be neutral, giving little indication of the Editor's opinion about the Budget?

4 What is a 'Plutocrat'? What was the significance of the 'Lloyd-Gorgibuster' cartoon? Write a short paragraph explaining the rhyme and the title of the cartoon.

5 Write a short paragraph summing up press opinion on the 1909 Budget.

TRADE BEFORE 1914

Free Trade

In the early years of the nineteenth century, trade with foreign powers was restricted by an intricate system of regulations, tariffs and duties. Only British ships could trade with the colonies, for instance.

Manufacturers said these regulations harmed Britain's industries, since tariffs or restrictions on the import of foreign goods (such as the Corn Laws which 'protected' the British farmer by controlling the import of corn – see page 2), encouraged foreign governments to retaliate. They did this by charging duties on the import of British manufactures. The Corn Laws also helped to make food dear in Britain, since cheap foreign grain was not allowed to compete on equal terms with British corn.

In 1839, the Anti-Corn Law League was founded and successfully brought pressure to bear on the Government, resulting in the repeal of the Corn Laws in 1846, despite the initial opposition of important politicians, like Benjamin Disraeli. This movement to release trade from all restrictions and import duties was called 'Free Trade'.

The final abandonment of 'protection' was masterminded by Gladstone in 1853, when he abolished the duties on many articles, such as soap, and drastically lowered them on others, such as tea. In 1860, he abolished almost all the remaining duties apart from those which brought in the greatest revenue, such as wine, tobacco, tea and spirits.

From that time onwards, until the 1930s, Britain traded freely with the rest of the world. The duties which still remained were designed not to discourage foreign competition, but simply to earn revenue to pay for government expenditure. It seemed to work. Britain's trade with the rest of the world expanded rapidly, although the problem of excessive dependence on imports and exports was brought home to people during the American Civil War, when Lancashire's cotton mills were starved of raw cotton from the American South. Mills closed and many thousands of workers were laid off.

The Balance of Trade

In the late nineteenth century, the volume of Britain's overseas trade continued to expand rapidly. But prices fell, and during the years of the Great Depression in agriculture (see Chapter 1), a change occurred in trade and business as a whole.

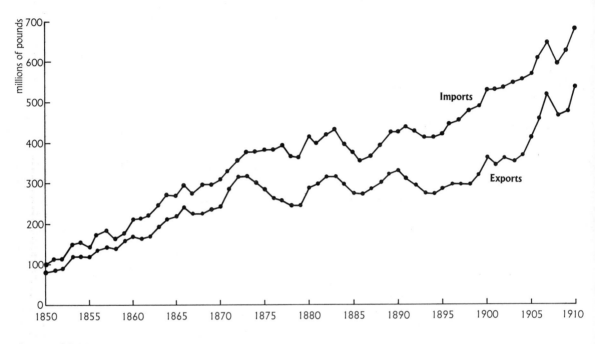

Graph of British trade between 1850 and 1910, showing exports and imports

1 *By how many times did the value of Britain's exports and imports increase between 1850 and 1910?*

2 *What fluctuations are there in the trend lines shown on the graph? How do you think these might have affected the lives of ordinary workers in mills, factories and other works dependent on the import of raw materials and the export of manufactured products?*

3 *Prices fell sharply between 1870 and 1900. How could this have affected the statistics shown in the graph? Does the graph exaggerate or understate the volume of trade?*

The value of imports continued to rise steeply, as did the value of exports, although the rate of increase between 1880 and 1914 (about 3 per cent a year), could be unfavourably compared with a rate of 5 per cent a year before 1870. As you can see, the value of imports always exceeded that of exports by a substantial sum (e.g. £523 million worth of imports in 1900, compared with only £354 million worth of exports). Victorians were worried by this lack of balance in trade, even though the difference between the payments made for imports and the payments received from other countries for exports (called the 'balance of payments') was more than made up for by earnings from other sources. As you have seen, British banks and investors earned interest and dividends on their huge overseas investments and insurance business ('invisible' exports), whilst merchant shipping companies earned huge profits from trade.

So long as the world wanted the products of British industry, and used British ships, financial services and capital, there seemed little to fear. Yet the nature of that trade was changing. As you saw in Chapter 1, Britain was becoming increasingly dependent on foreign food supplies at the expense of British agriculture.

In the 1860s, cotton and woollen textiles still dominated Britain's export trade, accounting for 62 per cent by value of all British exports. But, this dominance of manufactured products declined in the late nineteenth century, as machinery and raw materials (coal, iron and steel) supplied foreign industry, and increasingly took a larger share of Britain's export market.

---

1 *Why was this a threat to British industry?*

2 *Why did some economists believe it was better to export manufactured goods instead of raw materials?*

By the 1930s, textiles accounted for only 24 per cent of Britain's total export trade, compared with 12 per cent contributed by iron and steel, 15 per cent by cars and machinery, and 10 per cent by coal. By the 1970s, textiles accounted for only 4 per cent of Britain's total exports.

The Great Depression

As you can see from the graph on page 138, Britain's export trade suffered a succession of setbacks in the 1870s, 1880s and 1890s. Each time that trade declined, unemployment increased. For example, between 1888 and 1899, the highest rate of unemployment was 7.5 per cent in 1893, whilst the lowest rates of unemployment were 2 per cent in 1899 and 2.1 per cent in 1889 and 1890.

---

1 *Look at the graph of statistics on page 138. What happened to Britain's overseas trade in 1893, 1899, 1889 and 1890?*

2 *In which years between 1870 and 1888 would you have expected unemployment to be a problem?*

3 *Look at the picture on page 140 and read the extract below it. Why did temporary unemployment cause scenes of such great distress in the late nineteenth century?*

'The unemployed of London: "We've got no work to do!"', The Illustrated London News, 20 February 1886

'In Wolverhampton the suffering amongst the families of ironworkers is without precedent. The Mayor appeals for clothing for women and children, who are reduced, some of them, to one garment. Firms and individuals are contributing coal in boatloads, and ladies are distributing blankets. In this town above 700 able-bodied men are found work (stone-breaking) by the Poor-Law Guardians.'

The Illustrated London News, *11 January 1879*

Some Victorians thought of this period between 1870 and 1900 as a 'Great Depression' (see also page 4). A depression is a period when a decline or slump in demand for goods leads to falling prices, unemployment and a reduction in the amount of money invested in new factories and machinery. But there was little permanent unemployment in the late nineteenth century and wages even rose during this period. On average, the typical family was substantially better off in 1914 than it had been in 1880.

In general, the Great Depression made a much more lasting impression on the rich than on the poor, since its main effect was to reduce profits from land and industry. Profits dropped because prices fell sharply. Industries were still expanding and becoming more efficient, making goods cheaper to produce. But at the same time increasing competition between manufacturers caused prices to fall. Manufacturers also had to lower their prices to meet foreign competition, since imports paid no tariffs at the docks.

1 *What was the 'Great Depression'? How is it shown on the graph on page 138?*

2 *Average wages and average living standards rose at the same time that the profits of the rich fell. What effect do you think this had on the ownership of wealth in Britain?*

> **3** *Who do you think felt the effects of the Great Depression most? Was it the rich who suffered a permanent decline in profits or those members of the working classes who became temporarily unemployed?*

Fair Trade

Temporary unemployment, and the depression in overseas trade in the 1880s, aroused anger as well as causing distress. In February 1886, *The Illustrated London News* described the 'Riots at the West-End of London' after 'an open-air meeting of the unemployed and distressed men of the labouring classes' had been held in Trafalgar Square. Mr Peters (of the Fair Trade League):

> 'said that he hoped the rich would see the numbers wanting food, and was met by several voices exclaiming, "We want work, not charity." A set of resolutions was then moved requesting Her Majesty's Government to start useful public works for the unemployed; also that Parliament should encourage the use of British capital in British rather than foreign enterprises, and take measures to relieve our distressed agricultural interest; and that fair play should be given to British industry, against the disastrous effects of hostile foreign tariffs and of foreign State bounties on products imported into the British market.'
>
> The Illustrated London News, *29 October 1887*

'Meetings of the unemployed in London – the police and the mob: lowering the red flag in Hyde Park', The Illustrated London News, *29 October 1887*

1   *Look at the pictures of the unemployed and at the description of Wolverhampton on page 140. Do you think* The Illustrated London News *was sympathetic or unsympathetic to the unemployed? Quote your evidence.*

2   *What were the complaints of the unemployed? What did they want? What do you think the members of the Fair Trade League wanted?*

3   *What solutions were suggested to solve the problems caused by the Great Depression?*

Opponents of Free Trade pointed to the fact that most of the other countries of the world, especially Britain's chief rivals – Germany and the United States – had imposed tariffs on imports, making it difficult for British firms to sell their products overseas. Why should Britain allow foreign manufacturers unrestricted access to British markets?

'Our manufacturers are more and more excluded from the markets of the civilised world, not by fair competition, but by oppressive tariffs. At home they are met by the unrestricted competition of every article which can be made more cheaply in any country by dint of longer hours of work, lower wages, and a meaner style of living on the part of the workers.'

W. Farrer Ecroyd, 1881

1   *What reason was given for the growing exclusion of British manufactures from foreign markets? Do the trade figures on page 138 suggest this was true or an exaggeration?*

2   *What competition did the British manufacturer face at home in Britain? Why were foreign manufacturers said to be able to produce goods cheaply? What do you think a chemical worker (see page 47) would have thought of this argument?*

Members of the Fair Trade League wanted a 10 per cent duty on all foreign manufactures, in order to force other countries to agree fair trading methods. But the Fair Trade League lacked forceful leadership, and when trade picked up, support died down. However, it rose again under a new banner – Imperial Preference – in the early 1900s, under the dynamic leadership of Joseph Chamberlain.

Joseph Chamberlain (1836–1914)

Joseph Chamberlain made his name as Mayor of Birmingham in 1873–6, when he pioneered important municipal reforms directed at slum clearance and improvements in working-class living standards (see Chapter 6). He became an MP in 1876 and then, in 1895, Colonial Secretary in the Conservative and Unionist Government. Chamberlain thought it was nonsense that Britain should acquire a vast Empire without giving preference to the products from that Empire.

Joseph Chamberlain in 1886

But Imperial Preference, as this idea was called, was against the principles of Free Trade, and Chamberlain left the Government in 1903 to help start the Tariff Reform League.

The Tariff Reform League

Supporters of the Tariff Reform League argued that the 'civilised nations of the world' were engaged in a commercial war, which Britain was losing because of her Free Trade policy.

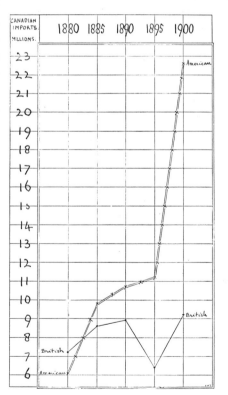

Graph showing Canada's imports from the United States and from the United Kingdom, 1880–1900

J. Holt Schooling used the graph on the left, to illustrate an article in *The Windsor Magazine*, in 1903, supporting Chamberlain's policy of Imperial Preference. He pointed out that foreign countries supplied about 40 per cent of the imports taken by the countries of the British Empire.

'I suggest that there is no country in the world except England that would be content to let foreign nations supply 40 per cent of a colonial demand.'

Yet at this time, Canada and Australia were self-governing dominions, virtually independent of Britain, and New Zealand and South Africa were shortly to follow suit in 1907 and 1910 respectively.

Chamberlain started his campaign in earnest with a speech on 15 May 1903, when he said:

'You want an Empire. Do you think it better to cultivate the trade with your own people or to let it go in order that you may keep the trade of those who, rightly enough, are your competitor and rivals?'

Chamberlain wanted 'to build up a self-supplying Empire, knit together by strong ties of common interest'.

1 *What do you think Schooling hoped to prove with his graph? Can you think of a good reason why Canada should take an increasing percentage of goods from the United States?*

2 *What difference in attitude can you detect between the comments of Chamberlain and Schooling?*

3 *Imagine you are living in Canada or Australia in 1903. What would your reaction be to these arguments?*

Collapse of Tariff Reform

Supporters of Free Trade pointed out that Britain, with its huge Empire, large merchant fleet and powerful Royal Navy, got far more out of foreign trade than did the foreign countries with whom she traded. In any case, the proposal to give preference to Canadian grain or New Zealand frozen lamb was hardly likely to benefit the British farmer. The vast majority of people in Britain wanted the cheapest food possible. In any case the colonies were already putting tariffs on goods imported from Britain, in order to protect their own infant industries. It was absurd for the Australians to export wool to Britain in return for imports of woollen cloth from Yorkshire and, as you have seen (page 44), Indian cotton mills were already beginning to threaten those of Lancashire.

Chamberlain and his supporters in the Conservative party made the mistake of thinking that the interests of the member-countries of the Empire were identical with those of Britain. The view that prevailed, even though foreign tariffs undoubtedly did hurt British exports, was that Britain would gain little from trying to force other countries to change their trading policy. Levying import duties would only harm industry, since it might start a trade war in earnest, with even higher foreign tariffs. Above all, Imperial Preference would increase the cost of food. It was this message which struck home with the voters, and in 1906, a Liberal Government was elected with a convincing majority over the Conservatives. The Tariff Reform Movement had been decisively beaten – for the moment.

THE FIRST WORLD WAR AND ITS AFTERMATH

Wartime Controls

The First World War (1914–18) was a major landmark in the development of the British economy. The requirements of wartime meant that the government had to introduce many controls and exercise powers (such as the running of the coal mines and the railways) which would have been unthinkable in pre-war days. Measures taken included the following.

- Britain went off the Gold Standard in 1914. This meant that banknotes could no longer be exchanged for gold.

- The amount of paper money in circulation increased and the value of the pound dropped, helping to cause inflation.

- Import duties were imposed in 1915 on a number of goods – a temporary breach in the policy of Free Trade.

- The gap between the value of imports and exports rapidly widened – factories were geared up to making arms and armaments, not exports, yet the need for imported raw materials was as great as ever.

- Many foreign investments were sold to pay for the huge cost of the war. In addition huge sums of money were borrowed from the United States and income tax rose to an unprecedented 6s in the pound (a rate of 30 per cent).

The Prince of Wales visiting the depressed areas in 1929

The Depression

Immediately after the end of the war in 1918, the British Government tried to carry on as if nothing had happened. But the First World War had changed Britain's trading position.

- Many traditional British export markets had been lost, huge debts had been incurred and industries, such as coal mining, which were already decaying in 1914, were now badly in need of re-investment and major overhaul (see Chapter 2).

- In 1925, the Government put Britain back on the Gold Standard but this only kept industry short of the very funds it needed to re-equip, since it restricted the amount of money in circulation. It also made the pound more expensive in relation to other currencies, making British exports seem overpriced to foreign buyers.

- A short post-war boom in trade in 1919 and 1920 proved to be only temporary, and a serious depression began in 1921 and 1922 when unemployment in Great Britain climbed to 15 per cent of the work force, compared with 2.4 per cent in 1920. From 1922 to 1929, it fluctuated between 10.5 per cent and 12.5 per cent, but it rose again in 1930 to nearly 15 per cent, by 1931 had topped 21 per cent, and in 1932 reached a peak of 22.5 per cent. Unemployment fell thereafter, but was never less than 11 per cent in the years up to 1939. For almost all of the inter-war years, then, at least one British worker in every ten was out of a job.

The worst unemployment occurred in the early 1930s, after the Wall Street Crash, in October 1929, triggered off a severe worldwide depression in trade and industry. Prices of shares on the New York Stock Exchange plunged in value and forced hard-pressed American banks to withdraw the huge investments they had made in Europe. Foreign governments levied higher tariffs to protect their industries. Britain, as the world's most important trading nation, suffered a disastrous setback.

The industries worst affected were those which normally exported most of their output abroad. Coal mining, iron and steel, and textiles all suffered severely. Since the Depression affected most countries in the world (including the USSR, Germany and Japan) there was a general decline in trade. Fewer cargo ships were needed, so Britain's shipyards got fewer orders to build new ships (see page 59).

The Abandonment of Free Trade

In 1931, foreign investors, suspicious of Britain's Labour Government, began to withdraw their money from Britain. This caused a run on the pound, which made the economic crisis worse. Instead of devaluing the pound, which might have solved the problem (since it would have made British exports cheaper), the Labour Government tried to negotiate foreign loans to keep up the value of the overpriced pound. The loans were agreed, but with strings attached – the high cost of unemployment benefit had to be reduced. Many of Ramsay MacDonald's Cabinet colleagues in the Labour party could not agree to the 10 per cent cut in benefit that was proposed. It looked as if MacDonald would have to resign.

But to everyone's astonishment, MacDonald agreed to lead a new National Government to deal with the crisis, consisting mainly of Conservative ministers and backed by the Conservative party in Parliament. Only a handful of Labour party members supported him in the House of Commons, the remainder forming the Opposition.

Immediately, the new National Government tried to restore confidence in the pound by introducing economy measures, including the 10 per cent cut in unemployment benefit and the introduction of the means test (see page 264). Public expenditure was reduced, chiefly by cutting the wages of various public employees, including teachers, civil servants and members of the armed forces.

The National Government in 1931

Banners displayed by civil servants on a protest march in October 1931 showed the intense anger felt by public employees: '23 CUTS IN 10 YEARS IS THIS EQUAL SACRIFICE?', 'YOU WANT LETTERS WE WANT FOOD', 'CUT CUT CUT THEY COME AGAIN'.

But MacDonald failed to save the pound. In September 1931, Britain went off the Gold Standard and the pound was effectively devalued, falling to about 70 per cent of its previous value. Newspapers tried to reassure their readers.

'What it means to the average man and housewife is simply: Business as usual. Britain just now is exceptionally well off in all the goods that make life pleasant and possible, she is unusually well stocked with food, and if any ill-instructed persons try to profiteer merely report them, for they have no excuse. And don't let us, any of us, act the giddy goat and start hoarding or running on supplies.'

Daily Sketch, *21 September 1931*

But there was another side to the story. A journalist on the *Manchester Guardian* watched a hunger march in Hyde Park, in 1932, and noted that that the sympathy of 'the crowd' lay less with the young and strong hunger marchers (chosen for their stamina) than with the local men 'of poor physique, with pale, pinched faces and a look of worry in their eyes – young men with the stamp of despair on them'.

---

1 *Why do you think the hunger marchers (many of them from Lancashire) aroused less sympathy than the local men at the demonstration in Hyde Park in October 1932? How much emphasis can be put on a source like this? Can we be certain that this was how 'the crowd' felt?*

2 *Was it the first time that the government had cut the pay of civil servants? Name one specific group of government employees who took part in the 1931 march.*

3 *What do you think the 1932 hunger marchers would have said to the Editor of the* Daily Sketch? *Write a letter to the newspaper, expressing the point of view of a member of the family of one of the men with 'pale, pinched faces'.*

The policy of cutting public expenditure was attacked by John Maynard Keynes, an economist who argued that only by increasing public spending could the Government pull the country out of the Depression. But this was too radical a view for the Cabinet in the 1930s, even though the success of Roosevelt's 'New Deal' programme of public works in the United States proved conspicuously successful between 1933 and 1936.

But the National Government did take one radical action. It abandoned the long-standing policy of Free Trade and, in 1932, passed the Import Duties Act which levied duties of 10 per cent on most imports and manufactures. This was later raised to 20 per cent on many goods (see also Chapter 1). The old idea of Imperial Preference was also revived in 1932 at the Ottawa Imperial Economic Conference. Britain agreed to give preference to Commonwealth goods – charging lower tariffs on imports from the colonies and dominions, and fixing quotas for goods from other countries.

British industry began to pick up once more under the protection of these new acts. Manufacturers were delighted that Britain was no longer to be a dumping ground for cheap foreign imports. But it was a false sense of security, since the protection it gave made it less likely than before that industries and the trade unions would change their working practices to become more competitive.

THE ECONOMY DURING AND AFTER THE SECOND WORLD WAR

The Second World War and its Effects

The Second World War saw a repeat of many of the economic measures taken more than twenty years earlier during the First World War. Motor manufacturers made tanks and aeroplanes, not cars for export. As a result many overseas markets were lost to the United States, particularly in South America. Yet raw materials, food and armaments were needed on a massive scale and had to be paid for – partly from the sale of overseas investments, partly from Britain's dwindling gold and foreign currency reserves, and partly from foreign loans. Money was borrowed from the United States under a special arrangement called 'lend-lease'.

At home, income tax was increased to a massive 50 per cent (10s in the pound) in 1941, and employers were later required to collect it themselves under the PAYE (Pay As You Earn) regulations of 1943. Purchase tax was imposed on many goods in 1940, partly to raise taxes and partly to control demand. The public was also encouraged to put money into National Savings and War Bonds, to provide further cash for the national war effort.

By 1945, Britain, like the other countries of Europe, was exhausted after six years of war. Apart from the large loss of life, the damage caused during the Blitz and the hardships imposed by six years of rationing, there were many grave financial problems to be tackled.

Lend-lease ceased immediately the war with Japan came to an end, in 1945. This caused immense financial problems for the incoming Labour Government. Massive investment was needed to revitalise industry, build new homes and rebuild city centres. Accordingly, new loans were negotiated and fresh American aid sought. This was forthcoming with the Marshall Plan in 1947, which pumped money into Britain and other European countries to aid post-war recovery. The Organisation for European Economic Recovery was formed to manage Marshall Aid and, since countries had to co-operate, it fostered the cause of European unity and a new approach to trade between friendly nations.

Devaluation

Despite foreign aid, the Labour Government felt obliged to devalue the pound in 1949 in order to make British exports more competitive. Foreign assessments of what the pound was worth were really based on their view of the British economy as a whole.

In 1948, the pound was worth $4. After devaluation in 1949, it was worth $2.80, and after another devaluation in 1967, $2.40. After 1972, it was allowed to 'float' (meaning that the British government did not fix the rate of exchange).

Its value dropped even further but gained some strength in the late 1970s when North-Sea oil contributed substantially to the nation's assets and the American economy suffered a temporary setback. But when oil prices fell drastically in the middle 1980s, the pound plunged to a new low. At one stage, in 1985, it was being exchanged in America at the rate of one dollar = one pound.

Economic Problems

Standards of living undoubtedly increased considerably after the war, whilst industrial output and productivity improved and British agriculture underwent a revolutionary transformation (see Chapters 1 and 2). But the improvements in industry were slower than in other countries, notably the United States, Germany, Japan and France. It was this relative decline which gave British governments most concern. In particular, Britain increasingly imported foreign manufactures, in preference to products made in Britain itself.

The excess of imports over exports in many of the post-war years led to a balance of payments problem, since it meant that the country was spending more than it earned. Governments reacted with the 'stop-go' policy – clamping down on spending, by increasing purchase tax and restricting credit. Then, when industries at home began to suffer from loss of orders, they cut taxes and relaxed credit restrictions to encourage spending once more. Not surprisingly, wage demands increased when prices rose (because of increased purchase tax). As a result successive governments fought a constant battle to keep wage demands down in line with prices.

Unemployment and Inflation

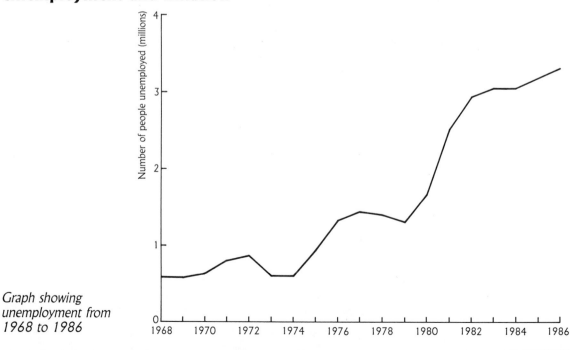

Graph showing unemployment from 1968 to 1986

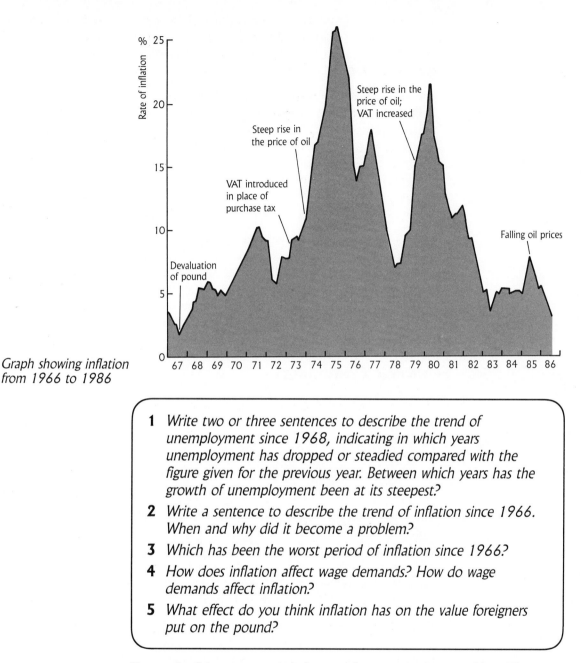

Graph showing inflation from 1966 to 1986

1 Write two or three sentences to describe the trend of unemployment since 1968, indicating in which years unemployment has dropped or steadied compared with the figure given for the previous year. Between which years has the growth of unemployment been at its steepest?

2 Write a sentence to describe the trend of inflation since 1966. When and why did it become a problem?

3 Which has been the worst period of inflation since 1966?

4 How does inflation affect wage demands? How do wage demands affect inflation?

5 What effect do you think inflation has on the value foreigners put on the pound?

For much of the post-war period, unemployment was not a problem. There was no immediate return to the 10 per cent unemployment levels of the inter-war years. In 1951 the unemployment rate was less than 1 per cent and in 1975, thirty years after the end of the war, unemployment was still below 5 per cent. But the oil crisis of the 1970s led to high rates of inflation and a depression in industry. One million people were out of work by 1976, 2 million by November 1980, 3 million by September 1982 and 3.3 million by the middle of 1986.

Unfortunately, levels of unemployment in 1986 varied as much between the different parts of Britain as they had done in the inter-war period. For example, 10 per cent unemployment in the South-east seemed low compared with 20 per cent in the North and 25 per cent on Teesside.

One of the reasons for the high rate of unemployment was fear of inflation. In the 1970s and 1980s, rising prices posed a serious threat to the economy, when the purchasing power of the pound fell dramatically. Goods which could have been bought for about £1 in 1945 cost £2 in 1965, £4 in 1975, £8 in 1980 and nearly £12 in 1986. Yet before the Second World War, inflation had not been a problem, except at time of war, and in the 1920s and early 1930s the purchasing power of the pound actually increased by 75 per cent (between 1920 and 1935).

In 1979, the new Conservative Government, led by Margaret Thatcher, Britain's first woman Prime Minister, treated inflation as the most important problem facing Britain. Public expenditure was cut and strict controls were imposed on the amount of money in circulation. Banks were made to charge high interest rates on loans to curb spending. This policy was called 'monetarism'. It had the desired effect of lowering inflation to less than 3 per cent in 1986, but at the cost of many jobs.

The European Economic Community

Since 1973, the United Kingdom has been a member of the EEC or Common Market and benefited from its trading policies. The six original member countries (France, Germany, Italy, Belgium, the Netherlands and Luxembourg) set up the EEC when they signed the Treaty of Rome, in 1957. The EEC made it easier for member nations to trade with each other. All tariffs and duties were phased out and goods traded inside the Community were free of customs duties.

The United Kingdom, originally invited to join the EEC, declined because British politicians feared the consequences of putting control of the British economy in the hands of a body representing several different countries. In addition they were worried about the effect that membership might have on trade with the countries of the Commonwealth, since many of these were partly dependent on the UK as the main market for their goods.

Instead, Britain became a founder member of EFTA – the European Free Trade Association – which came into being in 1959. The member countries – Austria, Denmark, Norway, Portugal, Sweden and Switzerland (and later Iceland and Finland) – agreed to remove the tariff barriers between them on industrial goods but not to seek the greater unity which was one of the aims of the EEC.

But the success of the EEC, and the growing independence of the Commonwealth nations, persuaded the British government to apply unsuccessfully for membership of the Community in 1963 and 1967, and successfully in 1973, when the admission of the United Kingdom, the Irish Republic and Denmark brought the number of member countries to nine. In Britain, the incoming Labour Government held a national referendum in 1975, to see if the British people actually wanted to stay in the EEC or not. They did – by a majority of two to one. In 1981, Greece became the tenth member of the Community, and Spain and Portugal made it twelve in 1986. The benefits of EEC membership are a matter of some controversy, but supporters point to these advantages.

- Many barriers to free movement between the member countries have been removed, such as the abolition of customs duties.
- Member countries share many common laws and regulations.
- People can seek work anywhere in the Community.
- There is a common European Parliament directly elected by the peoples of Europe.
- The EEC has an important say in world affairs.
- Trade has increased, bringing prosperity to the EEC.
- Food prices have risen, but they no longer fluctuate from year to year (see page 27) and the Common Agricultural Policy has prevented thousands of farmers from going out of business.
- European industries co-operate with one another and financial help has been forthcoming for depressed areas.

FURTHER QUESTIONS AND EXERCISES

THE PATIENT ASS.
THE INCOME-TAXED ONE MURMURETH.—"I DON'T GRUMBLE, BUT—I *SHOULD* LIKE JUST A LITTLE TAKEN OFF."

1 *(a) What was the point of this cartoon, published in* Punch *on 18 April 1896? Who was 'the patient ass'? Was income tax a burden at that time?*

(b) Write a paragraph outlining the history of income tax in Britain. When was it first imposed? Why was it re-introduced as a tax in 1842? When and why was it charged at a rate equivalent to half a person's income?

2 Thomas Jones noted in his diary in October 1931 that:

'In the recent crisis two English stockbrokers offered to pay their hotel bills in the French Riviera with Bank of England notes and were refused.'

What was the crisis and why were they refused?

3 Why were the effects of the Depression of 1929–34 so keenly felt in Britain? What problems lay at the root of the slump in British trade? How did the government attempt to deal with this problem and with what success?

4 What financial crises could have affected the life of a former Lancashire cotton weaver, celebrating her hundredth birthday in 1979? List the crises and show the effects they might have had on her everyday life and work.

Political poster in 1906. The 'fisherman' is shown with a worm labelled 'full employment' on the end of his line, and his basket is labelled 'protection'.

5 (a) Which political party is most likely to have been responsible for this poster? Who is the 'fisherman'?

(b) The bait is shown as being 'full employment'. How did the 'fisherman' hope to solve the unemployment problem?

(c) Why did the poster suggest that 'full employment' was the bait to attract the voter? What was the 'hook'? Explain the reasoning behind this argument.

(d) In what ways is this poster unfair to the politician represented by the 'fisherman'?

6 Write one or two sentences to say what is meant by each of the following terms. Add a note to say what part each has played in British financial affairs since 1850.

(a) invisible exports

(b) the balance of trade

(c) fair trade

(d) Imperial Preference

(e) lend-lease

(f) the European Economic Community

(g) the Gold Standard

(h) Free Trade

(i) devaluation

(j) inflation

(k) monetarism

(l) EFTA

7 Distinguish between (a) the 'Great Depression' of the 1870s, 1880s and 1890s, (b) the Depression of the 1920s and 1930s, and (c) the depression of the 1970s and 1980s. How did they differ from each other, and what were their different effects on the lives of the people of Britain?

8 Examine and explain the slogans used by these car workers. Whom or what did they blame for a cut in their jobs?

Protesting car workers
in the 1960s

Chapter Five

Population

INTRODUCTION

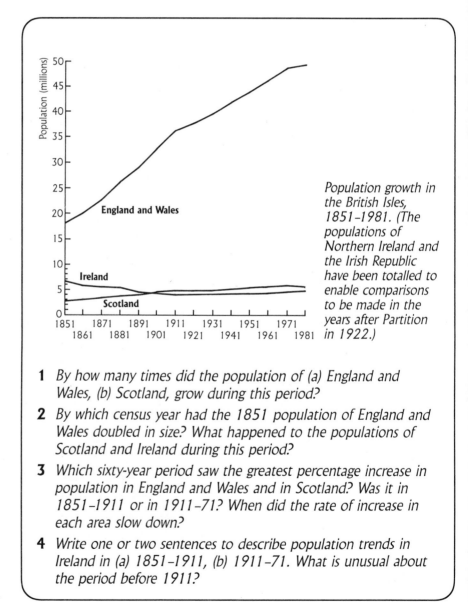

Population growth in the British Isles, 1851–1981. (The populations of Northern Ireland and the Irish Republic have been totalled to enable comparisons to be made in the years after Partition in 1922.)

1 *By how many times did the population of (a) England and Wales, (b) Scotland, grow during this period?*

2 *By which census year had the 1851 population of England and Wales doubled in size? What happened to the populations of Scotland and Ireland during this period?*

3 *Which sixty-year period saw the greatest percentage increase in population in England and Wales and in Scotland? Was it in 1851–1911 or in 1911–71? When did the rate of increase in each area slow down?*

4 *Write one or two sentences to describe population trends in Ireland in (a) 1851–1911, (b) 1911–71. What is unusual about the period before 1911?*

Basically there are only four reasons why the population of a town, county or country should rise or fall. These are increases or decreases in (a) the birth rate, (b) the death rate, (c) the rate of immigration, (d) the rate of emigration.

In this chapter, you will see how and why the birth and death rates have fluctuated since 1850, and how and why levels of immigration and emigration changed during the nineteenth and twentieth centuries. These changes had significant effects on the distribution of population in the British Isles and on the social and economic history of the period.

POPULATION GROWTH, 1851–1981

The Census

The first official census in Great Britain was held in 1801, and at first only simple questions were asked. As a result the early censuses lacked detail. But by 1851 the size and scope of the census form had been enlarged and obviously worried many householders – as you can see in the cartoon, 'Taking the Census of 1851'. The census forms were delivered by enumerators to each of the 200 homes on their lists. It was their job to see that they were accurately completed. The details were later re-classified by a huge army of clerks at the Census Office in London. Totals were compiled for different categories of age group, sex, occupation or marital status, and for different areas (e.g: parishes, towns, counties).

'Taking the Census of 1851', Windsor Magazine, 1897

1 *Where is the enumerator in this cartoon?*
2 *What was the point of the cartoon?*
3 *What serious doubts about the accuracy of the census are suggested by this cartoon?*

Birth and Death Rates

The basic cause of the rapid growth of population in Britain in the nineteenth century was an excess of births over deaths. But why this should have happened at that time is far from clear. For a long time, many historians thought that it must be due to the Industrial Revolution – mainly because the rapid rise in population coincided with an equally rapid growth in industrial production.

Nowadays historians are less sure. Some even think that the reverse may be true – that the growth in population had an important effect in stimulating industrial growth, since it created more mouths to feed and more hands to be employed. Almost all historians agree that there was no one single cause and that a number of factors played their part.

In the middle years of the nineteenth century, the death rate was always substantially lower than the birth rate. It usually rose or fell in line with the birth rate, because of the high level of infant mortality. The more babies that were born, the higher the death rate. But, after 1870, the birth and death rates began to change – as you can see from this graph.

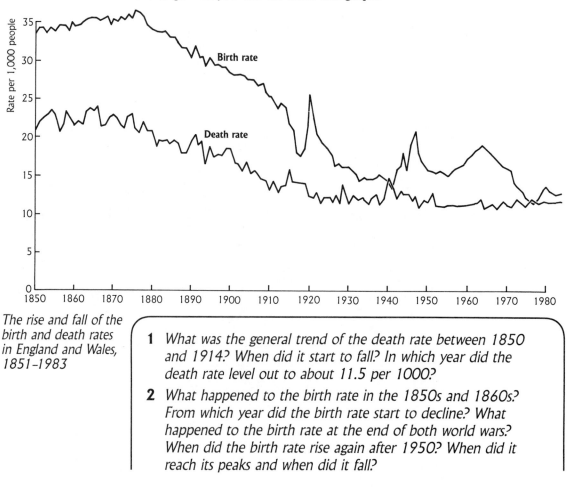

The rise and fall of the birth and death rates in England and Wales, 1851–1983

1 *What was the general trend of the death rate between 1850 and 1914? When did it start to fall? In which year did the death rate level out to about 11.5 per 1000?*

2 *What happened to the birth rate in the 1850s and 1860s? From which year did the birth rate start to decline? What happened to the birth rate at the end of both world wars? When did the birth rate rise again after 1950? When did it reach its peaks and when did it fall?*

3 What effect do you think a rise or decline in the birth rate would have on (a) schools, (b) factories making prams or baby foods, (c) the health services?

4 When did the gap between the birth and death rates start to narrow? In which years did the death rate match or exceed the birth rate? What would happen if this became a permanent feature in the future?

5 When would you expect the total population of England and Wales to have risen at a slower rate than in the past? Is this confirmed by the population graph on page 156?

6 Predictions of a catastrophic fall in population were forecast for England and Wales by 'experts' who assumed that a downward trend in the birth rate would continue. In which years (other than in wartime) do you think these forecasts were made? Why were they foolish to predict the future in this way?

7 Use the graph opposite and the one on page 156 to explain how and why the population of England and Wales has continued to grow, despite the overall decline in the birth rate.

REASONS FOR THE CHANGES IN THE BIRTH RATE

1. Young and Old Populations

As you have seen, the birth rate was high throughout the second half of the nineteenth century. This high fertility (as it is called) was due to a number of factors. The population as a whole was young – in 1851, roughly half the population of England and Wales was under 23. Young populations usually have more children than older populations.

In general, the growing industrial towns of the late nineteenth century held a higher proportion of young people than did the rural areas. Young people left the countryside to work in the towns where there were more jobs. Having a job meant they could settle down earlier and get married. Moreover, a large mill or factory, employing hundreds of workers, offered far greater opportunities to find a partner than did a country village.

As a result, the factory towns of the North and Midlands had a higher than average birth rate. This, coupled with the general lowering of the death rate, was one of the main reasons why they grew more rapidly than the country market towns (see Chapter 6). In 1897, Sheffield's annual birth rate of 34.4 per 1000 was substantially higher than the national average of 29.6 per 1000.

Since the 1930s, many of the older industrial towns, particularly those in the Lancashire cotton industry (such as Blackburn and Oldham) and on the South Wales coalfield (such as Llanelli and the Rhondda), some isolated rural areas and most seaside resorts (such as Bexhill, Bournemouth and Hove), have had a higher than average proportion of older people as residents. This has often meant a lower than average birth rate. In 1959, Sheffield's annual birth rate was only 15.4 per 1000 compared with the UK average of 16.5 per 1000.

Conversely, the New Towns (such as Harlow and Stevenage) and the rapidly growing, newer industrial towns (such as the steel town of Scunthorpe) have had a higher than average proportion of young families and an above average birth rate. You can see this in the table of town population statistics below.

Town	Population (1959)	Birth Rate (in 1959 per 1000)	Death Rate (in 1959 per 1000)	Population (1969)
Bexhill	26,610	11.1	20.3	33,470
Blackburn	105,900	15.0	15.4	100,010
Bournemouth	144,700	11.4	16.2	149,820
Harlow	45,250	29.8	4.1	76,240
Hove	69,930	10.0	19.1	71,190
Llanelli	31,430	12.3	14.3	27,570
Oldham	117,800	16.5	14.4	108,280
Rhondda	106,000	14.6	14.6	94,300
Scunthorpe	61,840	20.0	8.4	69,720
Stevenage	34,580	29.2	5.0	61,710

1 Locate these towns on an atlas map. Which towns (a) had a higher death rate than birth rate, (b) had a higher birth rate than death rate, (c) grew substantially between 1959 and 1969, (d) lost population between 1959 and 1969?

2 Why did the populations of Blackburn and Llanelli fall? Why did the population of Scunthorpe increase?

3 Why do you think Bexhill increased its population by 25 per cent at a time when its death rate was nearly twice its birth rate? Which other towns followed a similar pattern? Why? What would you say to someone who used these statistics to prove that it was obviously unhealthy to live by the sea?

> **4** What was unusual about the population statistics for Oldham and the Rhondda during this period? Suggest a possible explanation.
>
> **5** Was the growth of the New Towns entirely due to a higher birth rate than death rate?

2. Marriage and Employment

The overall fall in the birth rate partly reflects changing attitudes to childbirth and family life. As you have seen, the earlier that people married, the more likely they were to start a family. But in the twentieth century, many more young people have been able to stay on at school and follow a course of technical training or of higher education. Young people have been less likely to marry early and start a family. From 1960 onwards many more women continued their careers after marriage and by 1986 it had become normal for women to go out to work on terms of equality with their husband or partner. The widespread use of the oral contraceptive (since 1961) has made it easier to postpone having families.

3. Family Size and Family Planning

Contraceptive devices have been used since the eighteenth century, but only became widely available in the 1920s. At first they were frowned on by prudish Victorian society and opposed by many Church leaders. As a result their utility and availability received little publicity. Large families, with as many as ten children, were normal. Women continued to give birth to children throughout the fertile years of a marriage, especially since many infants died at birth or in the first five years of childhood. The larger the family, the greater the number of surviving children. Many mothers died in childbirth.

Reliable information about birth control was slow to reach the public, but in 1876 Annie Besant and Charles Bradlaugh published *The Fruits of Philosophy*, an American pamphlet advocating birth control as a means of limiting family size. They sold 200,000 copies but were fined £200 for publishing an 'obscene' book. In 1918, Marie Stopes (see page 328) aroused similar controversy when she published *Married Love*, a guide to birth control. She followed it by opening a birth-control clinic in London, in 1921.

Since contraceptives were expensive, their use was confined to the more affluent members of society. This may have been one of the reasons why professional people tended to have smaller families than unskilled workers in late-Victorian times. The average professional family had only 2.8 children in the 1890s compared with 5.1 children in the unskilled labourer's family.

As people became more affluent in the twentieth century, so they tended to have smaller families. By the 1980s, the average was 2.2 children per family. But exactly why growing affluence should be a reason for having smaller families has never been adequately explained. If anything, the sharp decline of the birth rate during the Depression years of the 1920s and 1930s, and the rise of the birth rate in the affluent 1950s and 1960s, suggest the opposite.

Nor does it explain why Queen Victoria, who was extremely rich, should have had nine children, whilst her own rich children should have followed the same downward trend as the rest of Britain, with 39 children between them (an average of 4.3 per family). Moreover, her great-grandchildren had only nine children – an average of 1.8 per family (in line with the general trend in Britain towards small families in the 1920s and 1930s).

---

1 *Find out from relatives and friends how many children their parents, grandparents and great-grandparents had. Work out the average family size for each generation.*

2 *Do your figures follow the national trend? If not, why not?*

---

4. The Effects of War and Peace

After the First World War there was a measurable decline in the number of young families in Britain, due in part to:

- the loss of 750,000 young men in the First World War;

- the high rate of emigration from Britain in the years before 1914 (see graph on page 175) – much of it by younger rather than by older people;

- the effects of the influenza epidemic in the autumn of 1918, which killed 225,000 people (many of them young).

These factors helped to deplete the number of potential parents in the post-war years and resulted in a marked lowering of the birth rate after the initial baby boom at the end of the war. The birth rate continued to decline during the Depression years, reaching its lowest point in 1941, during the Second World War. Luckily, this war had less effect in diminishing the number of potential parents, partly because many of the 460,000 casualties of the war were civilians and from an older generation.

Immediately after the end of the war there was a boom in the birth of babies, since many of the servicemen returning to Britain, were keen to start a family after six years of war. The boom reached its peak in 1947 with over 20 births per 1000, a rate higher than any since 1920. Then the birth rate declined steeply, until 1955, when it started to rise again (for no readily explicable reason) to a peak of over 18 per 1000 in 1964. This 'bulge', as it was called, in the birth rate, had an effect on school and medical provision, when these extra children made their way through the school system. Equally, the steep decline in the birth rate since 1964 has had a reverse effect, causing a rapid fall in school numbers and hastening the closure of some schools. As you can see from the graph on page 158, these fluctuations in the birth rate contrast sharply with a death rate that has been steady at about 11.5 per 1000 ever since 1950.

---

1 *Look at the graph on page 158. Imagine you were in charge of schools in your area from 1945 to 1980. In which years would you have had to make extra provision for pupils in primary schools (aged 5 to 11 years)?*

2 *When would you have been faced with falling numbers in secondary schools (aged 11 to 18 years)?*

THE DEATH RATE

Infant Mortality

A high birth rate is no guarantee, in itself, that the population will rise. What is really significant is the number of children who survive the perils of infancy. In the eighteenth century the chances of an infant surviving childhood were extremely poor. Even as late as 1899, over 16 per cent of the infants born in England and Wales died before the age of one.

Deaths of Infants under One Year Old

1850	16.2%	1900	15.4%	1950	3.0%
1855	15.3%	1905	12.8%	1955	2.5%
1860	14.8%	1910	10.5%	1960	2.2%
1865	16.0%	1915	11.0%	1965	1.9%
1870	16.0%	1920	8.0%	1970	1.8%
1875	15.8%	1925	7.5%	1975	1.6%
1880	15.3%	1930	6.0%	1980	1.2%
1885	13.8%	1935	5.7%	1983	1.0%
1890	15.1%	1940	5.7%		
1895	16.1%	1945	4.6%		

---

1 *Use the table to draw a graph showing the rise and fall of the infant mortality rate since 1850 (the statistics to 1980 are shown at five-yearly intervals).*

2 *From which date did the infant mortality rate start to fall steadily in England and Wales?*

3 *Do you think your graph can be used to predict that the infant mortality rate will fall even further in the future? Find out whether infant mortality rates have fallen in the years since 1983. Show these statistics on your graph.*

4 *How many infants celebrated a first birthday in 1896 out of every 100 babies born in 1895? How many 1983 babies did so in 1984? How many more children (in every 100 babies) would have lived into the twentieth century had the infant mortality rate in 1895 been the same as the rate for 1983?*

There are a number of reasons why the twentieth century has seen such a remarkable decline in infant mortality.

- The gradual elimination of slums and the construction of better homes (such as those to be found on the housing estates of any modern town) – see Chapter 6.

- Much higher standards of cleanliness – cleaner homes, cleaner streets, cleaner clothes and cleaner bedding.

- Better nutrition. Purer milk, purer water and more nourishing food have eliminated many of the diseases formerly carried by food and water (such as cholera, typhoid fever, tuberculosis) whilst higher living standards and welfare benefits have meant that fewer children have gone hungry. In fact, many experts now claim that the average modern child is overfed and that the type of food eaten by many children may well be harmful (see page 169).

- Higher standards of maternity care and infant welfare – with antenatal clinics, health visitors, paid maternity leave for working mothers, maternity benefit and child benefit. By 1986, almost all confinements took place in hospitals or in maternity homes; Caesarean operations had become commonplace in difficult cases; and the use of modern drugs, blood transfusions and the provision of intensive care units ensured a much higher survival rate for weakly infants.

- A much higher standard of education among parents (after the passage of the various Education Acts – see Chapter 9). Better-educated parents were more able to care effectively for their children. Moreover, compulsory schooling meant that teachers and school medical officers were able to monitor the health and condition of the children in their care. Physical education and games also played a part in increasing general physical fitness.

- Parliamentary legislation and the work of voluntary organisations. The Provision of School Meals Act of 1906 (see page 285) enabled Local Education Authorities to provide midday meals for poor children. Parliament legislated to prevent cruelty and neglect to small children. The London Society for the Prevention of Cruelty to Children was founded in 1884. It became a national society in 1889 and played a major part in getting

Parliament to pass an Act for the Prevention of Cruelty to Children in 1889 and an Act for the Better Protection of Children in 1890. The law provided that children, as of right, were entitled to be clothed, fed and properly treated. Voluntary organisations, such as the Salvation Army and Dr Barnardo's Homes also played an important part in improving the conditions in which slum children were brought up and bringing their plight to the attention of the public, the newspapers and the government.

The Effects of Medical Improvements

Many people think that the development of curative medicine (drugs, surgery, antibiotics) has been the main reason why the death rate has declined in the twentieth century and why the average person can expect to live a longer life.

Yet the statistics show clearly that the death rate from many diseases had already declined sharply, long before the development of antibiotics in the 1940s or the innovations in heart and transplant surgery of the last thirty years.

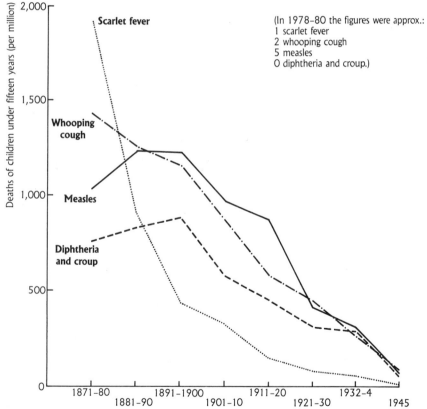

Deaths of children under fifteen years (per million)

Scarlet fever

(In 1978–80 the figures were approx.:
1 scarlet fever
2 whooping cough
5 measles
0 diphtheria and croup.)

Whooping cough

Measles

Diphtheria and croup

Deaths from the four main childhood diseases in England and Wales, 1871–1945

As you can see from this graph, the four most important childhood diseases of the late nineteenth century – scarlet fever, whooping cough, measles, and diphtheria and croup – have all ceased to be the threat they once were to the lives of children under fifteen years old. Some of the other main killer diseases of the nineteenth century were also declining before 1900, as you can see from the table below. Smallpox had been greatly feared at the end of the eighteenth century, until Jenner's demonstration of vaccination in 1795 brought a radical improvement in the death rate from this disease. In 1853, compulsory vaccination was introduced for all newly born infants and, by 1900, smallpox had ceased to be a problem in Britain.

	Average Annual Deaths (per million people)				
	— England and Wales —				*UK*
Disease	*1876–80*	*1891–5*	*1935*	*1958–9*	*1978–80*
Bronchitis	2,378	2,076	720	649	427
Tuberculosis	2,043	1,458	728	92	10
Smallpox	78	20	0	0	0
Typhoid fever	277	173	6	0	0
Typhus	34	4	0	0	0

1 *Draw a graph to show the statistics in this table. Write a paragraph explaining your graph.*

2 *Write a paragraph explaining the graph of childhood diseases on page 165. What does it tell you about these diseases? Did the death rates from these diseases decline steadily? When did those for measles and diphtheria start to fall?*

3 *Immunisation against diphtheria was not introduced into England and Wales until the 1940s, when health education posters warned, 'DIPHTHERIA is deadly – IMMUNISATION is the safeguard'. Vaccination against tuberculosis, whooping cough and measles were innovations of the 1960s and 1970s. Were these inoculation programmes the main reason why deaths from these diseases have been almost eliminated? Why are these inoculation programmes still important today?*

4 *Penicillin and other antibiotics, which have been in general use from about 1945 onwards, are used to treat bronchitis, tuberculosis and scarlet fever. Is this the main reason why the death rates from these diseases have declined? Why are antibiotics so important today?*

5 *By which years had typhoid fever and typhus ceased to be major health threats?*

6 *Write two or three sentences describing the part played by medical advance in the conquest of these diseases.*

Improvements in Hygiene, Sanitation and Water Supply

Victorian soap advertisement in 1890

Although advances in medical care and surgical techniques, and the discovery of life-saving drugs, have been of immense benefit to the human race, it is doubtful whether their effect on public health has been anything like as great as that of the improvements in sanitation, cleanliness, diet and standards of living, which have been so marked in the last hundred years. The contribution these made to public health was recognised in 1884.

> 'The Registrar-General's returns show the expectation of life is now about three years longer than for the period of 17 years ending 1854, which is probably due to abolishing the duty on soap and the window-tax, as well as to water supply, drainage, etc.'
>
> *Michael G. Mulhall,* The Dictionary of Statistics, *1884*

Another factor in the twentieth century has been the changeover from horse-drawn vehicles to motor vehicles, reducing the quantities of manure rotting in the streets.

The effect on the fight against disease has been startling. Better water supplies and cheaper coal meant there was less excuse for dirty clothes or for dirty bodies. Householders were more likely to boil water, to wash clothes and to scrub their homes. Cheaper coal also meant warmer, drier homes.

Typhus (carried by lice from unwashed clothes) killed many people in the slums in the early nineteenth century, as had typhoid fever and cholera (both of them carried by contaminated food or water). The terrifying cholera epidemics, such as those of 1831–2 and 1849, which killed over 100,000 people between them, disappeared – the last was in 1865 when 18,000 people died of the disease. The chances of catching these diseases diminished rapidly with the introduction of better working-class housing, effective rubbish and sewage disposal, piped water supplies from water purification plants, and general improvements in personal and domestic hygiene.

Bronchitis has been called the 'English disease' and is caused or aggravated by smoking tobacco, the smoke from millions of coal fires, fog, the cold damp climate and polluted air from factory chimneys. This is why the incidence of the disease has always been much higher in the industrial areas than in the countryside. Improvements in living standards and in nursing care helped to bring the death rate down in the early years of the twentieth century. In the last thirty years or so, the decline of heavy industry, the introduction of effective legislation to minimise air pollution and the use of antibiotics have all helped to reduce the incidence of the disease and the death rate still further.

Tuberculosis (or consumption) was a deadly disease in the nineteenth century. It was largely a product of crowded living conditions, particularly in the slums, since the disease was usually spread through droplet infection – by infected people coughing. Cleaner, less-crowded living conditions, better diet, an improvement in working conditions, better medical care, and the elimination of the worst slums all helped to reduce the incidence of the disease. Antibiotics have also been highly successful, since 1945, in lowering the death rate even further. The introduction of pasteurised milk and the systematic elimination of cows suffering from tuberculosis have also had a marked effect in reducing the spread of the disease. More recently, from the 1970s onwards, children have been routinely tested and vaccinated against tuberculosis.

Diet

Improvements in agricultural methods and imports of cheap food from abroad (see Chapter 1) meant that, in the late nineteenth century, many more people began to enjoy the benefit of a better, healthier diet – eating more grain, potatoes, meat, dairy products, fresh vegetables and fruit, and getting the protein, calories and vitamins needed to give them resistance to diseases. This was one reason why affluent families lived longer, on average, than poor families. People no longer had to rely on the success of the local harvest or on local farmers for their supply of meat, vegetables and milk. There was less starvation, since food could be taken to stricken areas by rail.

Yet, despite the improvements in food supply, many poor people still lived close to starvation level in the late nineteenth century and in the Edwardian period. Many were seriously under-nourished during the Depression years of the 1920s and 1930s. Lack of sufficient food of the right quality was a contributory cause of ill-health, since people suffering from malnutrition were more likely to catch epidemic diseases.

New Hazards

Parallel with these advances, however, has come an alarming increase in the death rate from heart disease and lung cancer. The number of deaths in England and Wales from heart disease rose from 49,000 in 1911 to 179,000 in 1981, whilst deaths from all types of cancer increased in the same period from 35,000 to 149,000 (due in part to the sharp rise in the number of deaths from lung cancer). In the forty years between 1931-5 and 1971-5, the death rate from lung cancer amongst men rose by over five times in England and Wales and by seven times in Scotland.

Paradoxically, the increase in the number of deaths from heart disease has been directly attributed to the same improvements in living standards which helped to eliminate the diseases which worried the Victorians. Many medical researchers claim today, that in the last forty years or so, three factors have been to blame for the steep increase in the numbers of people dying from heart disease (and also from strokes and certain types of cancer). These are (a) cigarette smoking, (b) an increase in the consumption of food containing saturated animal fat (such as the dairy products – milk, butter, cheese – and meat), and (c) a corresponding decline in the consumption of foods rich in fibre (such as potatoes, beans and wholemeal bread).

The relationship between the consumption of saturated animal fat and heart disease has been disputed by some of the national organisations responsible for the promotion of dairy products. Similarly, the tobacco companies have disputed that there is a direct causal link between cigarette smoking (a luxury of the affluent society) and lung cancer or heart disease, despite the research findings which led the Government to ban cigarette advertising on television and to insist that a government health warning be printed on cigarette packets.

By 1986, the spread of AIDS had also begun to arouse widespread concern, although its likely effect on public health, in the future, was still unclear.

1 *How many of your older friends and relatives are convinced that there is a strong link (a) between the consumption of animal fats or the smoking of cigarettes **and** heart disease, (b) between cigarette smoking **and** lung cancer? How many have altered their lifestyles accordingly (e.g. by stopping cigarette smoking, by becoming vegetarian, by eating more fibre-rich foods, or by cutting down on dairy products)?*

2 *What were the reasons for the decline in the nineteenth-century killer diseases? In each case was it **either** (a) the fact that a **cure** was found for the disease, **or** (b) that a method of **prevention** was discovered? Which do you think is more likely to cause a decline in the death rates from heart disease, lung cancer and AIDS – prevention or cure?*

THE CHANGING DISTRIBUTION OF POPULATION

Regions of the British Isles

The changes which took place in the growth of population in the British Isles were not evenly spread across the country. Population trends in England, Wales, Scotland and Ireland were all different. So, too, were the trends in the different regions of England. In 1871, Scotland had a population of 3.4 million people compared with 2.8 million in the Home Counties. A hundred years later, there were 5.2 million people in Scotland and 9.3 million in the Home Counties. You can see similar contrasts in this table. The areas shown are indicated on the map.

Region	*Population (in millions)*		
	1871	*1921*	*1971*
Scotland	3.4	4.9	5.2
Wales	1.4	2.7	2.7
North of England	1.4	2.6	2.6
Lancashire & Yorkshire	5.3	9.1	10.2
North & East Midlands	3.7	6.6	9.4
Ireland	5.4	4.3	4.5
South & West Midlands	1.7	2.0	3.2
East Anglia	1.0	1.2	1.7
West Country	1.6	1.7	2.3
Home Counties	2.8	4.7	9.3
London	3.8	7.4	7.4

1 Which areas (if any) declined or grew slowly in population (a) between 1871 and 1921, (b) between 1921 and 1971?

2 The population of which regions (if any) grew by less than 10 per cent (a) between 1871 and 1921, (b) between 1921 and 1971? Suggest reasons which may help to explain why.

3 Which regions grew rapidly (a) between 1871 and 1921, (b) between 1921 and 1971? In which parts of the British Isles are they situated? Suggest reasons which may help to explain why they grew faster than other areas.

4 Make two tracings of the map to show the growth of population (a) between 1871 and 1921, (b) between 1921 and 1971. Choose different colours or forms of shading to show those regions with a growth of population of less than 10 per cent, of between 10 and 40 per cent, of between 40 and 70 per cent, and of over 70 per cent.

5 Write a paragraph analysing the facts shown on your map.

Internal Migration

Most of the regional variations in the growth of population between 1871 and 1971 were the result of internal migration – people moving from one area to another – rather than variations in the birth and death rates (although these did exist). For example, in the 1870s Cornish people went to work at Barrow-in-Furness, in 1910 Scottish steelworkers went to the new iron and steel works at Corby in Northamptonshire, and in 1931 Ford workers moved from Manchester to Dagenham in Essex.

In 1961, over half the residents of Middlesex, Surrey, Hertfordshire, Buckinghamshire and West Sussex were born outside their respective counties. At the other extreme, only one person in every five living in Lancashire, Yorkshire, Durham, the Orkneys and the Shetlands had been born in another county.

> **1** *What do the counties with the highest proportions of people born outside their respective counties all have in common? Why do you think they have such a large proportion of residents born outside their county boundaries?*
>
> **2** *What do these figures tell you about internal migration in Britain in the twentieth century?*

Apart from internal migration from one region to another, there was also substantial migration from the countryside to the towns.

'The drift towards the town is continuous. We have long been aware of it. From north, south, east and west, with rare exceptions, comes the complaint that the young men are leaving them. The testimony on innumerable farms is that only the old men and the children remain. The depopulation of the land, and the overcrowding of the cities, are two related facts, and they must be considered together.'

'Depopulated England' by W. Stevens in The Leisure Hour, *1903*

Population of Selected Rural Counties (in 1000s)

County	*1861*	*1871*	*1881*	*1891*	*1901*	*1911*	*1921*	*1931*	*1951*	*1961*	*1971*
Dorset	189	196	191	192	200	221	225	239	291	313	362
Hereford	124	125	121	116	114	114	113	112	127	131	139
Norfolk	435	439	445	468	476	498	501	502	548	561	618
Shropshire	241	248	248	237	240	246	243	244	290	297	337
Suffolk	337	349	357	362	373	394	400	401	443	472	546
Caernarfon	96	106	119	116	123	123	128	121	124	122	123
Perth	134	128	129	122	123	124	126	121	128	127	127

1 To what extent do the statistics in the table support the author's argument in 'Depopulated England'? Was he overstating or understating his case in 1903? To what extent could he have made his statement with equal or greater accuracy in (a) 1931, (b) 1971?

2 Which counties (if any) suffered depopulation between (a) 1871 and 1901, (b) 1901 and 1931, (c) 1931 and 1971?

3 Draw a graph to show the statistics which you think best show how parts of the countryside have been depopulated.

EMIGRATION AND IMMIGRATION

GETTING BERTH NUMBERS.

GRAVESEND

Emigrating to Australia, The Illustrated London News, 12 February 1887

This is how *The Illustrated London News* described these emigrants in its issue of 12 February 1887.

'Men, women and children, the families keeping closely together, crowd over the deck, some fussy, excited and anxious, others with a listless and helpless air of being managed like a flock of sheep; a few silently weeping, because they have parted, it may be for life, from those most dear to them.'

Emigration overseas played an important part in population trends in the nineteenth century, accounting substantially for the decline in population in Ireland (shown in the graph on page 156). Over ten million people from Ireland, Scotland, England and Wales emigrated overseas between 1851 and 1900.

Decade	England & Wales	Scotland	Ireland	Total
1851–60	0.6	0.2	1.2	2.0
1861–70	0.7	0.2	0.9	1.8
1871–80	1.0	0.2	0.5	1.7
1881–90	1.8	0.3	0.8	2.9
1891–1900	1.3	0.2	0.5	2.0
1851–1900	5.4	1.1	3.9	10.4

Estimated Number of Emigrants from Britain (in millions)

Compare this table with the population figures shown in the graph on page 156.

> **1** What proportion of the total emigrants in each decade came from (a) England and Wales, (b) Scotland, (c) Ireland?
>
> **2** What percentage of the 1851 populations of England and Wales, Scotland and Ireland emigrated between 1851 and 1861? What were the equivalent percentages for the 1891–1900 decade? Which country suffered the greatest loss of population due to emigration?

The reasons for the growth in the numbers of people emigrating from the British Isles, in the nineteenth century, were partly 'push' and partly 'pull'. Distress and failure at home, notably after the Irish famine in the 1840s, pushed people out of Britain. At the same time, the attraction of 'a better land overseas' pulled them away from their roots. The discovery of the Californian and Australian gold-fields in 1849–50 added further incentives.

Emigration was deliberately fostered by the government and by emigration societies which offered free passages or cheap fares to make it easier for poor people to leave Britain. Improvements to sailing ships and to steamships (see Chapter 3) made their journeys safer, quicker and easier, although passengers still endured terrible hardships on the long voyages. You can find out more about the reasons for emigration if you look at these sources.

Source A

'Out of a population of 240, I found thirteen already dead from want. The survivors were like walking skeletons, the men gaunt and haggard, stamped with the livid mark of hunger, the children crying with pain, the women in some of the cabins too weak to stand.'

Description of the Irish village of Bunderagh, in 1847, by W. E. Forster

Source B

'The emigration is conducted in a very liberal manner, as the emigrants are clothed, have free passage, and are given a sum of money to start with on arrival at their destination. With such tempting conditions as these it is not astonishing that thousands of people who are leading a needy and uncertain existence on the land, and are liable to starvation, whenever there is a failure in the potato crop – should avail themselves of this opportunity to better their fortune by crossing the Atlantic.'

'Departure of Irish Emigrants', The Illustrated London News, *21 July 1883*

Source C

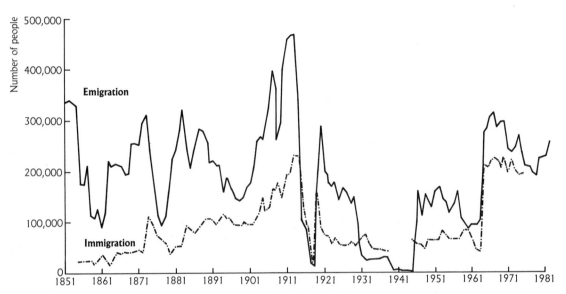

Emigration from, and immigration into, Britain between 1851 and 1982 (some of the fluctuations are due to a change in the methods of calculating the statistics)

Source D

'It cannot be doubted that a systematic plan of agricultural and industrial colonisation, with the removal to Canada, and other British dominions beyond seas, of boys and girls from our workhouses, after proper training, and with secure apprenticeship, might do very much to relieve the labour market in this country.'

'Immigrants in America', The Illustrated London News, *11 December 1886*

Source E

'Many have been led away by the highly coloured statements of emigration agents, and touts employed by companies who contrast this land of poverty and decay with the homes of freedom and plenty beyond the seas.

By such misrepresentation, thousands have been induced to leave comfortable quarters and good friends for dreary wastes or crowded cities. We know many individuals and families who have emigrated full of hope of improving their circumstances, and who have returned, after great expense and loss of time.'

Bibby's Quarterly *(a magazine for farmers), May 1899*

Source F

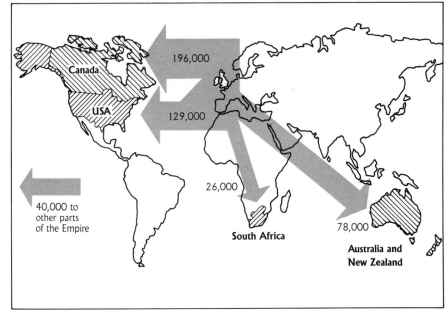

The destination of emigrants from Britain in 1913. This was the peak year for emigration with 469,000 people leaving the country.

Source G

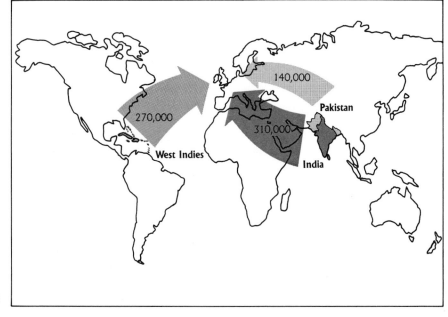

Main Commonwealth countries from which immigrants moved to Britain before 1971. (The totals given are cumulative to 1971 and **not** immigration figures for one year. Only people born overseas are included.)

1 What do these sources suggest as being some of the reasons why people emigrated in the nineteenth century? Why were some of these hopes unfulfilled? What inducements were offered to prospective emigrants? Support your answer with quotations from the extracts printed here.

2 *When were the peak periods for immigration and emigration (a) before, (b) after, the First World War?*

3 *To which countries did most of the emigrants from Britain go in the year immediately prior to the outbreak of the First World War?*

4 *In which years would you have expected Britain's population to rise or fall sharply as a result of emigration and immigration?*

5 *Extremists have complained about the extent of Commonwealth immigration into Britain in the 1950s and 1960s. Did Britain actually gain or lose population as a result of emigration and immigration during this period? From which countries did most of the immigrants come?*

6 *What social problems did the writer of Source D suggest could be overcome by emigration? What role did he have in mind for the dominions of the British Empire?*

7 *Write a short essay describing the graph and add comments to explain the fluctuations in these figures.*

As you can see from the graph on page 175, the scale of emigration from Britain has continued to fluctuate throughout the post-war years, although never reaching the scale of the years immediately preceding the First World War. In almost every year, there have been more emigrants than immigrants. But despite this, the Commonwealth Immigration Act, in 1962, effectively restricted new immigration to skilled workers and only permitted family members of immigrants already in Britain to join them.

FURTHER QUESTIONS AND EXERCISES

1 *Imagine you are an emigrant from Britain to America in the period 1901–14. Describe your feelings on the journey and explain why you have made this decision to start a new life in a country other than your own.*

2 *Explain, quoting actual examples, what is meant by each of the following terms:*

(a) the 'bulge'

(b) internal migration

(c) the birth rate

(d) curative medicine

(e) preventive medicine

(f) depopulation.

3 Look at these statistics showing numbers of children of school age (five to fourteen years) in England and Wales between 1881 and 1971.

Number of Children of School Age in England and Wales (in millions)

1881	1891	1901	1911	1921	1931	1951	1961	1971
5.9	6.6	6.8	7.2	7.2	6.5	6.0	7.0	7.7

(a) Draw a graph to show these statistics.

(b) How do you account for the steep rise in the number of children at school from 1881 to 1921, even though the birth rate had been dropping sharply ever since 1870?

(c) Why did the school-age population reach an all-time peak of 7.7 million in 1971?

4 What are the principal reasons why the expectation of life of an infant has increased dramatically in the twentieth century?

5 Write an essay explaining in detail why the population of England and Wales has grown in the twentieth century at a time when the birth rate has fallen.

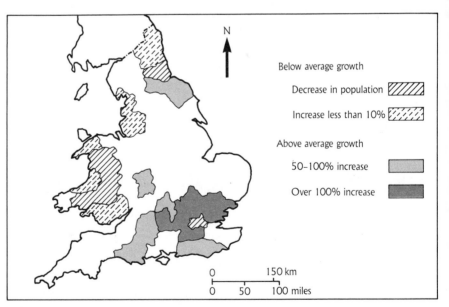

The growth of population in English and Welsh counties between 1931 and 1971

6 What does the map tell you about population trends in England and Wales in the period since 1931? Account for the fall in population in some areas and the rise in others.

Chapter Six

Urban Problems

INTRODUCTION

Providence Place, Stepney – a London court in 1909

Millions of working-class people in the nineteenth and early twentieth centuries lived in rows of small terraced houses or in courts like the one in the photograph – in badly built houses teeming with people, surrounding a narrow courtyard. Those built in the 1840s and 1850s often had only a standpipe to supply water and sometimes a communal earth lavatory to serve several families. In over-crowded, insanitary living conditions like this, it was hardly surprising that diseases such as typhus, tuberculosis, cholera and typhoid fever menaced the lives of the poor in the nineteenth century (as you saw in Chapter 5).

> 1 *What was a 'court'? Describe carefully the living conditions of the inhabitants of Providence Place in 1909.*
>
> 2 *Why are so many children to be seen in the photograph? Do the inhabitants of this court look happy or miserable?*

The speed with which towns grew in the nineteenth century posed enormous problems for the municipal authorities, especially since many councillors were reluctant to raise rates to improve living conditions. Early Victorian legislation, such as the 1848 Public Health Act, allowed them to make improvements but it did not usually force them to do so.

However, in the more progressive towns, such as Liverpool and Manchester, substantial improvements were made in the middle years of the nineteenth century, with the provision of amenities like street lighting, piped water supply, effective sewage and refuse disposal, public parks and public bathhouses. Later Victorian legislation, notably the 1875 Public Health Act, did force the municipal authorities to act, and even enabled them to build municipal housing and take over the running of public transport if they wished. Despite these advances, however, living conditions at the turn of the century were still bad.

As towns expanded in the twentieth century, with the coming of the motor vehicle and cheap public transport, the growth of the suburbs posed a new problem as towns threatened to turn the countryside into one continuous built-up area. Since 1945, much greater attention has been paid to town planning, the construction of adequate roads, the preservation of green spaces both within and outside the towns, and the elimination of pollution in all its different forms.

THE GROWTH OF VICTORIAN TOWNS

Growth in Population

The speed with which the Victorian industrial towns grew between 1851 and 1901 was astonishing. As you can see from the table on page 182, Middlesbrough shot from 8,000 to 91,000 in the space of fifty years and Cardiff from 18,000 to 164,000 in the same period.

But in the twentieth century, many of the older industries began to decline, and by 1951 several industrial towns were losing population (see page 182). In some cases this loss was to suburbs beyond the city boundaries (as in London between 1951 and 1985). In others the loss was permanent, as more and more young people left the district in search of employment elsewhere. By 1985, the distribution of large towns in Britain had changed very substantially from that of 1901, in just over eighty years.

1 *Look at the maps opposite showing the distribution of the major towns and cities in the British Isles in 1851, 1901 and 1985. How many towns were there in Britain with more than 100,000 inhabitants in 1851? By how many times had that number grown by 1901 and by 1985?*

2 On each of these maps, count the number of large towns situated (a) to the north, (b) to the south, of the line between the mouths of the Shannon (Ireland) and the Great Ouse (Norfolk). What do you notice?

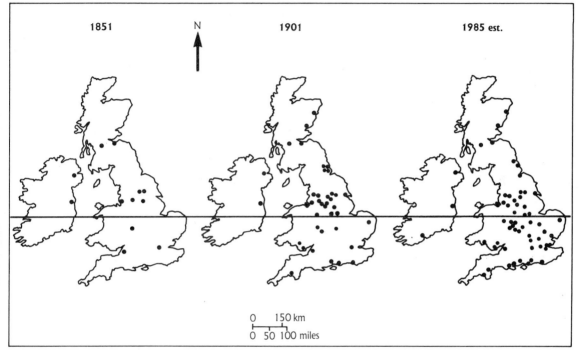

1851   N   1901   1985 est.

0   150 km
0   50 100 miles

Towns and cities with more than 100,000 inhabitants in 1851, 1901 and 1985

3 Use these maps to help you write a short essay describing and explaining the changing distribution and growth of large towns in the British Isles between 1851 and 1985.

4 Look at the table on the next page showing population statistics for a selection of towns in Great Britain. Find out briefly why these towns are or were important. By how many times (approximately) did the population of London grow between 1851 and 1901? Which of the other towns grew at a faster rate than this? Why? Which towns grew at a slower rate than London? Why?

5 How and why did the following pairs of towns grow at different rates between 1851 and 1985: (a) Middlesbrough and Peterborough, (b) Oldham and Bath, (c) Cardiff and King's Lynn?

6 *What do you notice about the growth of population in (a) Salford, (b) Bath, (c) Blackpool, (d) Coventry? Why did they grow in this way?*

7 *How many different patterns of population growth can you see in these statistics? Select one town from each group and draw graphs to illustrate your answer.*

Populations (in 1000s)

	1851	1901	1931	1951	1971	1985
Blackpool	3	47	123	147	151	148
Middlesbrough	8	91	138	147	155	150
Peterborough	9	31	44	53	70	138
Luton	11	36	90	110	161	164
Cardiff	18	164	224	244	278	274
King's Lynn	19	20	21	25	30	33
Coventry	36	70	167	258	335	317
Oldham	53	137	140	121	106	95
Bath	54	50	69	79	85	80
Leicester	61	212	239	285	284	282
Salford	85	221	223	178	131	98
Sheffield	135	409	512	513	520	477
Birmingham	233	523	1003	1113	1013	924
London	2685	6586	8216	8348	7452	6696

Growth of the Suburbs

London's suburbs were already growing in the early nineteenth century. In 1845, on each side of the New Road from Paddington to the City of London, there were:

> 'whole neighbourhoods, some of which were in their time detached villages and hamlets surrounded by fields. They are now thickly inhabited, and as the omnibuses pass along, a constant supply of passengers to and from the city is furnished by these neighbourhoods.'
>
> Chambers's Journal, *14 June 1845*

In 1867, Lord Shaftesbury warned that:

> 'the people of property and station are leaving the towns and are removing themselves from the working classes'.

In the 1840s and 1850s it was only the well-to-do who lived in the suburbs. But between 1871 and 1901, the population of London grew from an already massive 3,890,000 to a staggering 6,586,000 – an increase of 2,696,000 people in the space of only thirty years. The London of 1871 could not accommodate such a population, so the suburbs of London continued to grow outwards as new developments in public transport – the tram and the Underground – made it possible for more and more people to live at a distance from their places of work.

1   What evidence do these extracts provide about the growth of London's suburbs in the middle years of the nineteenth century? What did Lord Shaftesbury think they would do to the towns? Why was he worried? Were his fears justified?

2   What was London's percentage growth in population between 1871 and 1901? What problems do you think this posed for the local authorities in London?

3   Why did public transport (see page 203) play such an important part in the expansion of cities like London in the late nineteenth and early twentieth centuries?

LIVING CONDITIONS IN THE TOWNS

Pollution

This cartoon appeared in Punch *in June 1859. How has the cartoonist emphasised just how polluted the Thames was at that time?*

THE LONDON BATHING SEASON.
"COME, MY DEAR!—COME TO ITS OLD THAMES, AND HAVE A NICE BATH!"

Pollution was a serious problem in Victorian times. Busy streets were covered with horse droppings, despite the efforts of road sweepers to keep them clean. Horse manure attracted germ-carrying flies in summer, and this is believed to have been a possible reason why infantile diarrhoea (which yearly killed many babies) reached a peak in the hot summer months. In the 1850s, open sewers were common in many towns and even underground sewers emptied raw untreated sewage into rivers which were used as a source of water supply. The Thames was notorious in this respect. In 1852, *Punch* described the 'Pride of London'.

'Know ye the stream where the cesspool and sewer
Are emptied of all their foul slushes and slimes
Where the gas-works rain down the blackest of soot
Where the air's filled with smells that no nose can define,
And the banks teem prolific with corpses canine.'

There were complaints, too, about fog. In combination with the smoke from millions of chimneys, it created 'smog' – a near-lethal atmosphere which aggravated diseases of the lungs and left hundreds of thousands of people suffering from chronic bronchitis. When it killed several thousand people in the early 1950s something was done at last, and the Clean Air Act of 1956 helped to rid the industrial cities of this recurrent problem.

> 1 *What was the 'Pride of London'? How was it polluted? What evidence shows the extent and nature of this pollution?*
>
> 2 *See if you can find older friends or relatives who can tell you about the smogs of the 1950s. What other types of pollution can they remember from their childhood? Compile an oral history of urban problems since 1945.*

Traffic Congestion

Traffic congestion was also becoming a problem in busy towns like London. City-centre streets could not cope with rush-hour traffic. Victorian photographs of London Bridge and the streets outside the Bank of England show them crowded with cabs, carts, horse buses and pedestrians.

Traffic often came to a standstill and the time needed to travel across central London increased with each year. Not surprisingly there were frequent accidents.

Horse buses in central London in about 1890

Overcrowding – the Slums

Before the introduction of the horse-drawn tram in the 1860s and 1870s, and of workmen's trains in the 1870s, there was no cheap public transport in the towns. As a result, the vast majority of workers had to live within walking distance of the mills, factories and offices where they worked. Only the well-to-do middle class could afford to live in the suburbs and pay the relatively high cost of daily transport to and from work.

The labouring classes had to cram into the inner city. As a result, overcrowding became a major problem and helped to spread diseases like tuberculosis and scarlet fever. This was how a magazine article described the courts in a London slum in 1863.

> 'As foul a neighbourhood as can be discovered in the civilised world. The entrance to most of them is by a covered alley not wider than an ordinary doorway. At the end of this blind court there will be found a number of black and crumbling hovels forming three sides of a miserable little square.
>
> The miserable rooms are teeming with inhabitants. The water for some fourteen or fifteen houses is frequently supplied from one tap in a dirty corner, where it runs for only a short time every day; and the places are mostly undrained. Add to this the decay of vegetable matter, the occasional evidence of the presence of pigs and the result will represent a score of places in Bethnal-green.'
>
> The Illustrated London News, *24 October 1863*

Living conditions like this could be found in most of the great cities of Britain in the middle years of the nineteenth century – in Liverpool, Glasgow, Manchester and Birmingham as well as in London. Gradually, living conditions improved during the late nineteenth and early twentieth centuries, partly due to the efforts of local people, and partly due to government legislation, which increasingly began to tackle the problems of working-class housing and public health reform.

Yet, despite these improvements, the fundamental problem would not go away. This problem was poverty. Roughly one-third of the population lived at or below the poverty line – even in York, where Seebohm Rowntree's pioneering survey, in 1901, revealed that 28 per cent of the population could be classed as extremely poor.

In the 1880s, the middle classes became increasingly aware of the great social evil in their midst. A pamphlet called *The Bitter Cry of Outcast London* aroused the sympathies of thousands of well-to-do people, when it was published in 1883. The Salvation Army, founded by William Booth in 1878, and the work of early socialists like H. M. Hyndman, did much to publicise the plight of the poor. Charles Booth (no relation of William Booth) dismissed this as propaganda – until he started his own investigation in 1889. When his monumental survey, *Life and Labour of the People in London*, was published in 1902–3, it showed in graphic and exhaustive detail just how poor and squalid were the typical living conditions of the London poor, despite the fact that they lived in the greatest city in the world.

Booth made many constructive suggestions. He drew attention to the defects in existing housing – much of it cramped, neglected, badly built, insanitary, over-crowded, damp, stifling in summer, 'uncleanly' and overpriced. He said that crowded homes sent men to the public house and put poor children into the streets to live, play and even eat. Many of the houses were courts, like those in the photographs on pages 179 and 198. In some streets, homes were built back-to-back in terraces to economise on building walls, making it impossible to fit windows into rooms other than those at the front. Many homes had only two rooms, 'one up and the other down', and sometimes a washhouse. Outside in the courtyard hung the clotheslines, 'while the end of it is occupied by the closets and the dustbin'. Of Shelton Street (near Covent Garden), Booth said that:

> 'few of the 200 families who lived there occupied more than one room. In little rooms, no more than eight ft. square, would be found living father, mother and several children. Fifteen rooms out of twenty were filthy to the last degree. Not a room would be free from vermin. The little yard at the back was only sufficient for dustbin and closet and water-tap, serving for six or seven families. The water would be drawn from cisterns which were receptacles for refuse, and perhaps occasionally a dead cat.'

> *Charles Booth*

1 *Do you have a close relative (such as a great-grandmother) who was a child at the time when Charles Booth's final report was published in 1903?*

2 *Compare Bethnal Green in the 1860s (see page 185) with Shelton Street in the 1890s. Had living conditions improved in the thirty years separating the two reports?*

3 *What were the main conclusions to be drawn from Charles Booth's survey?*

4 *The cartoon and verse below were published at the time of the Jack the Ripper murders in London's East End. To what cause did the* Punch *cartoonist and poet attribute the growth of crime in the late nineteenth century? How relevant is this picture to the urban problems of the late twentieth century – a hundred years later?*

5 *Imagine you are a member of a well-to-do family in 1888. You have read about the work of the Salvation Army and know something of the problems of London's East End. Why would you be worried about poor living conditions in London at that time? Write a letter to your local MP, drawing his attention to the problems which worry you and ask him to take appropriate action.*

THE NEMESIS OF NEGLECT.

"THERE FLOATS A PHANTOM ON THE SLUM'S FOUL AIR, SHAPING, TO EYES WHICH HAVE THE GIFT OF SEEING, INTO THE SPECTRE OF THAT LOATHLY LAIR. FACE IT—FOR VAIN IS FLEEING! RED-HANDED, RUTHLESS, FURTIVE, UNERECT, 'TIS MURDEROUS CRIME—THE NEMESIS OF NEGLECT!"

Punch, *29 September 1888*

Slums in the Twentieth Century

Although living conditions have continued to improve throughout the twentieth century, the verdict of foreign observers has not always been encouraging. The Czech writer, Karel Capek, wrote in 1925 about London's East End, with its endless miles of dirty houses, noisy streets, 'poverty-stricken and down-trodden people' and 'storehouses for goods and storehouses for human beings'.

Even as late as 1951, the official census statistics showed that fewer than two homes in every five in the Rhondda, Merthyr Tydfil, Oldham and Rochdale had exclusive use of the five basic conveniences – piped water, flush lavatory, bath, kitchen sink and cooking stove – compared with over 97 homes in every 100 in relatively affluent London suburbs, like Coulsdon and Epsom.

PUBLIC HEALTH

The Spread of Disease

'Defective drainage, neglect of house and street cleansing, ventilation, and imperfect supplies of water, contribute to produce atmospheric impurities which affect the general health and physical condition of the population, generating acute, chronic and ultimately organic disease.'

Report of the Health of Towns Commission, *1845*

In 1845, the medical profession knew little about the causes of diseases or the reasons why they spread. The work of Pasteur and Koch on microbes and germs was still to come. Some doctors still believed the old theory that fevers were spread by 'miasmas'. These were the noxious vapours, gases, odours and stenches arising from decomposing organic matter.

> **1** *What was the most obvious 'miasma' to greet any visitor to a Victorian slum?*
>
> **2** *Why do you think doctors and public health officials rightly blamed overcrowding, bad drains and impure water as the main causes of these diseases, even though they had no knowledge of germs?*

The Public Health Act of 1848

The 1848 Public Health Act established a General Board of Health, to supervise the setting up of about 200 local Boards of Health with powers to require (if they wished) that all newly built houses in their areas should have proper drains and lavatories. They could require that other houses be linked to a main sewer. They could also enforce adequate standards of water supply, cleanse the streets, organise refuse collections and pay for these improvements with the aid of a local rate.

The trouble with the Act was that it was too weak and permitted, rather than compelled, towns to act – in the spirit of *laissez-faire*. The result was that some Boards of Health took little action to remedy the many serious problems with which they were faced at that time, and objected to government interference in local affairs. In 1850, *Punch* savagely attacked the:

> 'Boards of Health who pooh-pooh, And laugh to scorn doctors and drainers – Who self-government call, Not to govern at all – Of the great cause of dirt stout maintainers. Who, when orders come down, For cleansing the town, Wish to know by what right they're dictated to.'

1 *What were* Punch*'s criticisms of the Boards of Health?*

2 *What did* Punch *say was the Board's attitude to local government?*

3 *How did* Punch *attack the municipal authorities running London, in this cartoon published nearly thirty years later? See if you can find out why the name 'Bumble' was used then as a general term of abuse for a minor town official.*

THE COURT OF KING BUMBLE.

Water Supply

Although the early Victorian town reformers had no scientific evidence to confirm the link between bad drains, impure water and the spread of disease, there was no excuse for the later Victorians. The work of Pasteur and later of Koch (see Chapter 10) showed that diseases, like cholera and typhoid fever, could be carried by contaminated water. So long as London's main source of water, the Thames, was polluted by sewage, the problem of disease would remain. The earlier emphasis on cleanliness and effective sewers had not been misplaced.

In the early nineteenth century, towns had drawn their water supply from inefficient wells or through pipes installed by a water company. For many householders, this meant a tap outside the house, shared with several other families. It did not mean the luxury of piped water into the house. In many cases this water supply was contaminated. Worst were the wells polluted by seepage from a nearby cesspit. Even where lavatories drained into proper sewers in London, the raw sewage eventually emptied into the Thames – the source of the water supplied by the water companies. It was little wonder that visitors complained of the stench from the Thames.

This cartoon appeared in Punch *in 1849. What did* Punch *think about the quality of London's water in 1849?*

"WATER! WATER! EVERYWHERE; AND NOT A DROP TO DRINK."

Coleridge.

Purification of the Thames was essential, but it was not the responsibility of the private water companies that supplied London with its water. In fact, they were constantly expanding and improving their works to meet the needs of a rapidly growing population. But although improvements were continually being made, the technology of water purification was still in its infancy. Only in the late nineteenth century, when Pasteur and Koch showed the presence of bacteria in water, were scientists able to monitor the purity of water supplies accurately.

'Investigations in bacteriology have shown the necessity of excluding the lively, but to the naked eye, invisible microbe. This is attained by the use of a finer sand, though it has the drawback of holding up the water longer and necessitating the construction of larger areas of filter beds per million gallons of supply. The public, however, are adequately protected.'

Frederick T. Souden, The Windsor Magazine, *1898*

Some local authorities pioneered the building of huge reservoirs in the hills and the construction of pipelines to take water to their cities. Liverpool's municipal authorities created Lake Vyrnwy in North Wales in the 1880s, whilst Manchester took water from an enlarged Thirlmere in the Lake District, following the earlier lead of Glasgow, which used Loch Katrine in the Scottish Highlands as a reservoir.

Mains Drainage

In 1855, the Metropolitan Board of Works was given responsibility for sewage disposal in London, and under the direction of Joseph Bazalgette, its Engineer-in-Chief, the Board started work on the construction of a massive mains drainage scheme. The aim of this building work was to intercept London's sewage in its progress towards the Thames and to divert it, by covered channels, to points 22 km below London Bridge. There the sewage could be emptied into the river at the start of the ebb tide, causing it to be diluted and eventually swept out to sea.

This London Mains Drainage scheme involved the construction of about 80 km of brick-lined sewer underground, together with the pumping works necessary to carry it over rivers, canals, railways and roads. These pumping stations lifted 'whole rivers of liquid sewage from a lower to a higher level'. The Thames Embankment was also built at the same time to narrow the river and make it flow faster, thus scouring the channel.

By 1900, powerful processing plants had been installed near the outfall stations on the Thames. Here the raw sewage was treated with chemicals to separate the sludge from the clear, odourless effluent which was discharged into the Thames. The sludge left over was taken by boat and dumped at sea.

MUNICIPAL GOVERNMENT

The Growth of Local Government

Local government in the nineteenth century was chaotic, since a large number of different boards and committees had responsibility for the various services. Before 1888, it was said that the administration of local government in London was in the hands of no less than 427 different bodies, all elected in different ways, many not directly representing the people and none controlled by any central authority. In 1850, as many as 250 local acts were in force in the city.

The reorganisation of local government was an essential first step if improvements were to be made. But before 1875, most laws allowed, but did not force, municipal authorities to take action. Many Victorians believed in *laissez-faire*. Self-help was the key to success. Some people even thought that epidemic disease, hunger, the workhouse and dependence on charity were the penalties for idleness. Many local authorities responsible for sewers, water supply and highways took action only if they thought it absolutely necessary. In a few towns, however, progressive authorities did take effective action. For instance, in 1864, the Liverpool municipality was given the power to demolish over 20,000 slums through the Liverpool Sanitary Amendment Act.

In 1869, the Royal Sanitary Commission reported to the Government that the existing laws were ineffective and that major epidemics (such as the cholera epidemic which killed 18,000 people in Britain in 1865) would continue to threaten the growth of towns if there was no effective system of local government to deal with such emergencies. This is why the Local Government Board was established, in 1871, to ensure that local authorities carried out those Acts of Parliament which required them to take action.

The Public Health Act of 1875

The 1875 Public Health Act gave further teeth to these developments, by welding all the existing laws on public health into one major new law. Its main provisions were as follows.

● All local authorities had to appoint a Medical Officer of Health. In the past they had the option to do so, if they wished, and Liverpool appointed its first Medical Officer as early as 1847.

● The local authorities were made responsible for the organisation of refuse collection, mains sewers and drains, water supply and public health.

● They had to ensure that all new homes had a piped water supply and adequate sanitation – with good drains and lavatories (not necessarily flush toilets).

In the same year, the Artisans' Dwellings Act gave local authorities the power to pull down slums and to erect houses in their place.

> **1** *Why were these Acts of Parliament necessary? Why not leave the local authorities to act as they thought best?*
>
> **2** *Is there still a conflict in local government between those who try to do too little and those who try to do too much?*

Municipal Socialism

In Birmingham, substantial improvements were made under the strong leadership of Joseph Chamberlain, mayor of the city from 1873 to 1876 (see page 143). Slums were pulled down and working-class homes erected in their place. The local authority also took over the city's gas and water supplies and bought the sewage farm.

Several other local authorities took control of local services, like gas and water, which were normally sold to the public by private companies. This trend was called 'municipal socialism', since the local authorities were putting the provision of essential services (such as gas and water supply) into public ownership. Some cities, like Leeds, even took over the running of the trams and later the buses. It was a far cry from the early days of *laissez-faire*.

In 1888, the County Councils Act established the county councils and gave large towns (those with more than 50,000 inhabitants) a similar status as county borough councils. The London County Council (LCC), which was founded at this time became the largest and best-known local authority in Britain. *Punch* welcomed the LCC with this cartoon.

Punch, January 1889

NEW LONDON.

> **1** *Who is shown on the left in the cartoon on page 193? Who is shown on the right?*
>
> **2** *What hopes did the cartoonist hold out for the 'New London'? Why was he so optimistic? Write a paragraph explaining the thinking behind this cartoon.*

The new county borough councils were given the responsibility for the maintenance and building of roads and bridges within the borough boundaries. In 1902, they were also given power, as local education authorities, to take over elementary and secondary education (see Chapter 9). Understandably, many municipal authorities in the industrial towns took pride in their achievements and the rapid growth and success of the town's industries. This was symbolised in the many solid and impressive public buildings which were erected at this time – in magnificent town halls, new reservoirs, comprehensive mains drainage schemes, electric street lighting, public bathhouses, parks and open spaces.

> **1** *Find out how the local authority in your home district used its powers in the late nineteenth century. Did it build a town hall? Did it construct a public park?*

Local Government in the Twentieth Century

Since the Education Act of 1902, local authorities have acquired many other powers. But, the division into counties and county boroughs (outside the London area) lasted until 1972, when the Local Government Act (brought in by the Heath Conservative Government) redrew county boundaries and abolished county boroughs.

In their place, 39 non-metropolitan counties were created in England (divided into 296 districts), whilst six new metropolitan counties (Tyne and Wear, Greater Manchester, Merseyside, West Yorkshire, South Yorkshire and West Midlands) were set up to administer the six major conurbations (continuous urban areas) outside London. This was recognition that conurbations were convenient units for the administration of local government in heavily built-up areas. These metropolitan counties were further sub-divided into 36 metropolitan district councils, which were given separate powers, such as the control and administration of education.

Earlier legislation, initiated by the Macmillan Conservative Government in 1963, replaced the old London County Council in 1965 with the GLC (Greater London Council). The GLC shared power with 32 new London boroughs and with ILEA, the Inner London Education Authority. The GLC took over a much wider area than that covered by the LCC. It embraced the whole of the Greater London conurbation (including the whole of Middlesex and substantial parts of Surrey, Kent, Essex and Hampshire).

Ironically, another Conservative Government, in 1986, dismantled the metropolitan counties and the GLC because they were thought wasteful of public resources and an unnecessary extra layer of local government.

HOUSING AND TOWN PLANNING

It is still possible to see much of the urban housing built in the nineteenth century, although it is nowadays considerably improved and almost always equipped with the basic amenities of piped water supply, flush lavatory, bath and kitchen.

Victorian terraced houses in Leeds

Philanthropic Housing Schemes

At first the only substantial attempts to improve working-class housing were made by wealthy philanthropists, such as George Peabody, and industrialists, like Sir Titus Salt.

'The grand gift of a quarter of a million pounds bestowed on the poor of London by a generous American merchant is applied by the trustees to the building of healthy and comfortable dwellings for working-class families, let at a cheaper rate than the wretched apartments for which exorbitant rents are too often paid in the crowded parts of this city. Peabody-square, Islington, consists of four blocks of buildings, five stories in height, comprising 240 separate tenements of one, two, or three rooms, with baths and laundries, ample supplies of water and gaslight, shafts for the removal of refuse, and perfect drainage and ventilation, at rents of 2s 6d [13p], 4s [20p] or 5s [25p] a week.'

The Illustrated London News, *10 March 1866*

> **1** Who provided the money to build Peabody Square?
>
> **2** Why was it not built by the local authority?
>
> **3** How did the poor of London benefit from Peabody Square?

Other benefactors included Sir Edward Guinness whose Trust (1889) erected about 2,500 dwellings in London and Dublin, and Sir Sidney H. Waterlow, whose 'Improvement Industrial Dwellings Company' also helped to build thousands of homes in London. Octavia Hill was another worker in this field. She made her name buying up slum properties and then improving them, at first with the financial help and encouragement of the art critic, John Ruskin. Her aim was to put the running of the homes on a proper business footing, to enable money from rents to pay for further improvements. She explained her methods in 1899: (a) 'repairs promptly and efficiently attended to', (b) 'cleaning supervised', (c) 'overcrowding put an end to', (d) careful selection of tenants, particularly with a view to their co-operating with one another rather than fighting.

Model Towns

Some factory owners built model housing estates. Sir Titus Salt built a model village at Saltaire, where the 700 houses were:

> 'replete with every convenience conducive to the health, comfort and well-being of the inhabitants. On no account are they to suffer the air to be polluted by smoke, or the water to be injured or deteriorated by any impurity. Healthy dwellings and gardens, in wide streets and capacious squares – ample ground for recreation – a large dining-hall and kitchens – baths and washhouses – a covered market – schools – mechanics institution – a church: these are some of the characteristics of the future town of Saltaire.'
>
> The Illustrated London News, *1 October 1853*

Saltaire (woollen textiles) was followed by W. H. Lever's Port Sunlight (soap) in 1885 and George Cadbury's model housing estate at Bournville (chocolate) in 1895. In 1908, *The Sphere* described the new Brodsworth Hall estate near Doncaster, which had been built by a colliery company for its miners.

> 'The pit works are hidden from the village in a hollow at the furthest limit of the wood. Sixteen acres of the park have been converted into a village green. The remainder of the village is designed on similar lines to Bournville and Garden City. Trees have been left standing wherever possible, gardens and lawns abound, and the houses harmonise perfectly with their surroundings.'
>
> The Sphere, *24 October 1908*

Garden Cities

The garden-city movement was led by Ebenezer Howard and had an important influence on twentieth century housing. In 1898, Howard wrote a book called *Tomorrow*, in which he advocated towns surrounded by green belts and suburbs resembling country villages, with an emphasis on trees, lawns, gardens, villas and semi-detached villas, rather than monotonous brick terraces. His ideal city found fulfilment in the planning of Letchworth Garden City in 1903, Hampstead Garden Suburb in 1909 and Welwyn Garden City in 1920. But although there was no further development of new towns on garden-city lines, Ebenezer Howard's influence and that of the garden-city ideal can be seen in countless housing estates all over Britain.

---

1 Which parts of your nearest town most closely resemble the garden city?

2 Why were the tenants of Peabody Square charged relatively low rents for their homes in 1866? What type of modern building did Peabody Square anticipate?

3 Why did some of the great Victorian industrialists build model towns and housing estates for their workers?

Building Societies

Another important force for improvement in the nineteenth and early twentieth centuries was the growth of the building societies.

> 'The working man's building societies, which exist over the length and breadth of the land, have been of immense service in helping him to help himself.'
>
> Chambers's Journal, *September 1896*

By 1906, they had helped to finance the construction of nearly 50,000 homes in Lancashire and Cheshire alone. The dates of foundation of the building societies which are biggest today, show clearly when the movement first got under way – Woolwich (1847), Leeds Permanent (1848), Abbey National (1849) and Halifax (1853).

Municipal Housing

As you have already seen, Liverpool (after 1864) and Birmingham (1873–6) had begun to pull down slums and to erect working class housing in their place. The Artisans' Dwellings Act of 1875, gave all local authorities the power to pull down slums and erect houses in their place. But progress was very slow.

In 1884–5, the *Report of the Royal Commission on Housing* made dismal reading for those who thought that the problem of slum housing was being solved. In some ways it was getting worse and the Commission (which had the Prince of Wales as one of its members) provided fresh evidence of the appalling character of the slums, with poor families living in rotting and decaying houses and sharing a lavatory with several other families.

In 1890, the Housing of the Working Classes Act allowed town councils to force the erection of new houses in place of insanitary buildings. But progress was still far too slow, even though a progressive authority like the LCC could point to 11,000 new homes built between 1888 and 1900 and the fact that it was building or planning another 20,000. Unfortunately, during the same period, the population of London grew by over a million people.

Improvement was very slow and at the start of the First World War it was estimated that as many as 600,000 new houses were needed in Britain just to accommodate those people who were in desperate need of adequate housing. During the war years, when building work virtually stopped, the Government passed the Rent Restriction Act, in 1915, to prevent landlords raising rents to exorbitant levels. The continuing shortage of homes after the war led to the extension of this Act to peacetime conditions in 1920, and rent restriction became a feature of government housing policy until 1979. By the end of the war, the housing shortage had become acute, and a newspaper article made the forecast in 1919, that it 'will be necessary to erect 158,000 houses yearly until 1924'.

Court in Nottingham in 1931

> 1 What was the estimated housing shortage at the end of the First World War?
>
> 2 Compare this photograph with the one on page 179 at the start of the chapter, showing a London court in 1909. In what ways are the two pictures similar? How do they differ? Did the people living in this Nottingham court have indoor bathrooms in 1931?

The Addison Act of 1919

In 1919, the Lloyd George Coalition Government took steps to remedy the situation. Dr Christopher Addison, Minister of Health, brought in an act which not only gave those local authorities with more than 20,000 inhabitants the power to build municipal housing, but also positively *required* them to do so and gave them an incentive. This incentive was in the form of a government subsidy, to enable them to build the new houses which were badly needed at that time.

The new policy on housing was one of subsidising the cost of building good quality municipal housing, so that it could be rented cheaply to the less affluent members of society. It was recognised that without these subsidies, people on the poverty line would be unable to rent anything other than the worst type of slum dwelling. By now, it was accepted that new homes should be equipped with piped water, flush lavatory, kitchen and bath as a matter of course. If the cities were ever to get rid of their slums they would either have to build subsidised municipal housing or wait for the poor to get richer.

Over 200,000 homes were built under the provisions of the Addison Act and it was regarded as a success until abandoned at a time of public expenditure cuts in 1922.

The Chamberlain Act of 1923

In the following year, 1923, the Minister of Health in the new Conservative Government, Neville Chamberlain (a future Prime Minister and son of Joseph Chamberlain), brought in a new Act of Parliament, which provided a different type of subsidy and led to the building of over 400,000 homes, most of them by private builders.

The Wheatley Act of 1924

The Wheatley Act – the Housing (Financial Provisions) Act, 1924 – had as its objective the building of 2.5 million houses in the space of fifteen years, to be let at rents which the average worker could easily afford to pay. The act, which was introduced by the Labour Government, substantially increased the amount of government subsidy paid on each house – but only for local-authority housing. Nonetheless, half a million council houses were built as a result of this Act.

Slum Clearance

Slum clearance received a big boost when the new Minister of Health in the 1929 Labour Government, Arthur Greenwood, introduced his Housing Act in 1930. This forced local authorities to take steps to eradicate the slums. As a result, about 250,000 slum dwellings were destroyed before the outbreak of the Second World War. This was welcomed as a long-overdue development. 'The problem of the slums, with their terrible overcrowded and sunless homes is one of the greatest facing the country today,' wrote an author in 1935, welcoming 'this badly needed reform'.

Private and Public Housing Schemes

Another important factor in the improvement of housing between the wars was the continued growth of the building societies. They helped thousands of people to buy their own homes. Interest rates were low and houses were still relatively cheap.

By 1939, the housing programmes of the 1920s and 1930s had been so success-ful, that despite the Depression and the continued growth of population, Britain had a housing surplus even though thousands of homes were still classified as slum properties.

Many of the new housing estates were built on land next to the main roads leading out of the towns, since cheap public transport made it possible for most workers to live in the suburbs rather than near their work. Privately built houses extended on either side of the motor roads into the countryside – a process known as ribbon development. Similarly, estates grew up close to London Underground stations and near the suburban railway stations of London and other large cities. Long lines of suburbs extended into the countryside, radiating like a star from the city centre.

As well as houses, new blocks of flats were also built. In Leeds the Council built the impressive Quarry Hill flats in 1935 – a large curving block of dwellings, with multi-storey buildings on a site close to the city centre.

The success of these various housing schemes can be seen in the statistics displayed in the graph on page 201. Although many of the inter-war housing estates were ridiculed – particularly the detached and semi-detached houses with their pebble-dash walls, stained-glass windows, postage-stamp gardens and neat privet hedges – fifty years later they were still regarded as highly desirable residences, since the quality of the materials used was often of a very high standard indeed.

However, the main drawback to the new council houses, was that, despite subsidies, the controlled rents were often too high for the poorest tenants, whilst their remote position often made them inconvenient for ordinary working people, who had to rely on public transport to get them to work.

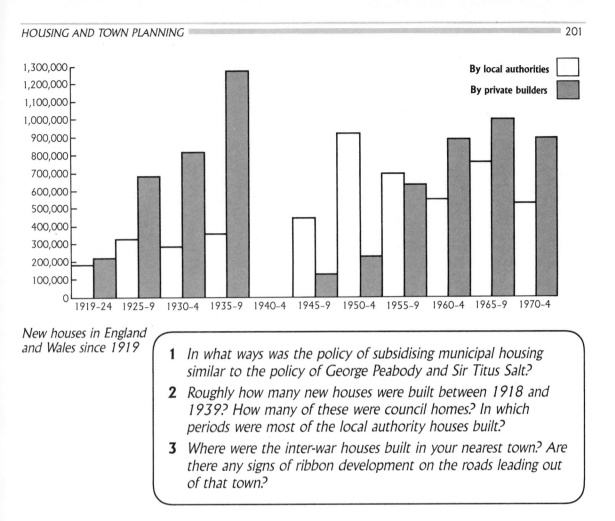

New houses in England and Wales since 1919

> 1 In what ways was the policy of subsidising municipal housing similar to the policy of George Peabody and Sir Titus Salt?
>
> 2 Roughly how many new houses were built between 1918 and 1939? How many of these were council homes? In which periods were most of the local authority houses built?
>
> 3 Where were the inter-war houses built in your nearest town? Are there any signs of ribbon development on the roads leading out of that town?

Post-war Housing

Recovery from the effects of bomb damage during the Second World War and a determination to eliminate the slums were two of the powerful motives which inspired a fresh housing programme after 1945. Aneurin Bevan was the Minister of Health at that time and began by erecting prefabricated houses (known as 'prefabs') to provide temporary accommodation for the homeless. These prefabs proved substantially stronger than anticipated, and some were still in use forty years later. In the immediate post-war years, however, shortage of building materials and resources curtailed the building programme. As you can see from the graph above, house building did not really begin to grow rapidly again until the affluent years of the 1950s and 1960s, when a major house-building programme began in earnest. Between 1955 and 1968 about 800,000 homes were pulled down and about two million people were resettled in tower blocks of flats and council houses. In some towns, a very high proportion of new homes were built by municipal authorities. A controversial innovation came in 1980, when the Thatcher Conservative Government brought in an act which gave council tenants the right to buy their own homes.

Town Planning

In the twentieth century, town planning gradually came to dominate the way in which towns were allowed to expand. It was recognised, at last, that haphazard, uncontrolled city growth created far too many problems to be either sensible or acceptable.

One of the major landmarks in this new approach was the Town and Country Planning Act of 1947. This introduced measures controlling the use to which the land could be put. In particular it developed the idea of the green belt – surrounding a town with an area of fields, farms and woods, in which planning permission would not be given for the construction of new housing or factories. In this way there would be limits to urban growth and the countryside would be protected.

Since provision had still to be made for the expansion of the population, the post-war Labour Government decided to build New Towns – usually around the core of an old village or small town. These New Towns were designed to accommodate people from the great cities (such as London, Manchester and Glasgow) who were displaced when the slums were cleared.

In 1946, the New Towns Act established Development Corporations to plan the construction of twelve New Towns in different parts of Britain. The Act was highly successful and further new towns were planned. By 1963, there were eighteen New Towns in Britain, at various stages of completion, such as those around London – Basildon, Bracknell, Crawley, Harlow, Hatfield, Hemel Hempstead, Stevenage and Welwyn Garden City. Other New Towns included Peterlee in County Durham, Cwmbran in Wales, Skelmersdale in Lancashire and Cumbernauld, Glenrothes, Livingston and East Kilbride near Glasgow.

New designs of houses, new ways of coping with the motor car and new types of city centre in these New Towns helped to stimulate similar developments in other towns.

City-centre Redevelopment

Many town centres were redesigned and redeveloped, with varying degrees of success, in the 1960s and 1970s, with new pedestrian precincts and indoor shopping centres. These schemes were generally profitable since they were essentially commercial developments in the most desirable part of town – the centre.

Even more controversial was the question of what to do with the inner city – the ring of decaying buildings, much of it Victorian, immediately surrounding the city centre. This presented a special problem, since some way of revitalising this area and making it prosperous once again (called 'urban renewal') was badly needed. Unfortunately, it was doubtful whether redevelopment, on the required scale, would ever pay its way. In the meantime, the houses rotted and decayed for want of maintenance, and inner-city crime rates soared (see also question 4 on page 187).

PUBLIC TRANSPORT

The Bus and the Tram

As you have seen, overcrowding in Victorian cities was partly due to the lack of cheap, effective public transport. Horse-drawn cabs and private carriages were strictly for the well-to-do, whilst horse buses were too expensive for the ordinary worker. In 1850, a bus or rail journey of 5 km cost about 1.25p – as much as most ordinary workers could earn in an hour.

The first significant step towards cheap public transport, came with the introduction of horse-drawn trams in 1860.

> 'The first street railway in England was opened on the 30th [August] in Birkenhead, with a success which scarcely leaves room for any doubt that the system will ere long be extended to all the great towns in the three kingdoms.'
>
> The Illustrated Times, *15 September 1860*

By 1890, London had about a thousand of these horse trams (forerunners of the electric tram). They carried 190 million passengers and covered 34 million km every year.

The first electric tram taking power from an overhead cable was introduced in Blackpool in 1889. The speed with which it replaced the horse tram can be seen in Leeds. There the first horse trams had been introduced into service in 1871 and were followed by steam trams in 1877 and electric trams in 1891. Leeds Corporation took over the running of the trams in 1894, withdrew all the horse trams from service in 1901, and closed down the steam trams in 1902. The electric trams continued in service until 1959.

Electric tramway at Northfleet in Greater London, The Illustrated London News, *6 April 1889. What type of tram was this? How do you think it picked up electric power?*

The London Underground

London pioneered a new and ingenious form of public transport, when the first stretch of track on the London Underground was opened by the Metropolitan Railway Company in September 1862. It was not yet a tube railway system, since it had been built as a shallow subway, sometimes open and sometimes covered, below the level of the street. But by 1884, the whole of the Inner Circle around Central London had been completed. The problems with steam and smoke which bedevilled the early underground railways, were dispelled in 1890, when the first electric underground locomotives were introduced, a vital and necessary advance, as you can see from these sources.

Source A

'Moorgate Street Station. As you enter the cheerless station in the early morning, a dark-red light appears like an eye in the cylinder of gloom which drives right into the bowels of London; and in a couple of seconds a workmen's train dashes forth from the blackness of the tunnel. Immediately a motley crowd of men and boys pour out of the uncomfortable carriages, and slouch along the draughty platform.'

P. F. W. Ryan, Living London, *1906*

Source B

'A heavy sulphurous smell, an atmosphere like a yellow fog in London, an orderly succession of earsplitting bangs, and the wave of a green flag. Man will give up much to save his precious time; he will consent to be half suffocated for ten minutes, and temporarily deafened for the sake of half an hour. Yet the most ardent admirer of the present railways cannot say it is joy to travel on them.'

G. E. Mitton, The Windsor Magazine, *1897*

Source C

Train journey on the Metropolitan Underground Railway, The Illustrated London News, *1862*

Source D

'THE CITY AND SOUTH LONDON RAILWAY

On Tuesday, Nov. 4, His Royal Highness the Prince of Wales formally opened the new underground electric railway, from the Monument, passing under the Thames, to Stockwell. This new railway provides South Londoners with an expeditious and economical means of reaching the City.'

The Illustrated London News, *8 November 1890*

---

1 *Why were fumes and smoke a problem in the early days of the London Underground? How did the railway companies try to get rid of them in the tunnels?*

2 *Why was electricity used to power the underground railway from the Monument to Stockwell, south of the Thames, in 1890?*

3 *What were the drawbacks to travelling on the London Underground in the nineteenth century?*

4 *Who used the London Underground? What effect was it likely to have on the growth of London?*

The electric underground railway was so successful it was followed by others, such as the Central London Railway, opened in 1900 from the Bank of England to Shepherd's Bush.

The Underground railway companies helped to colonise the suburbs. The Metropolitan Railway invited Londoners to 'Come live in Metro-land', as they extended their line into the countryside of Middlesex and Buckinghamshire to the north-west of the City. The Underground station at Golders Green in north London (featured in the poster) was opened in 1907. By 1914, over 14,000 people were living in the 4,000 new houses built at Golders Green after the station opened.

London Underground poster in 1912. What was the appeal of Golders Green to the early twentieth-century commuter?

In 1904, the first regular motor-bus service came into operation in London, in competition with horse buses and electric trams. In 1911, the London General Omnibus Company ran its last horse-bus service, and by 1914 the motor bus (see Chapter 3), had almost completely superseded the horse bus in the major cities.

Transport in Towns after 1914

The rise of the motor bus and the motor cab only made London's traffic problems worse. In 1915 a total of 35,342 vehicles passed a census point at Hyde Park Corner in the space of twelve hours, and another 34,561 did so at Trafalgar Square. A comparable figure at the biggest traffic bottleneck in mid-Victorian London was 13,090 vehicles in twelve hours on London Bridge in 1852.

'Horse v. Motor Obstruction: A panoramic view of the pandemonium at Ludgate Hill, the slow horse traffic impeding the swift motor', The Graphic, *26 May 1923*

'The problem of the London streets becomes more acute every year, partly on account of the increase of the population, and even more by the advent of motor traffic. Obstacles to be overcome are partly in the shape of bottle-necked frontages, as in the Strand and partly in the conflict between slow-moving horse-drawn traffic and motor vehicles. The motor is entirely conditioned by the speed of the horse traffic in front of it.'

The Graphic, *26 May 1923*

1 *How do you account for the huge difference in the traffic census figures between 1852 and 1915?*

2 *What bearing do these traffic census figures have on the claim that the slow horse was the main reason why London had a pressing traffic problem in 1923?*

3 *How can you tell from the behaviour of the pedestrians in the photograph that the traffic was virtually stationary?*

4 *How would you rate the traffic problem in 1923 compared with the traffic problem in any modern town today at rush hour?*

5 *How would a modern road engineer attempt to solve the problem illustrated by this photograph?*

> **6** *What were the fundamental reasons why London, like other major cities, had a traffic problem in 1923?*

In 1933, the London Passenger Transport Board was formed to control all public transport services in London (Underground railway, buses, trams, coaches), except the main-line railways. In the country as a whole, the bus gradually replaced the electric tram.

In the late 1950s and early 1960s, many cities, such as Leeds (1959) and Sheffield (1960), closed down their tram services completely, leaving public transport solely to the buses. But some urban areas, such as Tyneside with its Metro (opened in 1980), developed suburban and underground railway systems.

FURTHER QUESTIONS AND EXERCISES

1 *Use the graph to estimate the date of the photograph. Write a paragraph describing and explaining the graph. Why did London have fewer buses in 1911 than in 1906?*

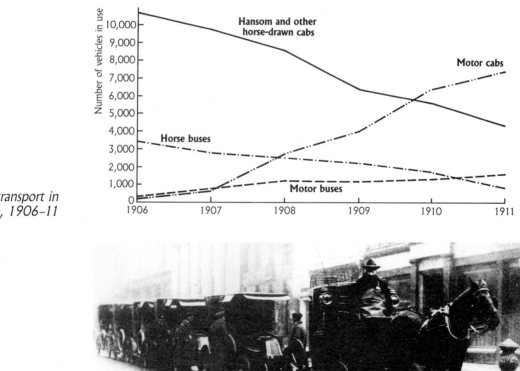

Public transport in London, 1906–11

'The Vanishing Horse Cab'

2 *Explain fully what was meant by each of the following and write sentences to include them in their proper context:*

(a) ribbon development

(e) Metro-land

(b) green belt

(f) back-to-back housing

(c) inner city

(g) garden city

(d) urban renewal

(h) conurbation.

3 *'The slum-dwellers did not make the slums, and for that reason you must help them. By so doing you are insuring the whole of the citizens against disease and crime.'*

(a) *How could the local authorities do something to help the 'slum-dwellers' in (a) 1875, (b) 1935?*

(b) *How could such action help 'the whole of the citizens'?*

(c) *Is it fair or unfair to suggest that the well-to-do middle classes only took action when they were afraid of disease and crime spreading from the slums?*

4 *What were the chief health problems in the Victorian towns?*

5 *Explain how the following pieces of legislation improved living conditions in the towns:*

(a) *the Public Health Acts of 1848 and 1875*

(b) *the Artisans' Dwellings Act of 1875*

(c) *the Addison, Chamberlain and Wheatley Acts of 1919–24*

(d) *the Town and Country Planning Act of 1947.*

6 *Write a short history of public transport in Britain since 1850 and explain its effect on the growth and development of the large cities.*

7 *What were the chief social problems created by the rapid expansion of London in the nineteenth century?*

8 *To what extent were the urban problems of London the same in the nineteenth century as in the twentieth century?*

Chapter Seven

Working-class Movements

INTRODUCTION

'The Unauthorised Programme of Labour – The Daily Meetings of the Unemployed on Tower Hill. It will be noticed that the police take notes of the speeches.' The Sphere, *12 December 1908.*

1 *Why do you think this meeting was held? Imagine you are a reporter working for* The Sphere *in 1908. Write a short description of the meeting on Tower Hill.*
2 *Why do you think the police took notes? Why were they there? What were the authorities afraid of?*

At least half the men and all the women in that crowd, in 1908, had no right to vote at a general election. This meant that they had no hope, through the ballot box, of getting Parliament to change the laws which they thought unjust. In the circumstances, it was hardly surprising that they should resort to demonstrations, petitions, and processions as a way of protest.

Throughout the period since 1850, strikes, demonstrations and riots have often provoked confrontations between workers and police (and occasionally between workers and troops). Yet despite the anger, frustration and despair, the prospect of a British rebellion has always seemed remote. The closest Great Britain ever came to revolution was probably at the time of the General Strike, in 1926, when the Government made military preparations. But strikers played football against policemen, little damage was done and everyday life for most people went on much as normal.

The causes of the anger which provoked the violence and protest were not hard to seek. In the nineteenth century and the early years of the twentieth century, unemployment, hunger, poverty and distress fostered socialism and spurred workers into developing effective trade unions. These working class movements reached fulfilment in the creation of a political party to represent labour (i.e. the workers) in Parliament and ultimately, in 1924, 1929, 1945, 1964 and 1974, to form the government.

THE REFORM OF THE ELECTORAL SYSTEM

Strictly speaking, the pressure to reform the electoral system came from many members of the upper and middle classes, as well as from leaders of the working-class movements. In particular, there were many aristocrats and professional women among the suffragettes. But, in practice, it was the working classes who suffered the gravest disadvantages by not being able to vote.

Electoral Reform before 1867

The Great Reform Act of 1832 made the electoral system more democratic by abolishing the old 'rotten boroughs' and giving the vote to male householders with a certain amount of property. In effect, this meant that only the middle class gained by the act, to the exclusion and fury of many members of the working class, who had expected to be given the vote. In 1832, only one man in every five had the vote in England and Wales and only one in twenty in Ireland.

In 1834, the passing of the Poor Law Amendment Act (see page 253) and the case of the Tolpuddle Martyrs created a working-class backlash which gave rise to the Chartist movement in the late 1830s and 1840s. It took its name from 'the Charter' – a six-point petition, signed by millions of people, which demanded specific electoral reforms – including the vote for every adult male, payment of MPs, secret ballots and annual Parliaments. The Chartists hoped this would lead to the election of working-class Members of Parliament, who could persuade the government to pass laws to improve the lot of the workers.

But Chartism had failed by 1850, and for the time being the working classes had no say in the election of the governments which taxed them, although some prospered sufficiently to qualify for the right to vote under the provisions of the 1832 Reform Act. Greater prosperity in the 1850s (see Chapters 1 and 2) meant that fewer people went hungry and demands to change the system met with only a muted response.

The National Reform League

National Reform League protest at Marble Arch in July 1866, contemporary print by W. H. Overend. The authorities had closed Hyde Park to prevent the League from meeting there; but the crowd pushed down the railings and met in defiance of the police ban.

The political demands of the Chartists were revived in 1865, with the formation of the National Reform League. Demonstrations, like the one shown in the illustration, helped to persuade politicians that there was a strong demand for the right to vote amongst the working classes. This time there were also more receptive ears in government, and Gladstone even said that every man of mature age had a moral right to the suffrage or franchise (i.e. the right to vote). He proposed, and Disraeli later implemented, the enfranchisement of a substantial proportion of the working classes.

Under Disraeli's Second Reform Act of 1867, the right to vote was given to many of the working men living in the towns. The act did not apply to people living in the country (who only qualified for the vote if they already met the existing qualifications laid down by the First Reform Act of 1832). Nor, indeed, did the act apply to women, not even to Mrs Disraeli! To qualify, a man had to be over 21, and either a householder or a lodger paying at least £10 a year in rent.

Thus, to take an imaginary example, a weaver renting a small terraced house got the vote as a householder but not his wife (since she was a woman), or his 22-year-old son, living with them (since he was not a householder), or his brother, aged 50 (since he only paid £5 a year in rent for his room).

As a result of the 1867 Reform Act, the electorate doubled to about two million men. It was still far from representative of the people of Britain as a whole, yet it did give some of the working classes in the towns their first say in the choice of government. But instead of voting Liberal or for working-class Members of Parliament, many voted Conservative – especially after the Liberal Government unwisely passed a law in 1871, which made peaceful picketing illegal (see page 218).

A contemporary print of working men voting during the 1874 general election

The Secret Ballot

Another electoral reform was introduced in 1872, when Gladstone's Liberal Government brought in the Ballot Act. Hitherto, votes had been cast openly at the hustings, on a wooden stand erected for that purpose in every constituency. Employers and landlords had been able to see how their employees and tenants voted – and to influence them accordingly! Although bribery was illegal, it still took place since open voting made it possible to check that those who had been bribed actually voted in the desired way. After the passing of the Ballot Act, voters were now able to cast their votes in secret (though many people were still worried that their employers and landlords might find out how they had voted).

The Third Reform Act, 1884

The Third Reform Act was also introduced by a Liberal Government led by Gladstone. It gave the vote to all adult male householders in Britain and to lodgers (provided they paid an annual rent of at least £10 for their accommodation). In effect this gave the vote to the working class in the countryside – mainly to farm workers, but also to many industrial workers, such as miners living in pit villages.

A cartoon from Punch, *17 October 1885, depicting the Conservative leader, Lord Salisbury, on the left and the Liberal leader, W. E. Gladstone, on the right. A 'New Rustic Voter' is shown between the two politicians. (N.B. A 'swain' is a lover or admirer!)*

THE CONTENDING SWAINS.

1 *What do you think was the point of this cartoon? Why are the two politicians shown on either side of the 'New Rustic Voter'? What are they trying to do?*

2 *How did the* Punch *cartoonist depict the 'New Rustic Voter'? Do you think he despised the country voter, poked fun at him, or only used this type of image to show that he was supposed to be a farm worker?*

3 *How can you tell that the picture on page 212 was drawn at a general election no earlier than 1874?*

Electoral Reform since 1884

In 1867, and again in 1884, many people hoped that women would be given the vote as well as men. Their protests led to the formation of the suffragette movement in 1903 (see page 318). Although this was not a working-class movement, it had the support of many members of the working class and most socialists.

But the Liberal Government led by Herbert Asquith (from 1908 to 1916) was afraid that by granting the vote to women, on the same terms as for men, they would simply be giving extra votes to the Conservatives, since only the well-to-do married woman (not otherwise qualified as householder or lodger) would be likely to own the property which could give her the right to vote.

The solution was the Representation of the People Act of 1918 which gave the vote to all men over the age of 21 and to all women over the age of 30. At one stroke, it trebled the size of the electorate from 7.7 million to 21.8 million. Its main effect was to increase the chances of the Labour party at the polls, since it gave the vote to a further third of the adult male population, many too poor to qualify under the earlier Reform Acts. Ten years later, the Equal Franchise Act of 1928 gave the vote to all women over 21 on exactly the same terms as for men. In 1948, the Representation of the People Act got rid of the remaining constituencies which allowed some people (such as university graduates) to vote twice at an election. Lastly, in 1969, a new Representation of the People Act gave the vote to everyone over the age of eighteen.

The effects of the four Reform Acts on the numbers of people able to vote at elections can be seen in this table.

Effect of the Reform Act of	*Number of Voters in every 100 Adult Males*		
	England and Wales	*Scotland*	*Ireland*
1832	20	12	5
1867	33	33	17
1884	67	60	50
1918	100	100	100

1 *Which Reform Act had the greatest effect in increasing the size of the adult-male electorate (a) in England and Wales, (b) in Scotland, (c) in Ireland?*

2 *Which types of people were still without the vote in 1885?*

3 *Approximately how many adults in England and Wales were without the vote in 1885? Was it (a) one in every three adults, (b) one in every six adults, (c) two out of every three adults?*

THE TRADE UNIONS, 1850–1919

The New Model Unions

In 1850, the trade-union movement was of little consequence. After the flurry of trade-union activity in the early 1830s, at the time of the Tolpuddle Martyrs, there had come a long period which had seen little effective trade-union action. In the 1850s, however, new trade unions were founded for the growing numbers of more affluent skilled workers. The first of these 'New Model Unions', as they were called, was the Amalgamated Society of Engineers (ASE), founded in 1851, with a membership of 12,000 which grew rapidly to 33,000 by 1868.

The New Model Unions had these features in common.

● They were organised by a centralised executive council, or committee, with paid officials based in a central headquarters, usually in London (like that of ASE).

● Their members were skilled workers, such as engineers and shoemakers. Higher than average wages meant they could pay the high subscriptions required to run these new and efficient unions. Engineers had to pay 1s [5p] a week – as much as 5 per cent of their income.

● The unions offered substantial welfare benefits to their members, including sickness benefit, unemployment benefit and provision for old age.

● Their officials cultivated a middle-class image. A New Model Union was respectable. Accordingly, its officials were more prepared to sit round the table and negotiate improvements in working conditions rather than try to force through higher wage claims with industrial action. When they did strike it was as a national union. Since the union's funds were held at the headquarters, only official strikes were approved and financed. In any case, this was a period when industry was booming. Employers were more inclined to settle a claim than lose potential profits during a prolonged strike.

Robert Applegarth (Secretary of the Amalgamated Society of Carpenters and Joiners), William Allan (Secretary of the ASE), and George Odger (an official of the Ladies' Shoemakers)

The Junta

The secretaries of several of the New Model Unions formed a powerful but unofficial committee, later nicknamed the 'Junta'. Its members included William Allan (Secretary of ASE), George Odger (Ladies' Shoemakers), Robert Applegarth (Amalgamated Society of Carpenters and Joiners), Edwin Coulson (London Bricklayers' Union) and Daniel Guile (National Association of Ironfounders).

They brought efficient business methods to the running of their trade unions and utilised the newly developed railway system to good advantage. They were opposed by the older style of trade unionists 'who objected to all connection between the Government and the concerns of working men' and who sought confrontation rather than agreement.

The Trades Councils

The co-operation of the different unions during a strike of the London Builders' Union, in 1859–60, resulted in the formation of the London Trades Council – a local conference of trade unions from different industries. Trade-union leaders like William Allan and Robert Applegarth recognised that the problems they wanted to solve were not specific to a particular trade or industry. There were many occasions when co-operation between the different unions was vital. Other regional trades councils were also formed, notably the Manchester and Salford Trades Council (which later took the initiative leading to the formation of the TUC).

The new image of the unions was beneficial in other respects, as well. Parliament passed the Friendly Societies Act in 1855, which seemed to give the unions protection of their funds. In 1859, the Molestation of Workmen Act permitted peaceful picketing. The unions had every reason to believe that many of the legal hurdles barring the way had been cleared. But two startling developments in quick succession threatened the very foundations on which the trade union movement then rested.

The Sheffield Outrages

A bomb attack on a blackleg saw grinder in Sheffield shocked the Government and the public, especially when the employers in the metal industries alleged that 200 further 'outrages' had also been committed by trade union members in Sheffield.

A Special Commission was set up to investigate the case and heard members of the Sawgrinders' Union confess to a number of other serious incidents of intimidation, such as sending threatening letters, putting gunpowder down a lighted chimney and even murdering a workman called Linley, who had broken the Union's rules.

In fact, the dispute was basically about the introduction of new machinery, which the unions claimed was unsafe. They wanted safeguards, the employers refused, so a strike began in 1866, supported by the Junta. But the Junta members were as appalled by the Outrages as the rest of the public, fearing their effect on trade-union aspirations. The Government set up a Royal Commission to 'inquire into the organisation and rules of Trades Unions' in general. It met at an opportune moment, since the judgment in the *Hornby* v. *Close* case meant that the legal position of the trade unions was in jeopardy.

The *Hornby* v. *Close* Case

This was a case in which the treasurer of the Bradford Boilermakers' Society had been sued for misappropriating £24 from the union's funds. But the Lord Chief Justice decided that, since the Bradford Boilermakers' Society was a trade union rather than a friendly society, it was not covered by the provisions of the Friendly Societies Act of 1855 and so the court case failed.

This was intolerable. The trade unions immediately wanted the law changed and took the opportunity to present a well-argued case for trade union reform to the Royal Commission. In particular, they wanted the trade unions to have the same legal rights as companies.

---

1 *Why were the Sheffield Outrages a serious blow to the trade-union movement in general, and to the New Model Unions and the Junta in particular?*

2 *What was the significance of the* Hornby v. Close *case? Why did the trade unions find this situation intolerable?*

3 *Why did they co-operate with the Royal Commission which was investigating the trade unions at this time? What did they stand to gain? What did they stand to lose?*

The First Trades Union Congress

As the unions prepared to give evidence, the Manchester and Salford Trades Council called a general trades union congress to consider 'the present Royal Commission on Trades Unions – how far worthy of the confidence of the Trade Union interests', and other matters of common interest, such as the law on picketing, the legal position of the unions, and the operation of the Factory Acts. They decided to meet annually. Initially, the members of the Junta declined to join this Trades Union Congress, which met for the first time in May 1868, with 34 delegates representing 100,000 members.

The Trade Unions and the Law

In 1869, the Royal Commission presented two reports. The majority of the members of the Commission felt that, provided trade-union membership was voluntary and that no coercion was put on other workmen or on blackleg labour, there was no reason to deny workers the right to be members of a trade union and the right to strike. The report of a minority of the members of the Royal Commission was even more favourable to the trade unions, having been heavily influenced by the members of the Junta.

The outcome was a new law, the Trade Union Act of 1871, giving the unions the legal recognition they wanted after the *Hornby* v. *Close* case. In future their funds would be protected by the laws of the land. But the Criminal Law Amendment Act, passed by Gladstone's Liberal Government in the same year, had the effect of making peaceful picketing illegal – to the consternation of the unions, since this was seen as one of the main ways of making a strike effective. The law was modified four years later, by Disraeli's Conservative Government, when the Conspiracy and Protection of Property Act, 1875, restored the trade unions' right to peaceful picketing.

The New Unionism

The New Model Unions had only organised the more affluent skilled workers. Unskilled labourers were much more difficult to organise effectively, since many of the jobs they did were on a temporary or casual basis. It was only too easy for employers to replace them with unskilled, blackleg labour (something they could not do as easily in the case of the craft unions).

Joseph Arch (see page 10) attempted to start an Agricultural Labourers' Union in 1872, but it ultimately failed. So it was one of the triumphs of the 1880s when Ben Tillett, John Burns and Tom Mann combined forces to achieve a remarkable victory in the London Dock Strike of 1889. This 'New Unionism', as it was called, was organised by militants (some of them socialist in their beliefs), to enable unskilled workers to fight for higher pay, shorter hours and better working conditions.

Procession of the match-girls to the Houses of Parliament during the celebrated strike in 1888, contemporary print by W. D. Almond

The first effective strike by manual workers was in 1888, when the match-girls went on strike. This caught the imagination, generosity and sympathy of the general public, largely because the action was taken by some of the poorest paid workers in London – the young working girls employed at a match factory in London. Annie Besant (see page 161) helped to organise this strike. In her *Autobiography*, she said she had collected facts about the grievances of the match-girls (such as the fines and deductions made from their already pathetically low wages), their working and living conditions, low income and expenditure, and had published these revelations under the title 'White Slavery in London', calling for a boycott of the company's matches.

Pressure was put on the match-girls to deny these facts and, when they refused, one of the girls was dismissed and the other 1,400 came out on strike. Annie Besant helped to publicise their case and their plight.

'We asked for money, and it came pouring in; we registered the girls to receive strike pay, wrote articles, held public meetings, got Mr Bradlaugh to ask questions in Parliament, stirred up constituencies in which shareholders were members, till the whole country rang with the struggle. We led a procession of the girls to the House of Commons and interviewed with a deputation of them, Members of Parliament, who cross-questioned them. The girls behaved splendidly, stuck together, kept brace and bright all through.'

Annie Besant, Autobiography, *1893*

In the end the employers gave way, the system of fines and deductions was abolished and the girls got a rise in pay.

---

1 *Why do you think the match-girls were successful in their strike? Quote evidence to support your answer.*

2 *What lessons do you think workers in other industries learned from this strike?*

The match-girls' strike was followed by one by the gas workers in 1889, demanding a reduction in the length of their shifts from twelve hours to eight hours for the same pay. This, too, was successful and gave hope and inspiration to the dockers when they went on strike later in the same year. John Burns said that it was the gas workers' victory which 'induced the strike of the dockers'.

'Engaging Dock Labourers at the West India Docks', The Illustrated London News, *20 February 1886*

The dock workers won their famous victory in the autumn of 1889, after going on strike for a wage rise from fivepence and hour to sixpence (the 'dockers' tanner'), and for improvements in working conditions. They were greatly assisted in negotiating a settlement by a sympathetic public, the efforts of the Lord Mayor of London and Cardinal Manning, and by a generous contribution of £30,000 from sympathisers in Australia.

Growth of Union Membership

Trade union membership tends to reflect the state of the economy and the level of employment. During periods of depression it falls, during boom periods it rises. This had been true of the Great Depression of the 1870s and 1880s (see page 139), when membership of the unions fell to under half a million.

But this series of successful strikes in 1888–9 helped to publicise the effectiveness of trade-union membership. The number of new members soared during the period of the match-girls' strike, the strike of gas workers and the London Dock Strike. By 1890, TUC membership had risen to about 1.5 million, but then a further depression in trade (see Chapter 4) and the successful resistance offered by a number of employers to further strike action, produced demoralised workers and TUC membership fell to below one million by 1894.

The tactic used by many employers in the 1890s was the 'lock-out' – refusing to employ workers if they threatened strike action. In their place they employed blackleg labour to take over the jobs of the workers who were locked out.

This was illustrated in 1893, when a major strike in the coal-mining industry had tragic consequences. The price of coal had fallen with the decline in trade (see page 139), yet wages in the industry had risen by 40 per cent since 1888. The pit owners wanted to cut wages in line with the fall in prices. The miners resisted.

When blackleg miners were used on the Yorkshire coalfield, violent demonstrations took place and the Home Secretary, Herbert Asquith, sent soldiers to the district to help the police keep order. On 7 September 1893, tempers flared up at Featherstone Colliery when a large crowd of strikers began to damage Lord Masham's pit, burning buildings and throwing the wreckage down the pit shaft. Troops were called in and a magistrate ordered them to clear the site. What happened next is described in the following sources, both written some time after the event.

Soldiers firing on striking miners at Featherstone Colliery, West Riding of Yorkshire, 1893, Cassell's History of England, 1896

Source A

'Of course no blame could be attached; the colliery was in danger of being entirely wrecked, and the action of the mob, whatever its excuse, was not technically defensible . . . the soldiers were justified in firing; and the whole matter could only survive as one more grievance of the socialists against capital.'

Source B

'At Featherstone two miners were shot dead by soldiers, a piece of brutality long remembered against the Home Secretary, Asquith.'

---

1 Which phrases betray the political leanings of these historians? Which account was written by a left-wing historian? Why is it difficult to be objective about an incident like this?

2 Write a sentence which you think both historians might have agreed was a fair summary of the incident at Featherstone Colliery in 1893.

The Taff Vale Case and its Consequences

In 1900, a relatively unimportant railway strike in South Wales had another epoch-making effect on the trade union movement. The Taff Vale Railway Company sued the railway unions, claiming damages for losses incurred during the strike. The court decision went in the company's favour and the Society of Railway Servants was ordered to pay £23,000 in damages. The judge said that since the law said the union could own property and employ people, it could obviously be sued if it authorised actions which caused loss or damage.

This affected all trade unions, since it meant they might all be liable to pay damages to employers when they called a strike. As a result, it spurred the unions into supporting the young Labour party (see page 228), in order to put pressure on Parliament. In 1906, they were successful. The Liberal Government, supported by Labour MPs, passed the Trades Disputes Act, which laid down that, in future, a union could not be sued by an employer for losses incurred during a strike.

There were many other serious strikes during the Edwardian period, as you can see from the graph on page 231. At this time, some trade unionists (including Tom Mann) were syndicalists, following a European theory that a social revolution could be achieved if the working classes would only assert their power in industry, by means of alliances between unions and by general strikes. As it happened there were a number of related strikes at that time, including those of the seamen and dockers in 1910, and the railwaymen in 1911. But syndicalism as such never took hold in Britain.

Some of these disputes led to serious confrontations, with the use of troops at Tonypandy in South Wales, in 1910, on the order of the Home Secretary Winston Churchill. An incident during the national railway strike at Llanelli in

South Wales, in 1911, resulted in the death of two demonstrators. The jury at the inquest thought that the incident would have been better handled had the officer in charge chosen some other means of dispersing the crowd.

There was yet another major coal strike in 1912, but by this time trade-union leaders were becoming aware of the benefits that could come from large unions or from joint action between unions. In 1912, the General Railway Workers' Union and the United Signalmen and Pointsmen joined forces with the Amalgamated Society of Railway Servants to form the National Union of Railwaymen (NUR). More ominously, in 1914, the NUR linked up with the Transport Workers' Federation and the Miners' Federation to form the Triple Alliance, with the objective of taking common action in any future disputes concerning any of their three unions.

During the First World War, the trade unions and the employers declared a truce, although this did not prevent the workers in many industries from striking – despite the Munitions of War Acts which specifically banned strikes. By the end of the war, the unions were fast gaining strength through mergers.

THE ORIGINS OF THE LABOUR PARTY

The Social Democratic Federation

THE TEMPTER.

SPIRIT OF ANARCHY.—"WHAT! NO WORK! COME AND ENLIST WITH ME,—I'LL FIND WORK FOR YOU!"

Punch,
27 November 1886

When the cartoon on the previous page was reprinted, in a collection of *Punch* cartoons in the early 1900s, the Editor explained that:

'The prevalence of poverty and lack of work at this time afforded an opportunity to the more violent Socialists to thrust themselves forward as champions of the poor and to make inflammatory appeals to the unemployed.'

1 *Give an example of an 'inflammatory appeal to the unemployed'.*

2 *How does 'anarchy' differ from 'socialism'? (Look up both these terms in a dictionary if you are not sure of the difference.)*

3 *Why do you think the* Punch *cartoonist confused the two terms in 1886? What was he afraid of?*

4 *Could a similar cartoon be drawn today? How might a right- or left-wing newspaper alter the drawing and the caption to make it fit the news today?*

As you saw in Chapter 4, unemployment became a problem in the 1880s during a period of temporary depression in industry and commerce. At that time, there was no social security or unemployment benefit, and people out of a job had to seek poor relief from the local Guardians of the Poor (see page 253). It was in these circumstances that the early socialists began to gain recruits for their cause.

The influence of left-wing political thinkers was already being felt, particularly after the publication in 1867 of the first volume of Karl Marx's book, *Das Kapital* – the source and inspiration of world communism.

One of the first attempts to create a socialist party in Britain was in 1881–4, when H. M. Hyndman, a convert to Marxism, founded the Social Democratic Federation. It quickly attracted middle-class intellectuals and trade unionists, and became the leading force in the early socialist movement in Britain. The Federation organised frequent processions and demonstrations, such as the socialist meeting in Trafalgar Square, in November 1886, when the crowd carried red flags and banners which bore slogans such as 'Work for All', 'Be not Slaves', and 'Solve the Labour Question'. A year later, on 'Bloody Sunday', 13 November 1887, the Social Democratic Federation helped to organise the biggest demonstration yet, as you can see in the sources which follow.

Source A

'The subject which most commends interest just now is the battle of Trafalgar Square on Sunday 13 November. The so-called "unemployed" & a good contingent of roughs had taken possession of the space round Nelson's Column in Trafalgar Square since the middle of October & had persistently slept there & held meetings assisted by the

Socialists & the extreme Radicals. Sunday, 13th of November arrived, & some Radical & all the Socialist Clubs from all parts of the town set off, followed by the whole criminal population & vast numbers of sightseers, for Trafalgar Square.'

Source B

'Riots in London on Sunday, Nov. 13', The Illustrated London News, 19 November 1887

Source C

'Sunday November 13, 1887, will be a day memorable in London history for a set conflict, in which, happily, no lives were lost or any permanently serious injuries, so far as we know, inflicted on body or limbs, though hard knocks were exchanged by the combatants on both sides.'

Source D

'In November 1887, Cunninghame Graham and Burns vainly attempted to storm Trafalgar Square against the police at the head of the unemployed; Alfred Linnell, the first English Socialist martyr, died of injuries received from the police in the conflict.'

Source E

'At a quarter-past four o'clock loud cheers were given by the crowd nearest Whitehall and the word flew round that the military were approaching. After a brief interval the bright cuirasses [pieces of metal body armour] and helmets of the 1st Life Guards came in sight, and a detachment of 200 troopers entered the square, under the command of Colonel Talbot, by whose side at the head of the regiment rode Mr Marsham, one of the Metropolitan Police Magistrates. The troops trotted slowly round the cordon of police amid cheers and cries, groans and hisses. By six o'clock all danger of further disturbance was at an end.'

Source F

'Several desperate rushes were made to break through the cordon of police. They were, however, driven back and after a series of severe scuffles, in which two men were so injured that they subsequently died, and a policeman was stabbed, two squadrons of Life Guards, with a magistrate at their head ready to read the Riot Act, appeared in aid of the constabulary. They rode round and round the Square. This display of force cowed the mob, and within half-an-hour the police had cleared the square.'

Source G

'In December a man named Alfred Linnell, who had been injured in the fight, died. His funeral on 18th December [1887] was attended by a huge but perfectly orderly crowd.'

Source H

'The Life Guards Keeping the Square', The Illustrated London News, *19 November 1887*

1 *Which picture shows Mr Marsham? Why did he go to Trafalgar Square? Who was Alfred Linnell?*

2 *Which sources provide evidence that there was (a) police violence, (b) crowd violence?*

3 *Which extracts describe the events portrayed by the artist? How do contemporary pictures like these differ from photographs, as sources of historical information? What would you want to know first before treating them as reliable historical evidence?*

4 *Which of these extracts may have been actual eyewitness accounts of 'Bloody Sunday'? How can you tell that some were written at least four weeks after the event?*

5 *In what ways do these accounts differ from each other? How do you explain the differences?*

6 *Make a list of the words which tell you what the authors themselves felt about the rights or wrongs of the demonstration on 'Bloody Sunday'. How have some of the authors allowed their political opinions to colour their judgment? Which sources appear to have been written without bias either way?*

7 *Imagine you are one of the 'sightseers'. Write your own 'eyewitness' description of the day's events using these extracts and pictures as your sources of information.*

The Fabian Society

The fear that riots and demonstrations might turn to revolution was shared by some left-wing supporters of the working-class movement. This is one reason why a group of well-known intellectuals formed the Fabian Society in 1884. They included George Bernard Shaw, Annie Besant, and Sidney and Beatrice Webb. They wanted to create a democratic and socialist society by gradual means – by continually pressing for progressive social reforms. They renounced the idea of a sudden socialist revolution on Marxist lines. They believed that socialism was inevitable but advocated a cautious approach. They wanted a peaceful transition period in which power would be transferred to the people.

The Fabian Society took its name from Quintus Fabius Maximus, a famous Roman general who was called 'the delayer' because his successful tactics against Hannibal were to avoid a major confrontation on the battlefield, whilst continually harassing and pressing the enemy.

The Labour Representation League

As you have seen, many working men got the vote in 1867, but this was not followed by a flood of working-class MPs, since Members of Parliament were not paid until 1911 and few working men had the resources to enable them to give up a paid job to become an MP. Those who were elected to the House of Commons owed their support to the Labour Representation League, which was founded in 1869. In Parliament they were called 'Lib-Labs', because they sat as members of the Liberal party but represented Labour (meaning the labouring classes).

This was not to the liking of many socialists, who therefore gave their support to Keir Hardie when he helped to found the Independent Labour Party (ILP) in 1893, after his election to Parliament in 1892 as an independent Labour MP for West Ham. The ILP wanted nationalisation, unemployment benefit and a minimum wage for an eight-hour working day. But it was not the infant Labour party. For one thing it lacked the support of the trade unions. Without TUC backing it could have no significant effect on party politics, since the TUC alone had the funds to support the national organisation needed to fight a general election with a wide choice of candidates. The leaders of the ILP were as yet unable to convince the moderate members of the TUC that there was any real need to form such a party, since many of the leaders of the craft unions distrusted socialists and their motives.

The Labour Representation Committee

Nonetheless, the intellectuals in the Fabian Society, the socialists, the ILP and many trade unionists felt the time was ripe for a political party which would genuinely represent the interests of the working class. At the Trades Union Congress in 1899, members voted to support a motion proposing a conference which would discuss ways and means of increasing the number of working-class MPs. They wanted to see 'a distinct Labour group in Parliament'.

At the conference in 1900, the TUC and the ILP jointly agreed to support a new Labour Representation Committee to try to get representatives of Labour elected to Parliament. In the 1900 general election, they made a modest start, fielding candidates in fifteen constituencies and getting two of them (Keir Hardie and Richard Bell) elected as the first Labour MPs.

Any doubts that moderate trade unionists had about the need for a Labour party, however, were quickly dispelled when the implications of the Taff Vale judgment became clear (see page 222). It was now vital for the trade unions to seek Parliamentary representation. Within three years, the number of supporters of the Labour Representation Committee reached one million, and the trade unions had agreed to charge a levy of one penny on each of their members, to help pay Labour MPs a salary.

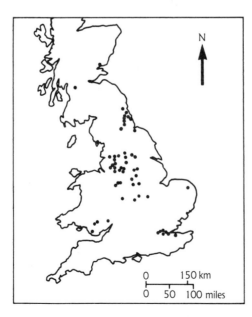

The first big test came with the 1906 general election, when the number of Labour candidates was increased to 51 and 29 Labour MPs were elected. Together with the Lib-Labs (in the Liberal party), this brought the number of Labour sympathisers in Parliament up to 57.

Constituencies of MPs supporting Labour party policies in the 1906 Parliament. Twenty-nine were Labour Representation Committee candidates.

1 Where did most of the Labour party supporters in Parliament in 1906 come from? What did these areas have in common?

2 Look at the table of statistics below, showing the progress made by the Labour party in the first fifty years of its existence. Why did the electorate (the total number of people eligible to vote) increase so dramatically at the 1918 and 1929 general elections?

3 Look at the column showing the percentage of the total electorate which voted Labour in each election. Did the Labour party gain or lose by the increase in the electorate in 1918 and 1929?

4 Between which elections do you think the Labour party gained most ground? When did they suffer major setbacks?

5 Draw two graphs to illustrate the growth of the Labour party using the statistics showing (a) the number of Labour MPs elected, (b) the percentage of the total votes cast for Labour candidates. Explain how and why the graphs differ.

Growth of the Labour Party, 1900–50

Year	Size of electorate (millions)	Number of Labour votes (millions)	Labour MPs elected	Percentage of total votes won by Labour	Party elected to form government
1900	6.7	0.06	2	1.8	CONS
1906	7.3	0.33	30	5.9	LIBERAL
1910	7.7	0.51	40	7.6	LIBERAL
1910	7.7	0.37	42	7.1	LIBERAL
1918	21.4	2.39	63	22.2	COALITION
1922	21.1	4.24	142	29.5	CONS
1923	21.3	4.44	191	30.5	LABOUR
1924	21.7	5.50	151	33.0	CONS
1929	28.9	8.39	288	37.1	LABOUR
1931	30.0	6.65	52	30.6	NATIONAL
1935	31.4	8.33	154	37.9	NATIONAL
1945	33.2	12.00	393	47.8	LABOUR
1950	34.6	13.27	315	46.1	LABOUR

The Osborne Judgment

The first Labour MPs had to rely for their incomes on the trade unions, since there were no salaries for MPs at that time and, unlike the majority of Liberal and Conservative MPs, they had no private incomes. As part of his or her union membership subscription every trade unionist had to pay a compulsory 'political levy', which went to support Labour MPs. But some objected to this, and in 1910 a railwayman called Walter Osborne, a Liberal, successfully got a court ruling that union levies of this type were illegal.

This immediately created a crisis for the Labour party and its parent the TUC, since it appeared to deprive them of the only method they had of giving the necessary financial support to working-class Members of Parliament. However, the Liberal Government introduced a new law paying MPs a salary in 1911, and followed it up in 1913, with the Trade Union (Political Funds) Act, which authorised political levies, provided that members of the trade unions concerned could 'contract out' of paying the levy, if they wished.

THE LABOUR MOVEMENT SINCE 1914

In 1924 Ramsay MacDonald, leader of the British Labour party, then a minority party in Parliament, formed a Government with the support of the Liberals. Although his Government lasted only ten months, MacDonald and his colleagues proved that the British working-class movement could produce leaders capable of governing the country.

After the 1924 general election, the Conservatives formed a Government led by Stanley Baldwin. It was this Government which provoked and dealt with the effects of the 1926 General Strike (see page 233).

The Trade Unions

When the First World War ended in 1918, the trade union movement was in a strong position, with nearly 40 per cent of the total labour force enrolled in trade unions. During the war, many of the skilled jobs of men in the forces had been taken by unskilled workers. As a result, there was a levelling-up of workers' pay, with less of a gap after the war between the skilled and unskilled. This strengthened the power of the unions and of the Labour party.

Significantly, the period 1920–1 also saw the formation of the two biggest unions in Britain today – the Amalgamated Engineering Union and the Transport and General Workers Union (TGWU). The TGWU was led by a remarkable union secretary, Ernest Bevin, later a Cabinet minister. His success in fighting for the members of his union earned him the title of 'the Dockers' K.C.'.

This period, the early 1920s, was also one of industrial unrest on a scale never experienced in Britain before or since.

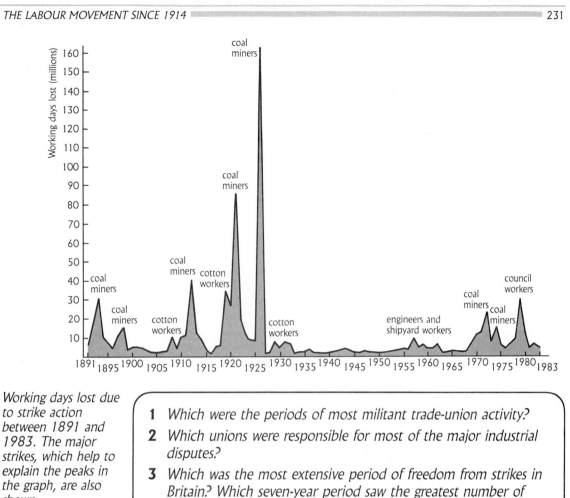

Working days lost due to strike action between 1891 and 1983. The major strikes, which help to explain the peaks in the graph, are also shown.

1 Which were the periods of most militant trade-union activity?

2 Which unions were responsible for most of the major industrial disputes?

3 Which was the most extensive period of freedom from strikes in Britain? Which seven-year period saw the greatest number of working days lost due to industrial disputes between 1891 and 1983?

As you have already seen, the mine workers, railwaymen and the transport workers formed a Triple Alliance, in 1914, with the aim of ensuring joint action if any one of the three unions came under attack from the employers. But the Alliance failed its first test when the railwaymen and transport workers refused to back the miners in their strike of 1921.

The coal-mining industry was in a bad way after the war (see page 54). The mines were unable to produce coal at competitive prices at a time of strong foreign competition and a decline in world coal demand. Something had to be done.

The Government and the pit owners rejected the idea of nationalisation, whilst the miners rejected cuts in wages and a proposal to lengthen the working day to improve productivity. There were strikes in Yorkshire in 1919, and throughout the country in October 1920, when the stoppage caused thousands of workers to be laid off due to shortage of fuel.

Then, in 1921, came the biggest industrial dispute in British history to that date, when over a million miners refused to accept cuts in wages proposed by the employers and were 'locked out' of the collieries. On 9 April 1921, *The Sphere* printed photographs of the tents in Kensington Gardens, 'where a Brigade of Guards had been encamped in view of the stoppage of the mines'. Hannen Swaffer, a well-known journalist, even claimed in an article in the same magazine, that:

> 'England, this week is nearer revolution than it has ever been. Never before has there arisen a crisis which cancelled all naval leave and marshalled troops in our peaceful parks in peace-time – just as though invasion were expected every hour.'

Soldiers drafted to South Wales during the miners' strike of 1921

The miners warned their partners in the Triple Alliance:

> 'Make no mistake. It will be your turn next. The miners are locked out in the great war on wages. You meet today, conscious that everyone of your own sections is threatened. The miners' lock-out is the first battle. Are you going to refuse them support? Your place is in the firing-line. Your safety, your standards, your wages, depend upon action now.'

1 *Since the nearest coalfield to London is over 100 km away in Kent, why did the Government bring troops into central London in April 1921? What were they afraid of?*

2 *How can you guess from the style of the miners' warning that it was written shortly after the end of the First World War?*

3 *Why was the warning issued? What did the miners want?*

4 *What arguments did the miners use to try to persuade the other unions that the dispute concerned them as well?*

At first, the National Union of Railwaymen and the Transport Workers' Federation (as the TGWU was then known) agreed to come to the assistance of the miners, saying that unless an offer was made to the miners which they could 'feel justified in recommending them to accept, a stoppage of the Railwaymen and Transport Workers will begin'. In this they had the backing of the Labour party and the TUC.

But on Thursday, 14 April 1921, the Secretary of the miners' union rashly indicated that a compromise might be reached. Although this was later denied, it was sufficient to allow the moderates in the other two unions to abandon the proposals for a strike in sympathy with the miners. They announced their decision on 'Black Friday', 15 April 1921.

The General Strike

Five years later came the biggest industrial dispute of all, when the miners were again involved in an argument with the mine owners, resulting in the loss of 145,000 working days in the mining industry and starting Britain's first and only general strike. It lasted nine days from 3–12 May 1926, and was the nearest Great Britain has come to a revolution since the Civil War, in the middle of the seventeenth century. Over two million workers closed down factories and transport services. Moderate trade-union leaders, politicians (including some from the Labour party) and Government ministers feared there might be riots, serious bloodshed, or even a revolution. In fact they had little to fear.

The origins of the the dispute were in 1925, when the mine owners made fresh proposals for wage cuts in the coal-mining industry and an increase in the working day from seven to eight hours. But they got a dusty reply from the miners' leader, A. J. Cook, when he retorted, 'Not a penny off the pay! Not a minute on the day!'

*Volunteer bus drivers
and policeman as
escort*

As in 1921, the TUC was afraid that, if the mine owners were successful, employers in other industries would follow suit and expect lower wages for longer working hours. So there were renewed threats of joint action and of a possible general strike – a move which alarmed the Government.

On 'Red Friday', 23 July 1925, Stanley Baldwin, Prime Minister in the Conservative Government, intervened in the dispute and said that the Government would subsidise the coal industry (so that wages need not be cut), whilst an official commission, led by Sir Herbert Samuel, would try to come up with a solution. Some people believe that Baldwin was merely buying time to allow the Government to make preparations to withstand a general strike (such as building up coal reserves and creating the Organisation for the Maintenance of Supplies, which was to be run on military lines).

In the end, the *Report* of the Samuel Commission pleased neither the miners nor the mine owners, since it supported the longer shift and the cut in wages but told the mine owners to modernise their pits. Talks between the miners and their employers broke down. The miners called a strike for 1 May but were 'locked out' anyway when the mine owners closed the pits.

The TUC held a special conference on 1 May 1926, and delegates celebrated May Day by voting by about 70 to 1 in favour of a general strike, scheduled to begin at midnight on Monday, 3 May 1926. Negotiations between the TUC and the Government continued, however, but broke down when printers on the *Daily Mail* refused to print an edition containing an article which was highly critical of the trade-union movement.

Accordingly, on 3 May 1926, the General Strike began when workers in the key industries (transport, heavy industries, printing, power supplies) stopped work. They had been chosen by the TUC to make the maximum possible impact.

The newspapers, affected by the printing strike, tried many ingenious and different ways of getting their papers into print and some were just duplicated sheets of news. Few ran to more than a single page. Most were pro-Government in tone, so the TUC published its own newspaper, *The British Worker*, partly in response to a Government newspaper, *The British Gazette*, which was edited by Winston Churchill. You can follow what happened during the General Strike if you read the following extracts from some of these makeshift newspapers.

Source A

'Ready response volunteers in provinces. In Poplar and Canning Town last night gangs held up and damaged motor-cars. Police made baton charges.'

Northern Daily Telegraph, *Wednesday, 5 May 1926*

Source B

' "General" Busses running now with two conductors, and each one with a policeman on guard.'

The Strand Gazette, *Thursday, 6 May 1926*

Source C

'WORKERS CALM AND STEADY – Firmer and Firmer Every Day of Strike – BLACKLEGS FAIL – HOW THE "B.W." CAME OUT – A Sudden Police Raid – and After – AMAZING SCENES – The detective inspector explained that they had a warrant from the Home Secretary to search for and seize all copies of the DAILY HERALD of May 4. It was quickly made clear that what really interested them was less the DAILY HERALD of May 4 than the BRITISH WORKER of May 5.

The British Worker, *Thursday evening, 6 May 1926*

Source D

'VITAL SERVICES IMPROVING – All Obstacles Being Progressively Surmounted – Defeat Of The Attempt To Silence The Press – RESULT OF THE STRIKE NOW BEYOND DOUBT – The attempt of the Trade Unions to silence the Press is being defeated. Over half a million copies of the *British Gazette* were this morning delivered throughout all parts of the country.'

The British Gazette, *Friday, 7 May 1926*

Source E

SUNDAY · PICTORIAL
SALE <u>MORE THAN DOUBLE</u> THAT OF ANY OTHER SUNDAY PICTURE PAPER

MAY 9th, 1926.   TWO PENCE.

STRIKE SCENES AND INCIDENTS PICTURED

TOP: Mounted London policemen with their staves engaged in clearing streets during one of the minor disturbances which have marked the strike in the area of the Elephant and Castle where a number of omnibuses driven by volunteers have had rough and stormy journeys, but where conditions have now become more peaceable.

BOTTOM LEFT: JollyNavy men with their equipment arriving in London in readiness for strike emergency service. So far it has not been necessary to make much call on the handy-man of all jobs, but the bluejackets are standing-by to keep services going if they are needed.

BOTTOM RIGHT: Military men on guard at an omnibus depot during the work of preparing the vehicles for the road. The volunteer drivers are being assisted in placing barbed wire guards along and around the bonnets of the cars to safeguard them against possible attempts to reach and damage the engines while on the streets.

Front page of the Sunday Pictorial, Sunday, 9 May 1926 (the front side of a single-page sheet)

Source F

'Nothing could be more wonderful than the magnificent response of millions of workers to the call of their leaders. The General Council are especially desirous of commending the workers on their strict obedience to the instruction to avoid all conflict and to conduct themselves in an orderly manner. Their behaviour during the first week of the stoppage is a great example to the whole world.

The General Council's message at the opening of the second week is "Stand firm. Be loyal to instructions and Trust Your Leaders."'

The British Worker, *Monday, 10 May 1926*

Source G

'The TUC deny that men are going back, and declare that their front remains unbroken. Another denial is that of Mr Cook that the miners are seeking to find grounds to call off the general strike, and the statement of mediation through Sir Herbert Samuel is denied by both sides.

Another large convoy under the escort of armoured cars and regular troops wearing steel helmets and carrying rifles with bayonets fixed brought food supplies from the docks to Hyde Park yesterday afternoon. The procession was unmolested.'

The News Daily, *No. 4, Tuesday, 11 May 1926*

Source H

'ORDER AND QUIET THROUGH THE LAND – Growing Dissatisfaction Among The Strikers – INCREASING NUMBERS OF MEN RETURNING TO WORK – 850 Omnibuses In The Streets Of London – MORE AND MORE TRAINS – WORK AS USUAL'

The British Gazette, *Wednesday, 12 May 1926*

Source I

'THE GENERAL STRIKE CANCELLED – "VICTORY FOR COMMON SENSE" – National Rejoicing Over the Dramatic Decision – Miners Not To Go Back At Once – TEXT OF BASIS OF SETTLEMENT – Subsidy for "Reasonable Period": Reorganisation Guarantee – NATIONAL WAGE BOARD – The rumours that have been current for the last few days of the activity of Sir Herbert Samuel as an unofficial peacemaker in the industrial troubles were crystallised last night [after the announcement of the cancellation of the strike].'

The Daily Chronicle, *Thursday, 13 May 1926*

---

1 *Why were volunteers recruited? What jobs did they do?*

2 *Which sources show that both the Government and the strikers attempted to stop newspapers reaching the public? Had either any right to talk about the freedom of the press?*

3 *How did the newspapers treat the General Strike? Which (if any) of these newspaper extracts appear to you to be (a) biased in favour of the trade unions, (b) biased in favour of the Government, (c) unbiased, (d) directly contradicting each other? Quote the sources used to support your answers.*

4 *Write a detailed chronological account of the General Strike, using these extracts and the pictures as your main sources of information.*

Negotiations behind the scenes continued throughout the strike, although the miners chose not to take part in them. Sir Herbert Samuel slightly modified the original proposals of the Samuel Commission on the coal mining industry, which had precipitated the crisis. On 10 May, the moderate union leaders on the TUC General Council decided that the Samuel Memorandum was acceptable and called on the Miners' Federation to agree. When the miners' representatives refused to do so (on the grounds that their original complaints still stood), the General Council members called on the Prime Minister, on 12 May, and told him of the decision to call off the strike. 'I thank God for your decision,' said Mr Baldwin. But the miners continued their strike until November, when hunger and distress forced them back to work, embittered against their fellow workers in the other unions.

Relative Decline of Trade Unions

An immediate result of the General Strike was disillusionment with the General Council of the TUC, bitter inter-union quarrelling and harsh, new trade-union legislation. In 1927 the Government brought in the Trade Disputes and Trade Unions Act which banned general strikes, the closed shop (union insistence in a factory that all employees belong to the same union), and strikes by the police force and other public servants.

> 'It is hereby declared that any strike is illegal if it has any object other than or in addition to the furtherance of a trade dispute within the trade or industry in which the strikers are engaged; and is a strike designed or calculated to coerce the Government either directly or indirectly or by inflicting hardship upon the community.'

The act also laid down that trade unions could not use membership subscriptions and union dues to contribute funds to political parties (e.g. the Labour party) without their members first giving notice, in writing, of their willingness to contribute. In other words, the onus was on the member to 'contract in' rather than to 'contract out'.

Trade-union membership fell sharply in the next few years – partly because of the disillusionment of some workers with the trade-union movement after the General Strike, and partly because the sharp rise in unemployment meant there were fewer workers in industry anyway. The 5.5 million members in 1925 had dwindled to 3.75 million by 1930.

The second Labour Government between 1929 and 1931 was dependent on the Liberals for support, so there was no immediate opportunity to repeal the Trade Disputes and Trade Union Act of 1927. Instead, the drastic economic measures which Ramsay MacDonald felt obliged to take (see page 146) caused a massive split in the Labour party and resulted in the break up of the Labour Government. The Labour party now found itself in the unusual position of forming the opposition to a Government which was run by its former leader. Not surprisingly Labour made a disastrous showing in the 1931 general election and had only partially recovered by 1935.

The Trade Unions since 1945

In 1945, the Labour party was returned to power with a huge majority – the first Labour Government able and willing to implement a full-scale programme of socialist reforms (see page 268). Early on in its life, in 1946, MPs voted in favour of legislation repealing the hated 1927 Trade Disputes and Trade

Union Act. The trade unions had recovered their former strength during the war years and membership was climbing. Between 1930 and 1948 membership more than doubled to about eight million, and increased by half as much again in the period up to 1980.

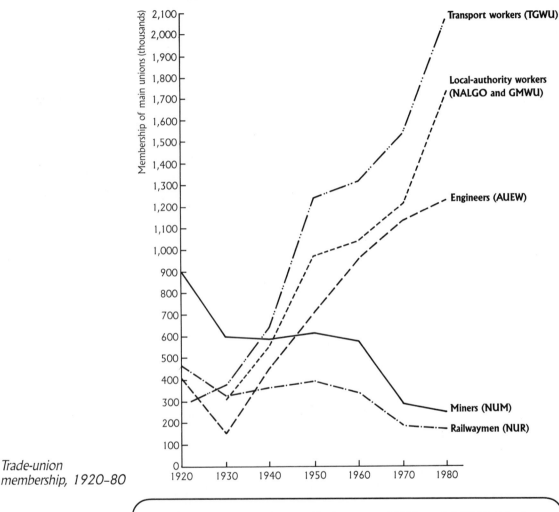

Trade-union membership, 1920–80

1 *Which unions grew steadily between 1920 and 1980? Why? Which unions declined between 1920 and 1980. Why?*

2 *Write a paragraph describing and explaining this graph.*

In 1900, only 12 per cent of the labour force had been members of a trade union. By 1984, the proportion was just under 50 per cent. At the same time, the number of separate trade unions fell as the process of mergers and amalgamations between unions continued in the post-war years. In 1960, there were 184 trade unions in the TUC with about eight million members. Twenty years later, there were 109 unions with twelve million members.

Since 1945, successive governments have tried to curb the activities of the trade unions – sometimes by persuasion, sometimes by legislation. In addition, several legal cases have resulted in decisions which have restricted the activities of the trade unions. In the 1960s, the Labour Government attempted to do so with a programme of legislation, entitled *In Place of Strife*. The White Paper outlining the proposed reforms caused dissension in the Labour party and in the trade unions. Richard Crossman, a senior Cabinet minister, described one of the proposals – to allow the Government to order unofficial strikers back to work – as 'dictatorship' and said that the TUC objected 'strongly to the right to impose strike ballots before an official strike'. Not surprisingly, the unions could not agree to support the proposals in the bill and it was shelved.

The Conservative Government of the early 1970s, under Edward Heath, was no more successful. Their Industrial Relations Act of 1971 was bitterly opposed by trade unionists. After Edward Heath's Government had been brought down, in 1974, following a confrontation with the coal miners, the incoming Labour Government repealed the act. However, the Labour Government itself was only marginally more successful, and in 1978–9 suffered a major setback when the 'Winter of Discontent' strikes by public employees in 'dirty jobs' (e.g. refuse collection) turned many people against the Labour party at the 1979 general election.

By 1986, the new Conservative Government, led by Margaret Thatcher, had introduced new, controversial trade-union legislation (e.g. on strike ballots and secondary picketing), but the Government's success in curbing trade-union activity had as much to do with the fact that widespread unemployment made employees reluctant to take industrial action, as with any deterrent posed by the new trade-union laws.

The miners' strike in 1984

The only really major strike in the period between 1979 and 1986 was the strike of the National Union of Mineworkers (NUM), led by Arthur Scargill, in 1984–5 (see page 70). Huge stockpiles of unsold coal, coupled with a major split in the miners' union, the well-organised policing of those pits which continued to work, an absence of concrete support from other unions (however sympathetic to the miners' cause) and a hostile national press, enabled the Government to ride out the strike. These were some of the newspaper headlines when the strike ended on 3 March 1985.

- 'TRAITOR! Even Scargill's hard men scorn him as strike is called off' (*Daily Star*)

- 'THE BITTER END "Traitor" taunt as Scargill orders a return to work' (*Daily Mirror*)

- 'SURRENDER After 12 months Scargill's army calls off the strike' (*Daily Mail*)

- 'FACE OF DEFEAT "Traitor" taunt as Scargill caves in' (*The Sun*)

- 'STRIKE ENDS BUT FIGHT GOES ON, WARNS SCARGILL Tears at vote to work Ban on overtime stays' (*Daily Express*)

- 'STRIKE ENDS BUT SCARGILL DEFIANT Fight against closure of "uneconomic" pits likely to continue' (*The Times*)

- 'MINERS CALL OFF STRIKE Battle for sacked men goes on, says Scargill' (*Daily Telegraph*)

- 'PIT STRIKE ENDS IN DEFIANCE AND TEARS Delegates vote 98–91 for return to work' (*The Guardian*)

---

1 *Which of these newspaper headlines do you think justifies the use of the phrase a 'hostile national press'?*

2 *What do these headlines tell you about the reasons for calling the strike in the first place and why it ended in defeat?*

3 *Write an explanatory oral history of the 1984–5 coal-miners' strike using the information you can obtain from friends and relatives. Did they approve or disapprove of the actions of (a) the NUM and Arthur Scargill, (b) the Nottinghamshire miners who continued to work, (c) the National Coal Board, (d) the Conservative Government?*

By 1984–5, membership of many trade unions had fallen off as a result of high unemployment and a substantial decline in the number of people employed in the older industries. Membership of the Transport and General Workers' Union had fallen to 1,434,000 (1985), the Amalgamated Engineering Union to 975,000 (1985), the National Union of Mineworkers to 208,000 (1984) and the National Union of Railwaymen to 143,000 (1984). Overall, only two workers in every five were trade-union members in 1985.

FURTHER QUESTIONS AND EXERCISES

1 *Match each of the activists in the list below (on the left) against the event (on the right) with which they are best remembered. Did they achieve their objectives?*

   Annie Besant   the coal-miners' strike, 1984–5
   A. J. Cook   the match-girls' strike, 1888
   Arthur Scargill   the General Strike, 1926
   Ben Tillett   the London Dock Strike, 1889

2 *What was the importance of each of the following in the history of the working class movement:*

   (a) Hornby v. Close *case*   (f) *Fabian Society*
   (b) *Taff Vale dispute*   (g) *Labour Representation Committee*
   (c) *Sheffield Outrages*
   (d) *New Model Unions*   (h) *Osborne judgment*
   (e) *New Unionism*   (i) *Social Democratic Federation?*

3 *What would you say were the three most significant events in the history of the working-class movement since 1850?*

4 *Write an essay explaining the reasons for the calling of the General Strike in 1926. Outline the course of the Strike, explain how and why it ended, and assess its impact on the working-class movement in the 1920s and 1930s.*

5

1868	118	1919	5,284	1960	8,128
1890	1,470	1930	3,744	1970	9,402
1900	1,250	1939	4,669	1980	12,173
1910	1,648	1948	7,937	1984	10,082

Draw a graph to show these statistics of TUC membership and write a short essay explaining in detail the reasons for the variations in your trend line.

6 *Trace the history of electoral reform since 1830, explaining how and why the electorate was widened during the period up to 1969.*

THE PROBLEM-PICTURE OF 1921.
HOW TO MAKE THE TAIL WAG. *Punch, 20 April 1921*

7 *Who or what was represented by the three dogs? What was the 'problem'? What was the outcome? Write a detailed, explanatory caption for this cartoon.*

8 *Look at this cartoon from* Punch, *15 March 1879.*

'Mr Punch – "Well, my Lord, you educated your 'Party' up to that [pointing with umbrella]! Don't you think you might educate 'em up to this [pointing with right hand]!!!"'

CAD AND CLOD.

(a) *Who is 'my Lord'?*

(b) *At whom was Mr Punch pointing with his umbrella?*

(c) *Which of the two customers at the tavern got the vote in 1867? When did the other customer get the vote?*

(d) *What was the point of the cartoon?*

(e) *On the evidence of this one cartoon, do you think* Punch *was in favour of widening the franchise, or not? Give reasons for your answer.*

Chapter Eight

Social Welfare and Reform

INTRODUCTION

'Relief of the
Unemployed in London:
Giving out Soup Tickets
in 1886', The Illustrated
London News,
13 March 1886

1 What were soup tickets and why were the unemployed fighting
   to get them in 1886?

2 Using this picture as your guide, say whether you think these
   people were entitled to receive a soup ticket as a right, or
   whether you think they were dependent on charity.

3 Look carefully at the faces and expressions of the people in the
   crowd. How has the artist depicted the plight of the
   unemployed in London in March 1886?

Nowadays, people take it for granted that if they lose their jobs, they will be entitled to draw unemployment benefit, because they and their employers have paid National Insurance contributions. When they retire from work, they draw a retirement pension; when ill, they receive sickness benefit; when they require hospital treatment, it is provided free of charge.

We live in a Welfare State; the Victorians did not. There was no system of National Insurance then. Instead, the sick, elderly, widowed and unemployed had to rely on charity or throw themselves on the mercy of the local Guardians of the Poor. Under the Poor Law Amendment Act of 1834 they were classed as paupers and treated by many officials, and regarded by others, as inferior human beings. A writer, called Robert Sherard, deliberately visited the slums, dressed in worn-out clothes. He said that the degradation of the poor was aggravated by the treatment they received at the hands of those in authority.

> 'Because you are poor, because you are in receipt of gratuitous assistance, therefore you must be spoken to like a dog. [At a hospital] I went by mistake into the room where poor people are received for free treatment. A nurse here, asking me my business, spoke to me in such a tone that the surprise quite took my breath away.'
>
> The Leisure Hour, *1903*

In this chapter, you will see how Britain made the transition from a time when the State made only slight effort to ensure the welfare of the poor, weak, sick and unemployed, to a Welfare State which Labour politicians claimed, with some justice, looked after the individual 'from the cradle to the grave'.

THE FACTORY ACTS

One major source of hardship and poverty in the nineteenth century lay in the long working hours, dangerous working conditions and low wages paid, in factories, farms and workshops. But by 1850, a number of Factory Acts had already been passed, regulating working conditions for women and children in coal mines and textile mills.

In 1850, the latest of these Factory Acts specified a $10\frac{1}{2}$-hour working day in textile mills (then by far the biggest industry). Saturday afternoons were to be half holidays, in addition to Sundays, giving workers a $5\frac{1}{2}$-day week. This Act was followed by the Factory Act of 1864, which introduced safety regulations into dangerous industries (e.g. gunpowder factories). The Factories and Workshops Act followed in 1867. This applied the existing Factory Act regulations (for textile mills) to all factories. These were defined as any works with more than 50 employees. Smaller works with fewer than 50 employees were called workshops and escaped most of the effects of the factory regulations.

In 1874, Sir Richard Cross, Home Secretary in Disraeli's Conservative Government, introduced a new Factory Act which raised the minimum age for child workers to nine years and said that children between nine and fourteen could work only a half-day shift. He followed this up with an act in 1875 preventing the use of climbing boys by chimney sweeps.

In 1878, Cross introduced yet another Factory Act, this time bringing together all sixteen of the existing Factory Acts into one comprehensive Factory Act. In addition, his act raised the minimum working age to ten years and got rid of the distinction between factories and workshops based on their number of employees. In future, a factory was a place where mechanical power was used to manufacture products. In a workshop, hand labour only was used. This meant that many small factories had to obey the regulations set out in the Factory Act.

But it proved difficult to apply the regulations to the hundreds of thousands of workers who worked in small, backstreet premises, making clothes, matchboxes and other products in appalling working conditions, for low wages and long hours. This was called 'sweated labour' (see also page 51).

Sweated labour – a tailor and his family at work in a gloomy attic in Bethnal Green in 1863

---

1 *What work are the children doing in this Bethnal Green attic? Write a description of the working conditions of these children.*

2 *Why was it difficult to improve working conditions and control the hours worked by children in sweated-labour workshops?*

3 *Write a paragraph explaining what you understand by the term 'sweated labour'. How did it increase the amount of poverty in Britain in Victorian times?*

Gradually, the provisions of the Factory Act were applied to most industrial activities and the minimum working age was raised to eleven years in 1891 and to twelve years in 1901. In 1897, the Workmen's Compensation Act gave financial compensation to workers for injuries received at work. The 1901 Factory and Workshop Act brought the existing Factory Acts together, whilst the Trade Boards Act, in the same year, set up Trade Boards to try to establish minimum wages in the sweated-labour industries.

Further acts in the twentieth century reduced the length of the working week (for example, to an eight-hour shift in coal mines in 1908 and to a 48-hour week in factories for women and young persons in 1937). The Shop Act of 1911 introduced half-day early closing to protect the shop assistant. Other government measures have introduced health and safety regulations in places of employment (as in 1961, 1963 and 1974) and protected employees against unfair dismissal, through Industrial Tribunals (in the 1970s), and by making firms pay compulsory redundancy payments (since 1965).

POVERTY AND DISTRESS

The Extent of the Problem in Victorian and Edwardian Britain

Outcasts sleeping in sheds, The Illustrated London News, *13 October 1888*

When Charles Booth made his survey of the East End of London in the 1890s (see Chapter 6), he divided the 900,000 people in his survey into different categories according to their income and lifestyle. About 25 per cent were classified as being middle class or 'better paid workers'. About 40 per cent were 'artisans' with regular wages of between 22s and 30s [£1.10–£1.50] per week. The remainder, about 35 per cent of the survey population (over 300,000 people), were 'poor', 'very poor' or loafers and criminals. The 'poor' included those earning less than 22s a week and those with intermittent earnings from irregular jobs. Booth said 'their lives are an unending struggle and lack comfort'. Even this was an improvement on the lives of the 'very poor', who could only obtain casual work and were 'ill nourished and poorly clad'.

There were about 100,000 of the 'very poor' in Booth's sample, over 10 per cent of the population. Nationwide, the 'submerged tenth' (as 'General' William Booth, founder of the Salvation Army, called them) would have meant well over four million people on the poverty line in 1901.

Self-help

In Victorian times, people did not assume, as most people do today, that it was 'up to the Government' to do something about a problem. The spirit of *laissez-faire* still dominated the thinking of many people. If people were poor then it was their own fault. Some even thought it was God's punishment for being drunk or idle.

In 1859, Samuel Smiles published his popular best seller *Self-Help*, in which he claimed that thrift could help everyone, no matter what his or her circumstances were, to advance in the world. He said that:

> 'Help from without is often enfeebling [weakening] in its effects, but help from within invariably invigorates. Whatever is done for men or classes, to a certain extent takes away the stimulus and necessity of doing for themselves; and where men are subjected to over-guidance and over-government, the inevitable tendency is to render them comparatively helpless.'

To the middle classes, it was inconceivable that millions of people could live in appalling poverty at a time when Britain was the 'Workshop of the World' and the most powerful nation on earth. Some refused to believe that there was any problem at all.

Slumming

"SEEING'S BELIEVING." Punch, *1 December 1883*

1 *What was* Punch*'s answer to those who doubted the poverty to be found in the London slums at that time?*

2 *How did the* Punch *cartoonist depict a poor family and their problems in the cartoon below? What was the point of this cartoon? Who was being blamed for London's slums?*

"MAMMON'S RENTS"!!
HOUSE-JOBBER.—"NOW, THEN, MY MAN; WEEK'S HUP! CAN'T 'AVE A 'OME WITHOUT PAYIN' FOR IT, YER KNOW!"

Punch,
10 November 1883

This cartoon was printed shortly after the publication of the pamphlet *The Bitter Cry of Outcast London*, which shocked many Victorians with its descriptions of the misery of the poor, and the harshness of the landlords who derived rents from squalid and insanitary tenements. People were paid such low wages that they would have been unable to rent decent accommodation, even if it had been available to them.

Robert Sherard, in an article published in 1896, described the life and work of a slipper maker, who lived:

'in one of the worst parts of Leeds, namely in a courtyard which is never entered by the police except in couples. His cottage was one of the poorest I have yet seen, a two-roomed house with a cellar, looking out on a brick wall. There was little furniture in the downstairs room; the upstairs room served both as bedroom and workshop.'

Pearson's Magazine, *1896*

In the 1880s, when unemployment and social unrest were at their worst (see Chapter 7), it became fashionable to go 'slumming' – to visit the slums, ostensibly to 'do good', but often to satisfy curiosity. Slumming produced mixed blessings. In many cases it did, indeed, produce welcome benefits for the recipients of charity. Poor people in the countryside genuinely welcomed the hot soup or the hamper of provisions provided by the lady of the manor.

One social worker approved of slumming, since it drew the attention of the well-to-do to the appalling living conditions of the poor. Others were less charitable to the 'slummers', especially when they saw an advertisement in a London paper 'by a particular kind of tourist agency' offering 'to guide the curious amongst the worst slums of the metropolis'.

Drink

Some students of the slums attributed the problems of the poor to alcohol. Daniel Kirwan, an American visitor in the Whitechapel district, in 1870, said:

> 'Shouts and yells and curses came from drunken male brutes who passed us, and now and then a wretched looking outcast of a woman, hideous with filth and bloated with gin, stole like a shadow from some of the low public houses.'

There seems little reason to doubt the mass of evidence, like this, describing drunken brawls and helpless drunks. Drink offered the only release from the degradation and from the grinding, desperate poverty of the Victorian slums.

Scene in a London street on a Sunday morning, The Illustrated London News, *6 December 1856*

The solution to the problem of poverty, in the eyes of 'General' William Booth, was temperance. In his stirring book, *In Darkest England*, published in 1890, he described:

> 'A population sodden with drink, steeped in vice, eaten up by every social and physical malady, these are the denizens [inhabitants] of Darkest England.'

This is why children were encouraged to join the Band of Hope, and why, at the Labour Homes run by the Church Army, inmates had to 'sign' an agreement undertaking 'to obey cheerfully all the rules and regulations' and pledge themselves to be total abstainers.

Dr Barnardo's Homes

Whilst some social reformers tried to attack the roots of the problem, others attacked the effects of poverty. Dr Barnardo established homes for destitute children, those uncared for by society, many of them abandoned by their parents or orphaned at an early age.

In an interview in *The Strand Magazine*, in 1893, he said that he had first encountered the problem in the winter of 1866 when, as a student doctor, he asked a boy in rags where he lived.

> 'Don't live nowhere, sir!'
> 'Nowhere! Where's your father and mother?'
> 'Ain't got none, sir!'

Dr Barnardo said, 'For the first time in my life, I was brought face to face with the misery of outcast childhood.' He investigated further and found eleven lads sleeping on the roof of a building. With the help of Lord Shaftesbury, he opened and cleaned up a dilapidated house and filled it with 25 boys. By 1893, he had 50 homes and 5,000 children in care.

Church Missions

The churches also established missions in the poorer areas of London, in which committed Christians went to live in the East End to try to enlarge the opportunities available to the 'submerged tenth'. For instance, the University Settlement Movement helped to start a working-class club at Bethnal Green in the East End in 1884. You can get some idea of the work they did from this description written by the Revd James Adderley for *The English Illustrated Magazine* in 1893.

> 'It comprises, besides the club proper, a provident dispensary, a young men's institute, a mothers' club, a children's club, co-operative stores paying a good dividend and supplying goods to a thousand customers on a Saturday night, a library, a boot and shoe productive society, a cabinetmaker's productive society, a book shop, athletic, dramatic, debating, dancing societies, and a band.'

> **1** *Why were they called 'missions'? Why do you think these Christian workers thought of themselves as missionaries?*
>
> **2** *What was their 'mission'? What did they hope to achieve from clubs like the one described in the extract?*
>
> **3** *Why was the need for Dr Barnardo's Homes so pressing in late-Victorian Britain?*

The churches and various charities also established homes for the homeless. For example, the London Congregational Union had a home for destitute men in London's dockland. In 1900, you could see a long queue outside the hall every night at six o'clock – 'Five or six hundred in number, they form a strange string of humanity.' Every one of the 343 wooden bunks (long boxes on the floor) was occupied and all the applicants, whether admitted or not, were given 'a substantial lump of bread-and-butter'.

THE POOR LAW

The Poor Law System after 1834

Sketches at a casual ward, The Illustrated London News, *19 November 1887*

Despite the work of the various charities, churches and missions, legal responsibility for the care and welfare of the poor already rested with the Guardians of the Poor, elected for each district in Britain. But people had to apply for 'poor relief', as it was called, it was not automatically granted, and it was designed to offer only the minimum comfort necessary. As a result many paupers (very poor people) preferred to fend for themselves, sometimes through crime, or by scraping a living from what they could find on refuse tips, from begging, and from odd jobs.

Paupers who lived in the Union workhouses, which were run by unions of neighbouring Guardians of the Poor and financed out of local rates, were said to be in receipt of **indoor relief**. Those who received other benefits from the Guardians of the Poor, but were allowed to live in their own homes, were said to be in receipt of **outdoor relief**. The harshness of the workhouse system can be seen from the recommendations of the Poor Law Commission in 1834 (later incorporated in the Poor Law Amendment Act of 1834).

> 'That except as to medical attendance, all relief whatever to able-bodied persons or to their families, otherwise than in well-regulated work-houses, shall be declared unlawful. At least four classes are necessary: (1) The aged and really impotent; (2) The children; (3) The able-bodied females; (4) The able-bodied males.
>
> It appears to us that both the requisite classification and the requisite superintendence may be better obtained in separate buildings than under a single roof. Each class might thus receive appropriate treatment; the old might enjoy their indulgences without torment from the boisterous; the children be educated, and the able bodied subjected to such courses of labour and discipline as will repel the indolent and vicious.'
>
> Report of the Poor Law Commission, *1834*

In order to 'repel the indolent and vicious', these new workhouses were to provide living standards which would be below those enjoyed by 'independent labourers' outside the workhouse. The workhouse was to become the last resort of the pauper, not the first. This was known as the 'workhouse test', since it was assumed that anyone desperate enough to live in the workhouse was obviously in genuine need of relief.

1 *How did the Poor Law Commissioners seek to deter paupers from applying for poor relief?*

2 *What happened to a family of ten (grandmother, mother, able-bodied father, four small sons and three young daughters) if they sought poor relief after 1834?*

Penalties, such as putting the offenders on a diet of bread and water or making them wear special punishment clothes, could be imposed by the workhouse master for offences such as swearing, uttering insults or threats, uncleanliness, malingering, playing cards, misbehaving during prayers, or (if a man) entering the women's ward. More severe penalties (such as imprisonment) were imposed for major offences like drunkenness, acts of indecency, assault, mischievous damage and wilful disobedience.

At its worst, it was indeed a vindictive system, segregating pauper families by age and sex, and providing the minimum amount of food and shelter – there were cases of starvation and maltreatment of inmates – in return for strict discipline and hard labour. To the unemployed wage earner it was a living hell. But to many aged and infirm paupers, it provided a haven of sorts in which to end their days.

Dinner in the St Marylebone Workhouse in about 1900

In 1870, an American called Daniel Kirwan visited the Workhouse of St Martin-in-the-Fields (near Trafalgar Square). He said it looked 'like a vast prison, stern, gloomy, and frowning'. The men wore 'a grey, rough, shoddy uniform' and the women were in coarse cotton gowns and wearing white caps. 'They all had a vacant, listless look', he said, and greeted the Master of the Workhouse with the 'most servile of salutations', bowing and rising from their seats whenever he entered a room. The Master told Kirwan that many of them had the idea, 'once a pauper, always a pauper'.

To the aged who could look after themselves, the Poor Law system provided a meagre income. A writer explained how it worked to readers of *Harper's New Monthly Magazine*, in April 1883, when he described the prospects of an elderly farm worker.

'Probably he has not laid by anything; he has not even joined one of the 'benefit societies' common among labouring-men. In his old age he is entitled to relief from the parish: to accept it, says Mr Thompson [a farmer], is no disgrace. It is his share of the wealth of England, said Mr Ford [another farmer]. After the age of sixty, when in infirm health, the labourer draws about 3s [15p] weekly from the parish, and depends upon charity and the help of his children. Before the age of sixty out-door aid is not granted, but the poor must go to the workhouse, where the sexes are separated.'

1 What was a 'benefit society'? Was this an alternative to receiving relief from the parish?

2 What would you have said to a farmer who claimed that a pittance of 3s a week was your 'share of the wealth of England'?

3 Did Daniel Kirwan provide any evidence to contradict the view that it was 'no disgrace' to accept poor relief?

4 What effect did the Workhouse of St Martin-in-the-Fields appear to have on the inmates who lived there? Why?

5 Where was the nearest workhouse to your home in the nineteenth century? What is that building used for today?

In time the administration of the Poor Law system was softened, and the original rule about making relief conditional on the recipient entering the workhouse was ignored in many parts of the country, particularly in the industrial areas. Here, so many people applied for help at times of unemployment that they were able to get outdoor relief in return for labouring on a project, such as road building, street paving, or laying drains.

Ironically, despite separation from their families, children in the workhouse were often better cared for than those in the streets. The workhouse schools provided pauper children with the education that others did not get, as of right, until the 1870s and 1880s (see Chapter 9). The Unions also appointed medical officers to take care of their old, handicapped and sick 'inmates'. As a result, the health of the workhouse paupers was sometimes better looked after than that of the 'independent' poor outside the workhouse, who usually had to pay for medical care.

But since the workhouses had so many different people to look after – such as the mentally ill, the chronically sick, healthy infants and infirm octogenarians – they were almost always unable to cope effectively on the meagre funds provided out of local rates. In addition, they had to cope with the 'casuals' – travelling paupers who did not live in the parish but could be admitted to the workhouse for one or two nights' stay, provided they earned their keep.

The Royal Commission on the Poor Laws, 1905-9

In 1905, the Government appointed a Royal Commission to investigate the operation of the Poor Law system. But, in 1909, the Commission had to report a major disagreement between its members. This is why the *Report of the Royal Commission on the Poor Laws* was published in two parts: (a) the *Majority Report* (the recommendations of most of the members); and (b) the more radical *Minority Report* which was greatly influenced by the socialist reformers, Beatrice and Sidney Webb, who were prominent members of the Fabian Society (see page 227).

Both *Reports* had much in common but the *Majority Report* placed greater emphasis on the need to make use of the voluntary organisations, which had done good work, as you have seen, in providing homes for the homeless. They wanted to abolish the 643 Boards of Guardians and put responsibility for the Poor Law in the hands of Public Assistance Committees.

The *Minority Report* deplored the fact that the doles and allowances provided under the system of outdoor relief were grossly inadequate. They wanted a 'national minimum of civilised life', together with a well-funded system of specialised care for children, the sick, the handicapped and the elderly, to be administered by the county councils and the county borough councils.

Both *Reports* showed that the Poor Law system had changed since the harsh days of 1834. One chairman of a London Union even told the Commission that there was nothing to deter paupers from entering the workhouses in his district. 'There is no test of work and inmates are better off and more comfortable than outside!' In many rural workhouses, almost all the inmates were of retirement age. Many Unions had built infirmaries, where the standard of care and treatment was said, by one doctor, to be 'higher than in the general hospitals'. But there were also devastating criticisms. In particular, the *Minority Report* of the Commission reported that however 'sumptuous or squalid' the workhouse:

> 'these institutions have a depressing, degrading, and positively injurious effect on the character of all classes of their inmates, tending to unfit them for the life of respectable and independent citizenship.
> That the institution is everywhere abhorred by the respectable poor, and that, in our judgment, the continued incarceration within its walls of the non-able-bodied or dependent poor, who are admittedly incapable of earning an independent livelihood, cannot be justified.'

---

1 *Quote evidence from the sources in this chapter to support these criticisms of the workhouse system.*

2 *Have the problems of the poor been adequately solved in modern Britain?*

Other defects criticised by the Commission included the lack of uniformity from one part of the country to another, the apathy of many electors when electing Guardians of the Poor, and the fact that there seemed to be little co-operation between the charities and the Boards of Guardians. In particular, they deplored the rising cost of the service which did not appear to correspond to any increase in its quality.

In the end, only two of the main recommendations of the Commission (labour exchanges and national insurance) were actually implemented by the Liberal Government, despite the fact that John Burns, the once-fiery socialist agitator of the 1880s was President of the Local Government Board which received the *Report*. He had fallen out with the socialists and bitterly opposed the proposals to break up the Poor Law system.

LIBERAL REFORMS, 1906–14

In 1906, however, the Liberal Government did help to lay the foundations of the modern Welfare State with a number of major social reforms.

1. Labour Exchanges

Registering the unemployed at the Chelsea registration office in 1887

When this picture was published by *The Illustrated London News* on 17 December 1887, the accompanying text read as follows.

'The opening of registration offices for the unemployed workmen of various trades, and for labourers willing to do any simple work, in different quarters of London, has obtained general approval. Several ladies have volunteered to act as clerks or registrars during certain hours of the day; and rooms have been assigned for the purpose, in some instances, at the parish Vestry-Halls, or in other public buildings.'

But it was not until September 1909, that Parliament finally approved 'An Act to provide for the establishment of Labour Exchanges', making it easier for the unemployed to get information about vacancies and for people to move from district to district in search of work. In 1919, they were renamed Employment Exchanges.

---

1 *Why do you think it took Parliament twenty-one years to copy this simple voluntary idea to help the unemployed find jobs?*
2 *What is its modern equivalent called?*

---

2. National Insurance

In 1911, David Lloyd George introduced a major government national insurance scheme which initially aroused the anger and opposition of the privately run friendly societies and big insurance companies. In a speech in the House of Commons, he told MPs that the reason why a large number of working-class people did not insure against unemployment and ill health was because they could not afford to pay the premiums. Their wages were too low to insure themselves against the three most important risks – death, sickness and unemployment.

Only half the working class, at that time, had any health insurance and only one in ten could collect benefit when unemployed. Moreover, even when they did have an insurance policy, they often had to abandon it when they were sick or unemployed, since they could no longer afford the premiums then. Lloyd George said that new legislation was needed: 'There is a real need for some system which would aid workmen over these difficulties.' This is why he proposed to bring in:

'An Act to provide for Insurance against Loss of Health and for the Prevention and Cure of Sickness and for Insurance against Unemployment.'

The act was in two parts. The first part made provision for health insurance and was sponsored by Lloyd George. The second part made provision for unemployment insurance and was sponsored by Winston Churchill and, later, by Sydney Buxton.

Part I: Health Insurance

This part of the scheme was strongly opposed by doctors and by many Conservatives. Yet it was by no means comprehensive in its coverage. For instance, it did not apply to the self-employed, to the non-employed (e.g. wives of insured workers), to farm workers or domestic servants (they had to wait until 1936), to those already contributing to existing schemes run by private insurance companies, or to people earning more than £160 a year (raised to £250 after 1920). And it did not apply to women workers until 1920.

The act said that health insurance benefits were to be paid out of funds to which each week the employer (3d) and employee (4d) contributed seven-ninths and the government (2d) the remaining two-ninths. In 1918, the Ministry of Health was established to oversee the provisions of the act.

Benefits included free medical treatment and medicines, treatment in a sanatorium for tuberculosis and other diseases, sickness benefit of 10s [50p] a week for up to six months when absent from work, and disablement benefit if absent from work for more than six months. For many years afterwards, workers who were off work through sickness or ill health, told enquirers they were 'on the Lloyd George'!

Part II: Unemployment Insurance

Under the provisions of Part II of the National Insurance Act, a scheme of compulsory insurance was brought in, but only to help workers in those trades which were particularly subject to persistent seasonal unemployment. Insurance benefits were to be paid out of funds to which each week the employer ($2\frac{1}{2}$d) and employee ($2\frac{1}{2}$d) contributed three-quarters and the government the remainder.

The standard unemployment benefit of 7s [35p] a week could be paid for a maximum of fifteen weeks in any one year. But workmen had to prove, among other things, that they (a) were unemployed, (b) were capable of working, (c) were not on strike or involved in an industrial dispute, (d) had worked in 'an insured trade' for at least six months in the previous five years, (e) had paid five weekly contributions for each week's unemployment benefit drawn from the fund.

At first, the 'insured trades' covered by the act were restricted to the four million casual or semi-permanent workers in the building and construction, ship-building, mechanical engineering, iron founding, vehicle manufacturing and sawmilling industries. In 1920, the scheme was extended to cover another eight million workers (but not yet servants or farm workers). Many subsequent National Insurance Acts modified the scheme in the light of new developments in trade and industry and as unemployment rose or fell.

> 1 What were the main deficiencies of the 1911 National Insurance Act, Parts I and II?
>
> 2 In what respects was it a notable social reform?
>
> 3 Why do you think many people opposed the act? What possible objections could they have had to its provisions?

3. Children

Another major series of social reforms provided services and protection for children. In 1906, the local education authorities were given the power to provide subsidised school meals out of the rates and give free meals to poor children (see page 285). In 1907, the school medical service was founded, providing for regular health inspections in schools. In 1908, the Children's Act (called the 'Children's Charter') increased:

> 'the powers of societies for the prevention of cruelty. It deals with vagrant children, with homes for destitute children. It forbids the sale of cigarettes to persons under sixteen years of age and prohibits them from smoking them. Juvenile offenders are to be separated from adult criminals in separate courts and places of detention.'
>
> The Sphere, *29 February 1908*

It also prevented children entering public houses and prohibited the imprisonment of children under the age of fourteen.

4. Old-age Pensions

The question of old-age pensions and national insurance had been debated in Britain for over 25 years. Contributors to *Cassell's Magazine*, in 1883, debated the pros and cons of the topic 'Should National Insurance against Pauperism be made compulsory?'. As you have seen, many of the paupers in the workhouses and those receiving outdoor relief were old people. Without a State retirement pension they had to throw themselves on the mercy of the Guardians of the Poor.

The subject was topical, in 1883, because Bismarck had just introduced a revolutionary new compulsory sickness insurance scheme in Germany, to be followed by an accident insurance scheme in 1884 and an old-age pension scheme in 1889. British politicians examined them with interest and recommended them for Britain, but nothing was done about it until 1908.

At last, in 1908, the Old Age Pensions Act was passed. From 1 January 1909, old people were paid a weekly pension of 5s [25p] a week, provided they were British, over 70 years of age, resident in the United Kingdom, had not been in prison for ten years, were not already in receipt of poor relief and their annual

"SOMETHING LARGE
AND ROUND."

A Punch *cartoon published in 1899, after a committee of the House of Commons had reported in favour of old-age pensions of at least five shillings a week to needy persons over 65, the cost to be borne by the Exchequer and the local rates.*

income from all other sources did not exceed £21. However, if their income was above £21 a year the level of pension was reduced, and they got nothing at all if it was more than £31 10s [£31.50].

In the debate on the bill in the House of Commons, Will Crooks, the Labour Member for Woolwich, claimed 'these pensions as a right', as the first 'instalment to bring decency and comfort to our aged men and women'. He argued that small as they were, the new 'very old-age pensions' would give old people liberty, instead of forcing them to leave their homes to go into the workhouse.

'When the Old Age Pensions began, life was transformed for such aged cottagers. They were relieved of anxiety. They were suddenly rich. Independent for life! At first when they went down to the Post Office to draw it, tears of gratitude would run down the cheeks of some, and they would say as they picked up their money, "God bless that Lord George".'

Flora Thompson, Lark Rise to Candleford, *1939*

1   Write a paragraph to explain why the introduction of old-age pensions in 1909 had such an effect on old people. Quote evidence from some of the other sources and illustrations in this chapter to support your answer.

2   What was Will Crooks getting at when he referred to the new 'very old-age' pensions? How did the 1908 act differ from the proposals made in 1899?

3   In what respects was the old-age pension of 1909 an advance on the existing system of making provision for the elderly? What was its greatest virtue in the eyes of many proud pensioners?

Opposition to Social Reform

This flood of social reforms was not always well received, even by people who were basically sympathetic to the causes espoused by Lloyd George.

Some critics complained of the cost, others that the State was doing too much for the working class family – educating and feeding their children free of charge, paying them a pension in old age, and helping to insure them against sickness and unemployment.

What was the point of this cartoon, published in Punch *in 1912?*

"OLIVER ASKS FOR" LESS.

JOHN BULL (*fed up*). "PLEASE, SIR, NEED I
HAVE QUITE SO MANY GOOD THINGS?"
MR. LLOYD GEORGE. "YES, YOU MUST; AND
THERE'S MORE TO COME."

David Lloyd George (1863–1945)

David Lloyd George

David Lloyd George was the leading force behind the social reforms of the Liberal Government.

As Chancellor of the Exchequer from 1908 to 1915, he controlled the purse strings. As you saw in Chapter 4, it was his Budget of 1909 which caused a constitutional crisis, when it was rejected by the House of Lords. Lloyd George proposed to finance the new social reforms, such as old-age pensions and national insurance, by imposing extra taxes on the rich.

Later, in 1916, he became Prime Minister and led Britain to victory in the First World War. Remarkably, he continued to sit as an MP until 1945.

SOCIAL REFORM IN THE 1920s AND 1930s

Unemployment

'A Sure Index of Unemployment: The Filling Up of the London Lodging-House', The Graphic, 22 January 1921

As you saw in earlier chapters, the period of the 1920s and 1930s was one of widespread unemployment in Britain. Poverty left its mark on many families living in the North at that time, despite the unemployment-insurance scheme introduced by the Liberal Government in 1911.

At first conditions looked bright for the future and the Government extended the national insurance scheme to cover three times as many workers as those originally insured in 1911. All those earning up to £260 a year were now covered, apart from the self-employed, farm workers, domestic servants and civil servants. In addition, benefit was raised to 15s [75p] per week. In 1921, a new concession was made when benefit for a married man was increased by 5s [25p] for a wife and 1s [5p] for each child. In 1922, the period of payment was extended to 26 weeks in a year and by 1928, the benefits payable had risen to 17s [85p] a week.

But even this was inadequate to cope with the problems created by long-term unemployment. With over a million people unemployed in the 1920s, something had to be done to help those out of work for more than 26 weeks. This is why, in 1924, the Ministry of Labour was given the discretion to pay benefit to the unemployed beyond the maximum period, if:

> 'having regard to all the circumstances it is expedient in the public interest that benefit should be allowed.'

> **1** *What other help could an unemployed worker seek when out of work for over 26 weeks, if refused this extra benefit by the officials of the Ministry of Labour?*

Unemployment Assistance Board

By 1931, mounting unemployment had drained the national insurance scheme of funds, and contributions were failing to meet the cost of benefits paid out. In the financial crisis of 1931 (see page 146), pressure was put on the Labour Government to cut the level of unemployment benefit. Accordingly, the new National Government reduced the rate of unemployment benefit by 10 per cent – from 17s [85p] to 15s 3d [76p] a week for the maximum period of six months.

After that time, applicants had to apply for Public Assistance to the local Public Assistance Committees which had replaced the Boards of Guardians (see below). This extra financial help was called the 'dole' and payments were made dependent on the means test. This meant that applicants stood to lose benefit if they had any other income, any savings, or if any other members of their family had a job.

One man said that when you applied for the dole, officials came to the house, looking to see if there were any tell-tale luxuries, such as a wireless set. An unemployed worker in the Potteries refused to eat a thing on Christmas Day, simply because the chicken, jellies and ham had been supplied by his daughters who did have jobs. Because they brought money into the house, he was given dole of only 8s [40p] a week.

> **1** *Why did trade unionists say the means test 'penalised thrift'?*
> **2** *Why did it cause families to break up (e.g. grown-up sons and daughters leaving the home of their unemployed parents)? Why was it unfair?*

In 1934, the Unemployment Assistance Board was set up to administer the scheme on a uniform national basis, instead of allowing it to vary according to the generosity of the local authorities who ran the scheme. In future all unemployment assistance after six months was paid out of government funds, not local rates. Unemployment benefit was also raised at the same time to its 1931 level.

The hardships endured by the unemployed were vividly shown in January 1939, when *Picture Post* printed an illustrated article by Sidney Jacobson, describing a typical day in the life of a painter's labourer who had been unemployed for three years. Photographs showed Alfred Smith at the Labour Exchange queuing for half an hour to draw £2 7s 6d [£2.38] a week, looking for jobs in the reading room at the Public Library and coming home in the evening to a small, three-roomed basement for which he paid 14s 6d [73p] rent. Breakfast and supper consisted of tea or cocoa, bread and margarine, whilst dinner was 'stew or boiled fish, potatoes, bread, tea'. A photograph showed him tramping London's streets in the fog.

> 'The Picture Of Our Time: Alone, Walking for Miles, Trying to Find a Job. He is 35. He has strength, intelligence, humour. He has a wife and children whom he loves. He should be in the prime of his life. But he is unemployed. He lives on the charity of the State, which cannot find him work. But he wants to work, to be a man, not a number on a Ministry of Labour card. He is one of nearly 2,000,000.'

---

1 *How did the Second World War solve the problem of unemployment for the time being?*

2 *What remedies could the National Government have resorted to, between 1931 to 1939, to try to alleviate the problem of unemployment?*

Widows', Orphans' and Old Age Contributory Pensions Act of 1925

This social reform was introduced by the Conservative Government to provide contributory pensions of 10s [50p] a week for widows, plus 5s [25p] for the first child and 3s [15p] for each succeeding child. Orphans were to receive 7s 6d [38p] a week. The act also lowered the qualifying age for old-age pensions to 65 years, but required future pensioners and their employers to contribute 9d [4p] a week. In return they got their contributory pension as a right, without any reduction for other income.

The Abolition of the Poor Law System

In the early 1920s, the high rate of unemployment in many districts made it almost impossible for the Boards of Guardians to cope with the greatly increased demand for outdoor relief. Nationally, the cost of poor relief increased by three times between 1913 and 1925. Meanwhile, the antiquated workhouse system was obviously inadequate to meet the higher standard of care demanded at a time when gas, electricity, cars, radios and domestic appliances were becoming commonplace. Moreover, no workhouse could be expected to cater equally effectively for babies, pensioners, the handicapped, the mentally ill, the unemployed, or even the able-bodied layabouts.

In March 1929, the Conservative Government abolished the Boards of Guardians and transferred their functions to the county and county borough councils – the proposal made twenty years earlier by Beatrice Webb in the *Minority Report* of the Poor Law Commission of 1909. From 1 April 1930, the Poor Law became Public Assistance and a Public Assistance Officer and Committee was appointed in every county authority to administer the scheme. The term 'pauper' disappeared and with it the stigma of 'being on the parish'.

The Effects of the Social Reforms of the 1920s and 1930s

From 1934 onwards, school children were able enjoy a daily glass of milk at school at a subsidised cost of a halfpenny (poor children got it free). For the million children whose parents were unemployed, this bonus supplied some of the proteins, vitamins and calories which were otherwise missing from their diet. By 1939, maternity care in Britain had also been greatly improved, with a comprehensive system of antenatal clinics, midwives and welfare centres.

Subsidised milk at school in 1934

Surprisingly, despite the apparently grudging nature of many of the benefits paid to the unemployed, total expenditure on the social services rose to nearly £500 million by 1939, compared with only £63 million in 1910. In addition, this was a period of deflation when prices fell sharply (see page 152). This meant that the 15s unemployment benefit of 1920, which had risen to 17s by 1935, bought twice as much food and clothing fifteen years later. Britain was not yet a Welfare State, but it was already making hesitant steps in that direction when war broke out in 1939.

By 1936, there was evidence (from Seebohm Rowntree), that in York, poverty had been cut by 50 per cent since his earlier study at the start of the century (see page 186). People with jobs were earning higher wages at a time of falling prices, local-authority housing was much more widely available than it had been in 1900, families were smaller (see Chapter 5) and living standards were correspondingly higher. Cumulatively, the social reforms of the first 40 years of the twentieth century made a significant impact on the everyday lives of the people of Britain, however slight the individual improvements and reforms may have seemed at the time.

The Impact of the Second World War

During the war, rationing (which shared food and clothing equally between rich and poor) and full employment helped to restore the health and confidence of the working classes.

It is estimated that, in 1939, half the population may have suffered from some form of malnutrition. During the war they were much healthier. Government measures enabled free orange juice and Vitamin A and D tablets to be supplied to pregnant mothers and free milk and cod-liver oil to children. Together with rationing (which cut down the number of cigarettes smoked and the amount of butter, animal fat, meat and sugar in the diet), they played a major part in helping people to stay healthy, despite the war. In 1941, the means test was abolished, partly because full employment during the war made it unnecessary.

These wartime improvements convinced people that there could be no return to the Depression and means test of the 1930s, once the war was over. Even at the height of the fighting, when a successful conclusion to the war could not be guaranteed, there were moves by the wartime Government to set in motion plans for reconstruction when peace was declared.

THE WELFARE STATE, 1942–86

The *Beveridge Report*

In June 1941, Sir William Beveridge was appointed chairman of a special committee set up by the wartime Government to make a survey of the existing social-insurance schemes. His committee was asked to make recommendations which could be implemented when the Second World War was over. When the *Beveridge Report* was published in 1942, it said:

> 'Want is one only of five giants on the road of reconstruction and in some ways the easiest to attack. The others are Disease, Ignorance, Squalor and Idleness.'

The committee recommended a 'Plan for Social Security' – a system of national insurance in which benefits would be earned 'as of right and without means test' in return for regular weekly contributions paid into the scheme. They envisaged the payment of children's allowances, maternity grants, unlimited unemployment benefit, retirement and widows' pensions, comprehensive free medical treatment and funeral expenses. Above all they aimed to 'abolish want' by guaranteeing every citizen sufficient income to 'meet his responsibilities'.

1 What were the five 'giants'? How are they tackled by the Government, local councils and other official bodies today?
2 How were they tackled by the Victorians in about 1880?

The *Beveridge Report* got a mixed reception from many Conservatives. According to Tom Hopkinson, in an article in *Picture Post* on 6 March 1943, some of its opponents:

> 'spoke as though the basis of the Report were an attempt to cadge money off the rich on behalf of the not entirely deserving poor.'

Hopkinson said that the Government's reluctance to implement the *Report* in full was a sign that they still viewed the Britain of tomorrow as being a 'We' and a 'They'. But in 1944, the wartime Churchill Government took action to eradicate 'ignorance' (see page 287) and did something about 'disease', when it announced plans for a National Health Service in 1944. In addition, the Conservative caretaker Government, which ran the country immediately before the general election, passed the Family Allowances Act in June 1945, which provided for the payment of a child allowance of five shillings [25p] a week for each child other than the eldest, up to school-leaving age or up to the age of sixteen (if still at school). Despite this, the electorate returned a Labour Government with a large majority and a clear mandate to build a Welfare State on the lines suggested in the *Beveridge Report*.

The National Health Service

The National Health Service (NHS) was the 'baby' of Aneurin Bevan, Minister of Health in the new Labour Government.

Aneurin Bevan (1897–1960)

Aneurin Bevan

Aneurin Bevan was a Welsh MP, one of thirteen children of a Welsh miner, and a miner himself at the age of thirteen. He took an early interest in the trade union movement and played an active part in the General Strike of 1926 as leader of the Welsh miners.

He became a Labour Cabinet minister in 1945. After his successful introduction of the National Health Service he became Minister of Labour, but he resigned in 1951, when prescription charges were brought in. As the leader of the 'Bevanite' wing of the Labour party, he was a thorn in the side of the Labour party leadership in the 1950s.

Bevan had to face the determined opposition of many doctors and surgeons, opposed to State interference in medicine. Many feared they would be forced to give up their lucrative private practices and become government medical officials at the beck and call of the Ministry of Health. But their fears proved groundless. Those who wished to, could retain their private patients, as well as the NHS patients registered with them under the National Health Service system.

The National Health Act, which came into force in 1948, replaced the system initiated by Lloyd George, which had only covered half the existing population and made no provision for families or for the self-employed. The new NHS boasted a truly comprehensive service, embracing dentists and opticians as well as doctors, hospitals and surgeons. It immediately created a huge surge in demand for free spectacles, teeth, minor surgical operations, drugs, medicines and appliances. Twice as many people went to the dentist, for instance, and twice as many prescriptions were issued, after the NHS came into being in 1948.

In its initial stages, the NHS was the envy of the world. The improvements in medical care were clear for all to see, most noticeably in the maternity wards, where the infantile mortality rate fell sharply (as you saw on page 163). Older people benefited enormously from better-fitting teeth, the use of good-quality spectacles and effective hearing aids, and the results of many minor operations which they would otherwise have been unable to afford.

Nonetheless there was a price to pay. The NHS cost much more than had originally been anticipated and, since 1948, this cost has risen sharply to the alarm of successive governments. The National Health Act originally laid down that the services provided were to be free, except in certain cases where charges might be levied. But, in 1951, a political storm broke when the Labour Government introduced some charges to recoup part of the cost of the NHS.

The scope of the National Health Service has been further enlarged over the years, such as when the Abortion and Family Planning Acts were passed in 1967. Numerous attempts have also been made to make the system more efficient. There was a major reorganisation in 1973 and, in 1985, an attempt to run the NHS on business lines.

National Insurance

The second major social reform of the 1945–50 Labour Government, was the National Insurance Act of 1946, which greatly extended the existing system of national insurance by making it compulsory for everyone. In future, unemployment, disablement, sickness and maternity benefits, widows' and orphans' pensions, old-age pensions at 60 for women and 65 for men, family allowances and funeral grants would be paid.

People contributed to the new national insurance scheme, according to whether they were (a) employed, (b) self-employed, or (c) not employed. Half the cost was met by the government, two-tenths by employees and three-tenths by employers. The act was welcomed by all parties and by the general public, since it eliminated many of the injustices of the pre-war schemes.

National Assistance

In order to eradicate 'Want' by guaranteeing a basic minimum income to everyone (see page 267), the Labour Government passed the National Assistance Act in 1948, setting up the National Assistance Board, which had the power to make assistance grants to those in need – but not to workers involved in industrial disputes. The act also laid down that all local authorities were required to provide residential accommodaton for the aged and the handicapped, and to make temporary accommodation available for those who were homeless and in urgent need.

The Times said that the 'last lingering taint of "pauperism"' had disappeared with this act and that the National Assistance Board was now 'the citizen's last defence against destitution'. But it also gave a warning, asking whether the people of Britain could reap the benefits of the Welfare State 'while avoiding the perils of a Santa Claus State'.

The National Assistance Act guaranteed that, in future, every person living in the United Kingdom would be certain of a minimum basic income, no matter what their circumstances – unemployed, unemployable, sick or handicapped. In theory, there need never be any reason for scenes of poverty on the scale which disgraced the Britain of the 1930s or late nineteenth century.

The Welfare State since 1951

But, despite all the hopes and aspirations of the enthusiastic supporters of the Welfare State ideal, it was still possible to see real poverty in many urban areas in the 1980s – perhaps not on the scale of the 1930s, but certainly on a level sufficient to bring into question the effectiveness of the social security system as a whole. Beveridge's five 'giants' were still much in evidence, despite the massive expenditure on the Welfare State.

In 1986, over 3 million people were in receipt of unemployment benefit and a further 15 per cent of the population were entitled to a retirement pension. When the national-insurance scheme was originally envisaged by Beveridge in 1942, and implemented by the Labour party in 1945, there was little idea, that in a future British society, a decreasing proportion of wage earners would have to meet the huge cost imposed by rising numbers of pensioners and of people entitled to benefit. By 1980, the social services were said to be absorbing 25 per cent of the country's income.

Since 1950 there have been many amendments and adjustments to the National Health, Insurance and Assistance Acts of the 1940s. The introduction of a system of graduated pensions, in 1961, and of earnings-related supplements, in 1966, both modified the provisions of the National Insurance Act. At frequent intervals, too, the rates of contribution have been altered, the scope and extent of benefits has been narrowed or widened, and every year the benefits have generally (though not always) been increased roughly in line with inflation.

---

1 *Do you think Britain has successfully avoided becoming a 'Santa Claus State'?*

2 *What do your older friends and relatives think have been the main benefits and effects of the National Health Service and the systems of national assistance and national insurance since 1948? Write down their comments and use them to write a short oral history of the Welfare State.*

FURTHER QUESTIONS AND EXERCISES

Punch, *22 January 1859*

THE HOMELESS POOR.

1 *Who were THE HOMELESS POOR? What provision was made for their welfare in Britain in 1859? Why did 'General' William Booth, founder of the Salvation Army, call the very poor the 'submerged tenth'?*

2 *Which of the different social-welfare reforms, discussed in this chapter, do you think was the most important? Give reasons for your answer.*

3 *Imagine you are a journalist and have dressed as a tramp in order to spend a night in an Edwardian workhouse. Write a vivid account of your stay in the workhouse.*

4 *How did the Liberal Government help children, the elderly, the ill and the unemployed between 1906 and 1914?*

5 *Explain the contribution of each of the following to the creation and development of the Welfare State:*

   (a) the Poor Law Amendment Act of 1834

   (b) the Royal Commission on the Poor Law in 1909

   (c) the Beveridge Report of 1942

   (d) the National Assistance Act of 1948.

Small Eastendian. "'ELLO! *'ERE'S* A MASHER! LOOK AT 'IS COLLAR AN' 'AT!"

Contemporary cartoon from Punch

6 *What does this cartoon depict? Write a detailed paragraph explaining the background to the cartoon. In which year do you think the picture might have been drawn?*

7 *Explain clearly what was meant by each of the following: (a) the means test, (b) outdoor and indoor relief, (c) a pauper.*

8 *Write a short essay on the Welfare State. Explain what it is, how it began and how it developed. What was the contribution to the modern Welfare State of (a) the 1906–14 Liberal governments, (b) the 1918–39 inter-war governments?*

9 *What were the main proposals outlined in the* Beveridge Report*? How many of them were implemented, and in what form, by the Labour Government of 1945–51?*

10 *In the 1940s, socialists in Britain were extremely proud of the Welfare State they had helped to create. In the 1980s there was considerable disillusionment. Why? What were the virtues and faults of the post-war Welfare State?*

Chapter Nine

Education

INTRODUCTION

THE "MODEL" SCHOOL.

Punch, *4 November 1882 – Put THREEPENCE in this box, and the model will work. 'Works wonderfully well, eh?' 'Y-e-s. But I think you'll have to put in another penny or two, if you want to keep it going.'*

Twenty years after this cartoon was published, readers of *The Leisure Hour*, put forward their own suggestions for improving education.

> 'The present is a momentous time in our national history; our commercial supremacy is in danger, and those countries we have most to fear are splendidly equipped in elementary, secondary and tertiary education. A country which can spend so much on war and armaments, upon drink and sport, will surely not begrudge paying for an adequate and efficient system of national education!'
>
> *George Adsitt,* The Leisure Hour, *1902*

1 *What was the point of the* Punch *cartoon in 1882?*

2 *How was 'our commercial supremacy' in danger in 1902?*

3 *What did George Adsitt think was one of the causes of that decline?*

4 *Do these sources have any relevance to the position of schools and education today?*

How to finance elementary and secondary education in Britain has been one of the major political issues ever since the middle years of the nineteenth century. In this chapter you will see that the problem lay partly in the fact that, until 1870, Parliament had been content to allow the churches to provide elementary education for the nation's children. Education became compulsory everywhere in Britain only after 1880, and free only after 1891.

Yet other nations were developing effective systems of secondary and technical education as well, recognising that the future lay in the hands of an educated and skilled working class. It was not until 1902 that Parliament passed an Education Act providing secondary education, of a sort, for the working classes; and not until 1944 that the Butler Education Act offered promise that the educational system could provide equal opportunities for all.

STATE-AIDED EDUCATION IN BRITAIN IN THE NINETEENTH CENTURY

In 1850, most elementary schools were run by the churches, either the British and Foreign School Society (which was Nonconformist) or the National Society (which was Anglican). They were staffed by teachers and pupil-teachers (aged thirteen to eighteeen years) who were directly paid a yearly fee by the government, and also by the school managers paid out of charitable contributions and fees paid by the children (a few pennies a week).

The Newcastle Commission and the Revised Code

Government Inspector testing pupils, from a contemporary cartoon in Punch

In 1861, the Newcastle Commission, after investigating whether government expenditure on education was being well spent, recommended a system of payment by results. Robert Lowe, the minister responsible, introduced the Revised Code of 1862 with the promise, 'If it is not cheap, it shall be efficient; if it is not efficient, it shall be cheap'.

In future, the government grant would be made only after an annual inspection of the children of each school to see if they had made sufficient progress. After 1862, the government grant was paid in a lump sum to the school managers. They received 6s 6d [33p] for each child under six years, provided the Inspector was satisfied with the children's performance. Older children were divided into Standards I to VI and at each Standard were tested in reading, writing and arithmetic, the 'three Rs'. In this way each child could obtain a maximum of three passes. The school was paid 2s 8d [13p] per child for each pass, plus 4s [20p] if the attendance of the child had been satisfactory – making a maximum grant of 12s [60p] per child.

The test for Standard III, for example, specified that scholars passing this examination had to read a short paragraph from 'an elementary reading book used in the school', write out a sentence from the same paragraph (as it was dictated) and do a basic sum. The defects were obvious. Teachers trained children hard to pass the three Rs, ignoring other subjects such as history, geography, art, music and science. Some children were made to learn their reading books off by heart! They were bullied into coming to school on the day of the inspection, even though ill in bed. False entries were even made in attendance registers and there was sometimes cheating during the inspection. The Code was later amended, in 1867 and 1875, to widen the number of subjects tested to include history, geography and practical subjects, but, even so, it led to dull, boring, repetitive teaching. From the point of view of the Treasury, however, the Revised Code was highly successful. The government grant fell by about £175,000 in three years and there was a marked improvement in attendance.

The 1870 Education Act

During the 1860s, pressure for a national system of compulsory education came from many organisations. The National Education Union (Anglican) wanted Church of England teaching to continue. But the Birmingham Education League and other Nonconformist groups wanted undenominational education for all children, i.e. education taught in such a way that it could not be said to follow the creed of a particular Church. One of their spokesmen, Joseph Chamberlain (see page 143), said in 1869 that he, and other Nonconformists, wanted a national system of education which would be both free and compulsory.

The problem was that, although the Government sought to provide school places for every child – if necessary paid for out of local rates – it nevertheless wanted to use as many of the existing voluntary schools as possible. Nonconformists, however, objected to this method of subsidising the Church of England schools, which outnumbered the other Church schools. Equally, the

Church of England was opposed to the setting up of schools which would not be able to teach religious instruction according to the dictates of the Established Church. The bickering between the two sides over the role of religious education in schooling delayed the passing of the Education Bill.

"OBSTRUCTIVES."

MR. PUNCH (*to* BULL A1). "YES, IT'S ALL VERY WELL TO SAY, 'GO TO SCHOOL!' HOW ARE THEY TO GO TO SCHOOL WITH THOSE PEOPLE QUARRELLING IN THE DOORWAY? WHY DON'T YOU MAKE 'EM 'MOVE ON'?"

Punch, *2 July 1870*

> **1** *What was the point of this cartoon? Who were the people quarrelling in the doorway?*
>
> **2** *What do you think was the attitude of* Punch *and of many people in Britain to the quarrel between the Churches?*

W. E. Forster, the minister in charge of education in Gladstone's Liberal Government, introduced the new Elementary Education Bill, in 1870, saying that there were two main principles running through it. These were (a) 'that there shall be efficient schools everywhere throughout the kingdom', and (b) that there would be 'compulsory provision of such schools if and where needed, but not unless proved to be needed'. In other words, the existing British and Foreign Schools and the National Schools would continue to provide the bulk of the nation's education, provided they were good enough. If not, and in areas where there were no existing schools, then new ones would have to be built. The main points of the Education Act of 1870 were as follows.

- England and Wales were divided into 2,500 school districts.

- The Churches were given six months to decide whether they wanted to build new schools in the areas which needed them.

- Failing this, a School Board had to be elected by local people (both men and women), charged with the duty of building new schools, financed out of the rates.

- The old system of financing the schools would continue with children paying up to 9d [4p] a week in fees and the government paying grants, now increased but still subject to the requirements of the Revised Code.

- School Boards could provide free education for poor children out of the rates. In this way some ratepayers helped to subsidise the Church schools, to the annoyance of the Nonconformists.

- School Boards (but **only** School Boards) could make education compulsory for all pupils of 'not less than five years nor more than thirteen years' in their areas, if they wished. In London and in other cities, School Boards did make elementary education compulsory and provided it free of charge for poor children. The London School Board made attendance at school compulsory for all children between the ages of five and thirteen, but exempted pupils over ten if they passed Standard V and had to go to work to support their parents.

In this picture from The Illustrated London News *for 9 September 1871, London School Board officials are shown 'capturing truants' at 2.40 a.m.*

- School Boards could, if they wished, decide against religious instruction in the new rate-supported Board Schools. But if they went ahead, then they were required to see that religious instruction was undenominational. The act was amended by the adoption of a clause suggested by William Cowper-Temple, 'No religious catechism or religious formulary, which is distinctive of any particular denomination shall be taught in the school.'

- The voluntary Church schools could continue to provide an education according to the dictates of a particular religious denomination, but they had to allow children from other religious denominations living in the area to attend the school. A conscience clause gave parents the right to opt out of religious education.

The 1870 Education Act was a great milestone in social welfare, since for the first time it created a State system of education. In 1841 only half the women of the country could sign the marriage register. By 1883, this proportion had risen to 84 per cent. But there were defects as well as merits in the act.

> 'In regard to the compulsory attendance of children at school, the provisions of the bill are tentative and timid. The principle of direct compulsion is admitted; but it is to be applied only in those districts in which a school Board exists, and not necessarily even in them.'
>
> The Illustrated London News, *26 February 1870*

---

1 *What fault did the* The Illustrated London News *find with the proposed bill?*

2 *Was it compulsory (a) to elect a School Board, (b) for children under ten years old to go school in an area which already had adequate Church schools?*

3 *'He destroys nothing that is really doing its work.' Why was this said about Forster and the 1870 Education Act?*

The Dual System

The 1870 Education Act fudged the issue of religious education in schools and created the 'Dual System' of elementary education. In 1881, there were 14,370 voluntary Church schools with 2,008,000 pupils, and 3,692 Board Schools with 856,000 pupils. Since the Church schools were not controlled by the local School Boards, the Dual System created many difficulties, particularly if the Church school managers were at odds with the elected members of the School Boards. Increasingly, the Church schools found it difficult to pay their way, whilst the schools maintained by the School Boards could always rely on an increase in local rates to compensate for rising costs.

---

1 *What was the average size of a Church school? Was the average Board School bigger, smaller, or the same size?*

2 *Explain why it was called a 'Dual System'.*

> **3** Where do you think most of the voluntary Church schools were situated – in towns or in villages?
>
> **4** Did the educational system in 1880 provide equality of opportunity for all pupils? If not, why not?

The Education Acts of 1876 and 1880

Since areas with adequate Church schools did not have to elect School Boards, there was no means of making elementary education compulsory in those districts. Lord Sandon's Education Act in 1876, however, forced areas without School Boards to elect School Attendance Committees, with the power to make education compulsory, if they wished. It also said:

> 'It shall be the duty of the parent of every child to cause such child to receive efficient elementary instruction in reading, writing and arithmetic, and if such parent fail to perform such duty, he shall be liable to such orders and penalties as are provided by this Act.'

The act also prevented employers from taking into their employment any child who was under the age of ten years or:

> 'Who, being of the age of ten years or upwards, has not obtained such certificate of his proficiency in reading, writing and elementary arithmetic.'

Nonetheless, it did not compel attendance at school, nor did it provide the means to ensure that all parents carried out their obligations under the act. This was rectified in A. J. Mundella's Education Act of 1880, which made education compulsory for all children between the ages of five and ten, without exception. All children had to go to school (unless privately educated at home). Moreover, children aged between ten and thirteen also had to attend school, unless they could show they had reached a satisfactory standard of education.

Commendable though these new requirements were, they created great hardships for the poor. Many parents bitterly resented the operation of Acts of Parliament for which they had little sympathy, particularly since it deprived them of what income their children had been able to earn at work. At the same time, parents who were not classed as 'poor' had to pay a few pence each week to the school in fees. Even a penny a week was the equivalent of at least £1 a week to a modern parent. This was a lot of money to families unexpectedly on the poverty line through ill health or unemployment. This is why the London School Board decided to take action in 1886, demanding:

> 'the "school-pence" in advance, from every child before admitting the child to instruction. Every child who does not bring the money is to be instantly sent home.'

'Waifs and Strays of London: Raw Material for the School Board', The Illustrated London News, *9 October 1886*

---

1 *What effect do you think the Education Acts of 1870, 1876 and 1880 had on (a) poor children like those in the picture, (b) parents, (c) teachers, (d) employers?*

2 *Use information from earlier chapters in this book to explain why non-payment of school fees was likely to be a particular problem in 1886.*

Pressure to make education free for all children continued, but it was not until 1891 that the Goschen Act allowed elementary schools to claim 10s [50p] a head for every pupil in school if they stopped charging weekly fees.

In 1893, the compulsory school-leaving age was raised to eleven years and in 1899 to twelve years. Meanwhile the Revised Code, which had had such a restrictive effect on the curriculum, was abolished. In 1897, the annual examination of pupils by HMIs was replaced by half-yearly inspections, and in 1900 schools received a block grant based on the number of pupils, instead of a grant dependent on their success in a yearly examination. This was described as marking:

> 'a great epoch in the history of the education movement. It kills the mercenary motive, for it makes the school no longer a grant-earning agency.'

George T. Sampson, The Leisure Hour, *1902*

1 *How did the 'block grant' kill 'the mercenary motive'? What did it replace?*

2 *Why was this 'a great epoch in the history of the education movement'?*

3 *Look at the photograph. What evidence of late-Victorian education can be found in your area today?*

Elementary school in Wakefield, West Yorkshire, built in 1890

STATE EDUCATION IN THE TWENTIETH CENTURY

State Secondary Education before 1902

In 1888, the Cross Commission made a number of recommendations concerning the education of older pupils, including the setting up of a new Standard VII for pupils staying on at school after the age of thirteen years.

Some School Boards had already put their older pupils into higher-grade schools and some members of the Cross Commission wanted the Government to develop a new system of State-aided secondary education based on these local authority higher-grade schools. Others (the majority) wanted to see the existing endowed grammar schools used as the basis for such a secondary education system.

In 1895, another committee, the Bryce Commission on Secondary Education, also made a number of recommendations, including the proposal that the secondary-school system should be run by the county and county borough councils, under the direction of a Ministry of Education.

The Balfour Education Act of 1902

As you saw at the start of this chapter, by 1900 there was growing pressure to establish an effective system of secondary education in Britain. In 1900, a High Court case established that School Boards were not even legally entitled to charge a rate to enable older pupils to stay on at school. The Government had to take action if it intended to make secondary education available to all and not just to the children of those parents who could afford to send them to the existing, fee-paying endowed grammar schools or the public schools. At the same time, many of the voluntary Church schools in the Dual System were in financial trouble and finding it difficult to keep up standards compared with the Board Schools. The education system had become too complicated.

A. J. Balfour, shortly to become the Conservative Prime Minister, decided to replace the existing School Boards with new local education authorities, which would also have responsibility for secondary education. The main provisions of the Balfour Education Act of 1902 were as follows.

● It abolished the 3,347 School Boards and School Attendance Committees and replaced them with 315 local education authorities, based on the existing division of the country into county and county borough councils.

● It put the voluntary Church schools (if they wished) under the control of the local education authorities, enabling them to be partially financed out of local rates. The different Churches would still be responsible for religious education in these schools but the local education authorities would be in charge of non-religious education. They would pay the teachers, ensure they were properly qualified and provide the necessary books and equipment. As their contribution the Churches would provide the buildings and keep them in good condition.

- It enabled the new local educational authorities to provide secondary education legally out of the rates for pupils who were over the compulsory school-leaving age. They could also provide financial support for adult education as well, including the provision of teacher-training colleges and technical schools. Many of the old higher-grade schools now became separate secondary schools and many new grammar schools were built. Nonetheless, the vast majority of children continued to stay on at their elementary schools in the senior department until they reached the school-leaving age.

Council school in 1908. Write a paragraph comparing this classroom with a modern classroom. What are the chief differences? Do these differences have any bearing on the pupils' education?

Opposition to Balfour's Education Act largely centred on the proposals to aid the voluntary Church schools out of local rates. The Nonconformists had far fewer schools than the Church of England and the Roman Catholic Church. Their members resented the fact that they would have to pay local rates directly to support denominational religious education taught in these schools. Protest marches and meetings were held. One slogan read, 'Unwise for the children. Unfair to the teachers. Unjust to the Nonconformists'. The Passive Resistance League was formed and some of its members even went to prison after refusing to pay their rates. They were encouraged in this by Lloyd George and a number of other Liberal politicians, who objected to the use of public funds to support Church schools.

But the alternative of building new State schools would have been far too costly. In any case, it would have been unfair to scrap the Church schools, especially after they had spent so much of their time and money educating children in the period when government had very little to do with the educational system.

---

1 *Do you think the support given to the Church schools by the 1902 Education Act was 'unwise', 'unfair' or 'unjust'? Explain your reasons.*

2 *Why do you think the Nonconformists felt so strongly about using local rates to support the voluntary Church schools, even though they knew perfectly well that ever since 1862 the government had paid an annual grant to the voluntary Church schools (partly derived from income tax)?*

3 *Was it sensible to replace the School Boards with the new local education authorities? What were the disadvantages?*

The Effects of the 1902 Education Act

The Board of Education, under the influence of its public school-educated officials, insisted that the curriculum of the new secondary schools should be academic, based on the subjects taught in public schools (including Latin), rather than the more practical technical education which might have been of greater value to many of the pupils staying on at these schools. It was not until the formation of central schools from 1911 onwards, that practical courses became available for many pupils.

In 1907, new government regulations were introduced which provided a system of grants to the existing endowed grammar schools. These schools, many of them founded before 1600, were used mainly by middle-class children whose parents paid fees for an academic education similar to that of the public schools. In 1907, endowed grammar schools were given grants of £5 per pupil, provided they accepted at least 25 per cent of their pupils from the local elementary schools. The selection of these pupils at the age of eleven years led to the eleven-plus scholarship examination and the segregation of the more academic pupils from their less academic friends.

The Welfare of Pupils

Ever since the first Board Schools were built in 1870, teachers in the poorest districts of London and the great industrial cities of the North, had been faced with one insuperable problem – the extreme poverty of many pupils. As you saw in Chapter 8, as many as 3 to 4 million people were living on the poverty line in the late nineteenth century. The London School Board could force poor children to go to school but it could not, legally, ensure that they were adequately clothed or fed, or fit enough to last through a day's compulsory

'Free Breakfasts for Hungry Children' in Shoreditch, The Illustrated London News, *17 April 1886*

education. This is why the voluntary charitable organisations played an important part in raising money to buy or collect clothing for those children desperately in need, and in helping to provide school meals. A headteacher in 1900 pointed to 'two poor little lads – ragged, and not over-clean' and said:

> 'It's no use trying to work their brains when their stomachs are empty, but they will be back in a minute when they have got their bowl of bread and milk.'

Cast-off clothing was issued to children in need, although it has to be said that older people, recalling those times, said that children sometimes resented this – especially if the clothes were issued in public or made the recipients conspicuous, like one small boy in London's East End who had to wear an Eton suit.

In 1906, the Education (Provision of Meals) Act enabled local education authorities to provide school meals for those pupils, 'unable, by lack of food, to take advantage of the education provided for them'. Unfortunately, the act was permissive – it did not *compel* authorities to provide school meals. But, in Bradford, the schoolchildren were fed at six food centres to which 'solid, tasty, two-course dinners, consisting of broths, pies, vegetables, and puddings, with occasionally meat or fish', were taken by motor wagon from a large, central municipal kitchen. A writer in *The Sphere* for 29 February 1908, commented that this did:

> 'not settle the question of parental responsibility which is involved in the state feeding of children. Many writers have recently drawn attention to the huge growth of public doles to masses of the population.'

---

1 *What were the arguments for free meals? What were the arguments against?*

2 *Imagine you are a teacher in a London school in the slums in the 1880s or 1890s. Write an imaginative description of the scene in school at the start of the morning.*

The health of schoolchildren was another problem which aroused the concern of the local education authorities. In 1907, a new Act of Parliament made it possible to provide regular health inspections in schools. The benefits were soon apparent. In 1911, Bradford's School Medical Officer, said:

> 'The condition of the school children has vastly improved. Running ears, sore eyes, ringworm, and verminous condition of the head and clothing have become much less common. Infectious diseases are less prevalent. Diphtheria has not assumed epidemic form for some years back. Scarlet fever has declined steadily for three years.'

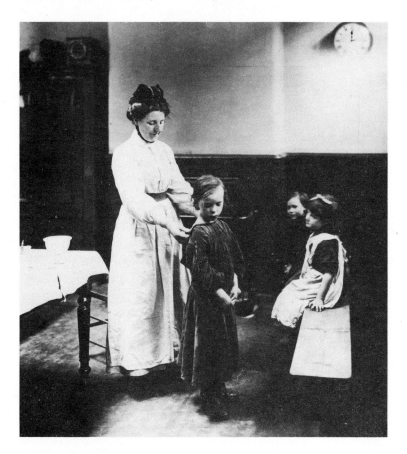

Medical inspection in a London school in 1912

The Fisher Education Act of 1918

In 1918, the Education Act introduced by H. A. L. Fisher, raised the school-leaving age to fourteen and further restricted the employment of children. The act also began an imaginative programme of further education, which would have meant that all pupils would have had to attend day continuation classes after leaving school, until reaching the age of eighteen years. Unfortunately, cuts in public expenditure in the early 1920s put paid to this advanced reform (which was still unrealised in 1986).

The Hadow Report

In 1926, the Hadow Report, *Education of the Adolescent*, advocated that separate senior schools should be built for all those pupils who 'failed' the eleven-plus examination and were not selected for grammar schools. The Hadow Committee recommended that the school-leaving age be raised to fifteen and said that these new 'modern secondary schools' could offer practical courses which would better fit pupils for employment when they left school. As you have seen, most pupils stayed on to the age of fourteen in the senior department of the elementary schools. The Hadow Report now proposed that these should become separate primary schools. As with many other such recommendations, the Government took no immediate action, since this was a time of cuts in public expenditure rather than expansion.

But, in 1936, the raising of the school-leaving age to fifteen years was scheduled to come into force in September 1939, although the outbreak of the Second World War caused these plans to be postponed as well.

The Butler Education Act of 1944

Despite the fact that the Second World War had not yet been won, the wartime Coalition Government took the remarkable step, in 1944, of attacking 'ignorance', one of the five giant social evils highlighted in the *Beveridge Report* of 1942 (see page 267). R. A. Butler, President of the Board of Education, introduced a radical new plan to reform education in Britain. This 1944 Education Act was a major social reform and an important step forward towards removing special privileges and ensuring equality of educational opportunity for all. Its main provisions were as follows.

- The President of the Board of Education was to become the Minister of Education, and the local education authorities were to be reorganised and reduced in number from over 300 to 146.

- The school-leaving age was to be raised to fifteen years with effect from 1947. It was also planned to raise it to sixteen years, in due course, although this was not actually implemented until 1973. All education was to be free of charge in State-maintained grammar schools. Henceforth only children passing the eleven-plus examination would be admitted. Hitherto, parents had been able to pay school fees to send their children to grammar school.

- Compulsory part-time education was to be introduced for all school-leavers up to the age of eighteen years (although this provision has yet to be implemented).

- All pupils would leave primary school at eleven years and go on to a separate secondary school. This meant that new secondary modern schools would have to be built to accommodate pupils from the old elementary schools and to allow for the raising of the school leaving age to fifteen.

- Subsidised school meals were to be provided in every school, together with free milk and a free dental and medical service.

- Almost all the remaining voluntary Church schools were to be divided into two categories. Firstly, the voluntary aided schools, in which the Church still contributed substantially to the cost of running the schools and in return retained control of religious education and the appointment of teachers. Secondly, the voluntary controlled schools, entirely paid for by the local education authorities but allowed to give a limited amount of non-compulsory denominational religious teaching each week.

- The act also specified that the school day should begin with an act of 'corporate worship' and that non-denominational religious education was to be taught in every school.

> 1　*What were the significant differences between the 1944 and 1902 Education Acts?*
>
> 2　*Which Education Act do you think made the biggest difference to the everyday lives of people in Britain – the Forster Act of 1870, the Balfour Act of 1902 or the Butler Act of 1944?*

Comprehensive Education

The building of the new secondary modern schools did not produce all the benefits the Government had originally intended. This was because many people assumed too readily that the grammar schools must be superior because of their academic results, despite the fact that many secondary modern schools were brand new and better equipped to teach practical subjects to those pupils who wanted a practical education. Nor was the eleven-plus examination an infallible method of selecting grammar school pupils. It was felt by many people to favour children from middle-class homes.

Equality of educational opportunity seemed as far away as ever to many members of the Labour party. Yet a new type of school – the comprehensive school for all pupils – had already been tried out with some success in Anglesey and by the London County Council. In the 1950s and 1960s, many other local education authorities followed suit, and by 1965 there were many successful comprehensive schools throughout Britain.

In 1965, Anthony Crosland, Secretary of State for Education in the Labour Government, unleashed a bombshell when he initiated a major new reform of secondary education, and told local education authorities to submit plans to his Ministry, indicating how they proposed to reorganise secondary education on comprehensive lines. By the time the Conservatives came back to power in 1970, many areas had already made definite plans for comprehensive education and the transition continued throughout the 1970s.

Independent Schools

Meanwhile, public schools, many of them founded in the Railway Age of the 1840s and 1850s, had developed an extensive and distinctive fee-paying system of education alongside that of the State-maintained sector.

After 1902, many of the old endowed grammar schools became part of the State system, when they chose to be subsidised through the government grant, in return for allocating a percentage of their places to local scholarship children whom they educated free of charge.

In 1926, a number of these schools elected to be paid directly by the government instead of getting their grants through the local education authorities. In return they guaranteed a minimum number of free places to local-authority children. These direct-grant schools built up a fine reputation for academic results, but were long regarded by the Labour party as unfair and divisive, since they tended to cream off the best pupils from the State schools. In 1974, the Labour Government abolished the direct-grant system, forcing most of these schools to go fully independent, although some were absorbed into the State system and became comprehensive schools.

New Examinations

Edwardian pupils in secondary schools could sit a bewildering number of examinations. These were simplified in 1917, when the School Certificate and Higher School Certificate examinations were introduced. In 1951, they were replaced, in turn, by the new General Certificate of Education (GCE) – the Ordinary (O level) examination replacing School Certificate and the Advanced (A level) examination replacing Higher School Certificate.

Pressure from parents for an examination below GCE O level led to the appointment of the Beloe Committee, which in 1958 set out to investigate secondary school examinations and eventually produced a new examination the Certificate of Secondary Education (CSE). In 1988, the GCE O level and CSE examinations were merged in a new examination, the GCSE (General Certificate of Secondary Education).

The Universities

At the start of the nineteenth century, there were only two universities in England and Wales – Oxford and Cambridge – serving a population of 12 million people although Scotland, with only 2 million people, had four universities (Aberdeen, Edinburgh, Glasgow and St Andrews). England and Wales desperately needed new universities. Those of Durham and London were founded in the 1830s, to be followed by Owens College in Manchester, in 1851. Colleges were also started in Leeds and Liverpool and these were linked with Owens College, in 1884, to form the Victoria University. Twenty years later, all three had become separate universities, at a time when other universities

Lecture by Professor Blackie at Edinburgh University, Cassell's Magazine, *1882*

were being founded as well – Wales (1893), Birmingham (1900), Sheffield (1905) and Bristol (1909). By 1960, new universities had also been opened in Reading, Leicester, Nottingham, Newcastle-upon-Tyne, Exeter and Southampton.

Even this was inadequate and the report of the Robbins Committee on higher education, in 1963, proposed a vast expansion of higher education places. The *Robbins Report* was immediately implemented with the creation of many new universities (such as those at Norwich, Canterbury, Lancaster and York), resulting in a doubling of university places. Technological education was also expanded and by 1982–3, there were over 300,000 university students and another 250,000 students in polytechnics and colleges of higher education.

In 1969, the Open University offered a radical new approach to university education when it began degree courses for students at home, using television, radio, summer schools and tuition by correspondence. This was probably the most inspired educational achievement of the post-war period. By 1982, it had over 100,000 students and was Britain's biggest university.

FURTHER QUESTIONS AND EXERCISES

1 *Write an imaginative account of the changes in education seen by a teacher. You begin work in 1860, as a pupil-teacher of thirteen years, in a country school. You retire in 1912, after teaching for twenty years in a large school in a poor part of London.*

CRAMMING VERSUS "CLEMMING!"

BOARD-SCHOOL MASTER.—"NOW THEN, BOYS, WE
MUST GET TO WORK AGAIN!"
ADVANCED SCHOLAR.—"PLEASE, SIR,—MAYN'T WE
HAVE SOMETHIN' TO RELIEVE THE CRAVINS OF
'UNGER FUST?"

Punch, *1 December 1888*

2 *What was the point of this cartoon? What attempts have been made to alleviate this problem since 1870?*

3 *Write about the importance and the effects on education of each of the following:*

   (a) Revised Code of 1862   *(c) Hadow Report of 1926*

   (b) Robbins Report of 1963   *(d) Labour party policy in 1965.*

4 *How did the following Acts of Parliament affect the development of education in England and Wales:*

   (a) Forster Act of 1870   *(d) Balfour Act of 1902*

   (b) Sandon Act of 1876   *(e) Fisher Act of 1918*

   (c) Mundella Act of 1880   *(f) Butler Act of 1944?*

5 *Read the following extract.*

> *'No scholar shall be required to attend or abstain from attending any Sunday school, or any place of religious worship, or to be present at any such lesson or instruction or observance, as may have been objected to on religious grounds by the parent in writing.'*

What was this called? When do you think it was written? To what does it refer? Write a short essay, explaining how and why religion has played an important part in the development of State education in Britain.

6 *Look at the following statistics.*

1902: 9 per cent of fourteen-year-olds and 2 per cent of seventeen-year-olds stayed on at school; 20,000 students went to universities.

1938: 38 per cent of fourteen-year-olds and 4 per cent of seventeen-year-olds stayed on at school; 50,000 students went to universities.

1983: 100 per cent of fourteen-year-olds and 18 per cent of seventeen-year-olds stayed on at school; 300,000 students went to universities.

What do these statistics tell you about the progress of education in the twentieth century? Write an essay outlining the major reforms since 1900, using these statistics to illustrate your answer.

Chapter Ten

Medicine, Health and Leisure

INTRODUCTION

Relief on a memorial to Florence Nightingale

This monument in London's West End depicts a scene in the hospital at Scutari (near Constantinople) to which Florence Nightingale and 38 nurses came, in 1854, to nurse soldiers wounded on the battlefields of the Crimea. Within a matter of weeks they had transformed the hospital and Florence Nightingale became the leading figure in a movement to improve the quality of nursing in Britain, an indispensable part of the medical revolution of the last 150 years.

The middle of the nineteenth century was a time when surgery and medicine made big strides. In 1847, James Young Simpson discovered that chloroform could be used as an anaesthetic in operations. In the early 1860s, Louis Pasteur conducted the important bacteriological investigations in France which resulted in the discovery of microbes and germs, and in 1867, Joseph Lister put them to practical use with the first antiseptic surgery. Together, Florence Nightingale, James Young Simpson, Louis Pasteur and Joseph Lister helped to lay the foundations of modern medicine, the subject of this chapter.

---

1 *What scene is depicted in the photograph?*

2 *Why do you think people often fail to recognise the importance of nursing in the history of medicine?*

3 *How do we recall the name of Pasteur today? What was his role in the history of medicine?*

MEDICAL DEVELOPMENTS

Anaesthetics

Before 1847, patients who underwent an operation in hospital did so as a last resort, since their chances of survival were very low. At that time there were no anaesthetics to dull or deaden the pain and no antiseptics to kill germs. Patients undergoing surgery had to be either physically restrained or given brandy to make them too drunk to feel the pain of the surgeon's knife. As a rule only rapid operations could be carried out.

But in 1847, James Young Simpson discovered that chloroform could be used as an anaesthetic in surgery and to ease the pain of childbirth. By using anaesthetics, surgeons no longer had to work rapidly and inaccurately. Careful and precise surgery, and complicated, deep-seated operations were possible at last.

Antiseptic Surgery

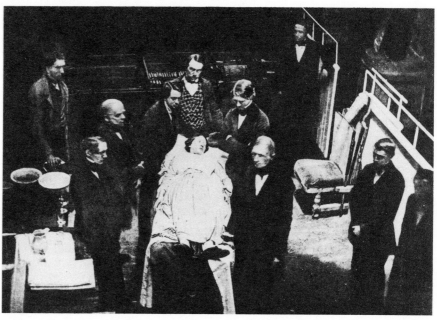

Hospital operation in 1847 – one of the first to use an anaesthetic on a patient. Make a list of the differences between this scene and what you would expect to see in a modern operating theatre.

Although many more patients were now able to undergo operations, anaesthetics alone did not mean that more people benefited from surgery. Many survived the operation, only to die a few days later from 'hospital fever', after poison got into the operation wound, causing it to putrefy. In many cases, abscesses and gangrene formed and the patient died. Few patients recovered from a serious operation in less than a month.

Joseph Lister (1827–1912), Professor of Surgery at Glasgow University, tried to discover the reasons for this disturbingly high mortality rate. At first, like most doctors, he associated the cause of diseases with bad smells and thought that some form of poison in the air was making the operation wounds putrefy. Then his attention was drawn to the work of the great French scientist Louis Pasteur, whose researches on germs were published in 1865. Pasteur showed that germs were living things and that these micro-organisms caused diseases and infections. It seemed clear to Lister that the 'hospital fever' in his surgical patients was caused by germs infecting the body both during and after the operation, causing poisoning (sepsis) and eventual death. This is what he wrote in 1867.

'When it had been shown by the researches of Pasteur that the septic property of the atmosphere depended, not on any gaseous constituent but on minute organisms suspended in it, it occurred to me that decomposition in the injured part might be avoided by applying as a dressing some material capable of destroying the life of the floating particles.'

1 What did he mean by the 'septic property of the atmosphere'?

2 How had Pasteur's researches shown that the theory of miasmas (poisonous vapours) was wrong? Which phrase in the extract means the same as miasma?

3 What deduction did Lister make as a result of reading Pasteur's work on germs?

4 Lister wanted 'some material capable of destroying' the 'septic' (poisonous) organisms. What do we call such a material?

FOR DISINFECTING USE "SANITAS" ONLY

'SANITAS' Is Fragrant, Non-Poisonous AND Does Not Stain

THE "SANITAS" Cº Lº LONDON E.

" 'Sanitas' is a valuable disinfectant, having certain advantages over all others."—*Medical Press and Circular.*
" 'Sanitas' now enjoys general favour as a disinfectant."—*Lancet.*
" 'Sanitas' has met with wide recognition and approval."—*British Medical Journal.*

"HOW TO DISINFECT" BOOK SENT FREE ON APPLICATION.

Advertisement for a disinfectant spray

Lister began to experiment, using carbolic acid applied to a surgical dressing. After successful trials with patients suffering from compound fractures (where the bone breaks through the skin) he started to use it as an antiseptic during operations. Sprays disinfected the operating theatre as he worked. Dilute carbolic acid sterilised his surgical instruments and his own hands before the operation. He cleansed the patient's skin with antiseptic before making an incision and continued to dress the wounds with carbolic dressings.

Remarkably, many more of Lister's patients began to survive his operations than had done so before. In 1864–6, the survival rate of his patients had been only 55 per cent of all those undergoing surgery. In 1867–9, the proportion of survivors increased to 85 per cent – a truly remarkable improvement.

Despite this convincing evidence, many surgeons refused to accept his findings and even Florence Nightingale rejected the theory because she had never seen any germs! But Lister triumphed in the end, saving countless lives with his revolutionary methods and becoming accepted as one of the greatest surgeons in the history of medicine. He was made Lord Lister in 1897.

Aseptic Surgery

Antiseptic surgery was quickly followed in the late nineteenth century by the development of aseptic surgery. Where Lister used antiseptics to kill germs, the aseptic technique was devised to prevent germs coming anywhere near the patient undergoing the operation. As a result there was no need to direct a spray of carbolic acid on the patient during the operation.

Instead, the patient was first bathed and shaved and the skin in the vicinity of the incision treated with antiseptics to make it sterile. Surgeons and operating theatre staff wore sterile clothing and masks, the surgical instruments and equipment were sterilised before use, and the operating theatres were equipped with special apparatus to keep out germs.

'Antiseptic surgery depends on the use of carbolic acid or some other chemical which prevents or, at all events, slows up the development of germs.

Aseptic surgery, on the other hand, depends on the use of dressings which are perfectly free from germs and block out the possibility of their entrance to the wound. Aseptic surgery is, in fact, almost universally practised today. Every possible precaution is taken to keep the operating theatres perfectly free from germs. Only air which has been well-washed with water and filtered through cotton-wool and warmed to a proper temperature is allowed to enter the theatre. To such an extent is the use of aseptic surgery carried that in one of the theatres no antiseptic has ever been used since the day it was first opened. Everyone who enters the room has to wear a long smock which has been sterilized.'

The London Hospital' by Rudolph de Cordova in The Strand Magazine, *1903*

> 1 Write two or three sentences explaining clearly the difference between aseptic and antiseptic surgery.
>
> 2 What were the advantages of aseptic surgery over antiseptic surgery? Were there any disadvantages?
>
> 3 Was aseptic surgery completely new or was it based on Lister's antiseptic surgery?

New Operations

The developments in anaesthetics, and in antiseptic and aseptic surgery, quickly led to new types of surgical operation being performed, to the benefit of patients, who would otherwise have been condemned either to death or to a life of pain or discomfort.

Brain surgery began in 1879 with the work of William Macewen, a pupil of Lister in Glasgow. The first successful removal of an appendix took place in Iowa, USA, in 1885. Pioneering operations became routine. Many other new types of operation were successfully developed; some with the aid of new tools, such as the laser beam (used in eye surgery), and some with the aid of new techniques, such as transplant surgery.

Nursing

The popular view of nursing in the early nineteenth century was typified by Sairey Gamp, a midwife and nurse in *Martin Chuzzlewit* by Charles Dickens, with her 'rusty black gown' and face 'somewhat red and swollen' from heavy drinking. In the middle years of the nineteenth century, good nurses were hard to come by, as you can see in this report from Scotland in 1865.

> 'At present nursing is the last resource of female adversity. Slatternly [scruffy] widows, runaway wives, servants out of place, women bankrupt of fame and fortune, from whatever cause fall back upon hospital nursing. When on a rare occasion a respectable young woman takes to it from choice, her friends most likely repudiate her, her relatives resort to various ways of concealing her whereabouts.
>
> Until our nurses have conferred upon them the dignity and morale of which a special education, special organization, firm and kind moral supervision, with high pay during active service, a home when not actually engaged, and a superannuation fund to look forward to in old age, we shall never have good nurses.'

Dr J. B. Russell, Glasgow's Medical Officer of Health, Introduction to First Hospital Report, *1865*

> 1 What were Dr Russell's complaints about the standard of nursing in Britain in 1865? Whom or what did he blame?

> **2** *What type of person did Dr Russell think was attracted to nursing at that time? Was it a respectable career for young women?*
>
> **3** *Were Dr Russell's suggestions for improving the standard of nursing in hospitals likely to produce the effect he wanted?*

Dr Russell's *Report* was published about ten years after the work of Florence Nightingale in the Crimea had drawn ecstatic praise from the British public.

Florence Nightingale (1820–1910)

Florence Nightingale

Florence Nightingale was born in Florence in Italy, the daughter of well-to-do parents. At an early age she visited the sick but, like other women of her class, she was restricted from training for a career in nursing or medicine. Society women were not supposed to work for a living. In any case, there were no nursing schools in Britain. This is why she trained as a nurse in Germany and France in the early 1850s and returned to Britain in 1853, to become Superintendent of a Home for Invalid Gentlewomen. In 1854, she led a team of nurses who took up the challenge in the Crimean War of a war correspondent who asked, 'Are there no devoted women among us able and willing to go forth to minister to the sick and suffering soldiers of the East in the hospitals of Scutari?'

There were – and when they arrived at the main British Army hospital at Scutari, near Constantinople, they found a forbidding barracks housing 10,000 sick men, with dirt and filth throughout the hospital. Patients were lying in the corridors as well as in the wards, many of them suffering from typhoid fever and cholera, as well as from battle wounds.

Florence Nightingale and her team of 38 nurses scrubbed the hospital clean; washed the sheets, blankets and towels; cleaned the hospital's kitchens; and prepared better, wholesome food for the patients. Most important of all, she got army engineers to repair the hospital's drains and improve its supply of drinking water. As a result the survival rate at Scutari rose sharply.

Newspapers and magazines sang her praises. On her return to England in 1856, she devoted her life to the training of nurses, and started the Florence Nightingale Training School and Home for Nurses at St Thomas's Hospital in 1860, with the aid of a fund of £50,000 subscribed by a grateful public. In that same year, her book *Notes on Nursing* was first published, to be followed by other influential books and articles in the years to come.

The example of Florence Nightingale, in starting a training school for nurses, was eventually followed by other hospitals and the standard of nursing care improved immeasurably, to the benefit of patients, doctors and surgeons alike.

Nurses at the New Hospital for Women in London's Euston Road, The Illustrated London News, 3 May 1890

1 *Which parts, if any, of Dr Russell's gloomy report of 1865 (on page 297) are confirmed by this account of the career of Florence Nightingale?*

2 *In what ways does the extract from Dr Russell's Report appear to be unfair to Florence Nightingale?*

3 *If Dr Russell passionately wanted to improve the standard of nursing, how might this affect the value placed on his Report, as evidence of low standards of nursing in 1865?*

Hospitals

Even though surgeons were making remarkable progress in developing new surgical techniques, the provision of hospitals for the poor left much to be desired. Most were dependent for their funds on charitable subscriptions from the public, and some would not admit patients (except in the case of an accident), unless they brought a letter from a subscriber. The extract on page 300, and the picture on page 301, were designed to encourage people to subscribe money to the London Hospital in the East End, which catered for the needs of about a million people. Patients who were poor got their treatment free of charge, but out-patients who could afford to do so, paid something towards the cost of the medicine supplied to them.

'Without the great general hospitals, with their medical schools, there would be no doctors, either for the rich or for the poor; and the great results, in the way of diminished mortality and of diminished suffering, which the last half century has witnessed, would not have been brought about. The hospitals which possess medical schools are truly national institutions, not only charities for the benefit of the poor, but of equal value to all classes, and which should, therefore, be supported by all. It would be impossible, in the interests of the State, for any Government to allow them to languish, if a time ever came at which sufficient voluntary support were no longer supplied.'

The Illustrated London News, *21 July 1888*

1 *What did the 'letter from a subscriber' prove? What would a modern patient entering a National Health Service hospital have to prove?*

2 *What reasons were given to persuade people to subscribe to the London Hospital in 1888? How did the London Hospital, and other hospitals which catered for the poor, also benefit the rich, who could afford to pay the fees demanded at more exclusive hospitals?*

3 *How did the London Hospital differ from ordinary hospitals? What does this tell you about the progress being made in medicine and surgery in the late nineteenth century?*

4 *Look at the picture opposite, showing one of the wards in the London Hospital in 1888. In what ways is it similar to a modern hospital ward? How was it heated and lit? What improvements would be needed to bring this ward up to the standard required by a modern hospital?*

5 *In Leeds, the Infirmary dates from 1868, the Cookridge Convalescent Hospital from 1869 and the Seacroft Infectious Hospital from 1904. See if you can find out when the hospitals in your district were built and whether any date back to the time of Simpson, Nightingale and Lister.*

Patent Drugs and Medicines

The reader of a Victorian newspaper may sometimes have wondered why such a fuss was made over hospitals, surgical techniques and better nursing care, when miraculous preparations like Holloway's Pills or Dr J. Collis Browne's Chlorodyne were available.

Ward in the London Hospital, The Illustrated London News, *21 July 1888*

Thomas Holloway invented a harmless pill (said to be made of soap, ginger and aloes) and advertised it as a miraculous cure on such a scale that the gullible Victorian public provided him with an income of £50,000 a year. Dr J. Collis Browne's Chlorodyne was widely advertised, in 1880, as a treatment (*not* a cure) for colds, bronchitis, coughs, asthma, tuberculosis, diphtheria, cholera, dysentery, diarrhoea, epilepsy, palpitation, spasms, hysteria, colic, neuralgia, rheumatism, gout, cancer and toothache.

'Dr J. Collis Browne's CHLORODYNE is a Liquid Medicine which assuages pain of every kind, affords a calm and refreshing sleep WITHOUT HEADACHE and invigorates the Nervous System when exhausted.'

1 *Why was Chlorodyne popular? What do you think it probably contained? What type of drug would it be called today? Suggest a possible reason why it was called Chlorodyne.*

2 *Aloes are bitter in taste and used as a laxative. Why do you think people thought Holloway's Pills must be good?*

New Drugs and New Treatments

Some of the major breakthroughs in medical science in the nineteenth century came from European scientists. The greatest achievements were probably those of Louis Pasteur who:

● founded the modern science of bacteriology, which led Lister to develop antiseptic surgery, enabled food scientists to develop the pasteurisation process to destroy harmful organisms in foods, and helped Victorian scientists devise effective methods of sewage disposal and water purification;

● developed the techniques which enabled successful immunisation programmes to be carried out, notably against rabies, and later (by other medical researchers) against diphtheria, tuberculosis, cholera and other diseases.

Pasteur's work in bacteriology was followed with notable success by the German bacteriologist, Robert Koch, who isolated the tuberculosis bacillus in 1882 and the cholera bacillus a few years later. In 1902, T. F. Manning said in an article:

> 'Until Dr Koch's brilliant discovery of the tubercle bacillus in 1882 we did not know the cause of consumption [tuberculosis], and believed the disease to be hereditary and incurable. Experiment has revealed the weak points of the microbe. It cannot exist in a moderately high temperature, for instance. It cannot contend against sunlight and pure air. Again, it has been found that the bacillus is rarely victorious in a vigorous person. Consequently, by taking pains to maintain a high standard of health, even those who are predisposed [more liable to catch the disease] can preserve themselves from invasion.'
>
> The London Magazine, *1902*

Deaths from Tuberculosis (per million people)

1840	3,897	1870	2,410	1899	1,326
1850	2,624	1880	1,869		
1860	2,564	1890	1,682		

---

1 *What did doctors think was a 'cure' for consumption before 1882? What was the 'cure' for tuberculosis in 1902?*

2 *How and why did improvements in housing, sanitation, clothing and food, and a general rise in living standards, help to lower the death rate from tuberculosis before Koch's discovery of the bacillus in 1882?*

In 1906, Leon Calmette and Camille Guérin began the experimental work which eventually led to the development of a tuberculosis vaccine, called BCG (*Bacille Calmette-Guérin*), first used in France in 1922 but not in Britain until the 1960s.

Another great step forward, in a different direction, came in 1895, when the German scientist Wilhelm Roentgen made a major breakthrough at Würzburg University, with his discovery of electromagnetic rays (X-rays) and his realisation of the use that doctors and surgeons could make of them in accurate diagnosis. Three years later, Marie and Pierre Curie discovered radium in Paris and afterwards used it to treat cancers.

Probably the greatest medical discovery of the twentieth century to date was that of penicillin and the other antibiotics. Penicillin was originally discovered by Alexander Fleming in 1928, when he noticed that mould had accidentally spread to a specimen dish he was using to cultivate bacteria. Fleming's interest was aroused by the fact that the mould (called *penicillium notatum*) had destroyed some of the bacteria. However, the successful use of penicillin as a 'miracle' drug in the treatment of wounds and many illnesses (such as pneumonia), derived largely from the work of two other scientists, Howard Florey and Ernest Chain who, in 1940, developed a method of purifying the mould for use in treating human patients. It was followed by the development of other antibiotics from different types of mould, such as streptomycin and tetracycline.

Other major medical developments of the twentieth century have included the study and treatment of viruses, the identification of vitamins, and the routine use of blood transfusions. These had been used successfully as long ago as 1825, but only became safe after the classification of different blood groups in 1900, by the Austrian scientist Karl Landsteiner.

PUBLIC HEALTH

Preventive Medicine

Curative medicine has undoubtedly played an often miraculous part in the history of medicine and surgery, but there seems little doubt that in the long run more lives are saved through the effective use of preventive medicine than by finding a cure.

Dr Edward Jenner's use of vaccination against smallpox, in 1797, was the first effective demonstration of immunisation as a means of preventing the spread of disease (see page 166). Improvements in personal hygiene, sanitation and water supply have all played their part as well, in improving public health (see pages 163–70). Britain has become a cleaner, less-polluted environment in which to live, partly as a result of new inventions and partly because living standards have increased dramatically. As you have seen in Chapters 5 and 6, this led to a remarkable fall in the death rate.

In Britain, the setting up of the National Health Service (see page 268) has also had an appreciable part to play in helping to make Britain a healthier place in which to live.

THE GROWTH OF LEISURE ACTIVITIES

Sports and Outdoor Activities

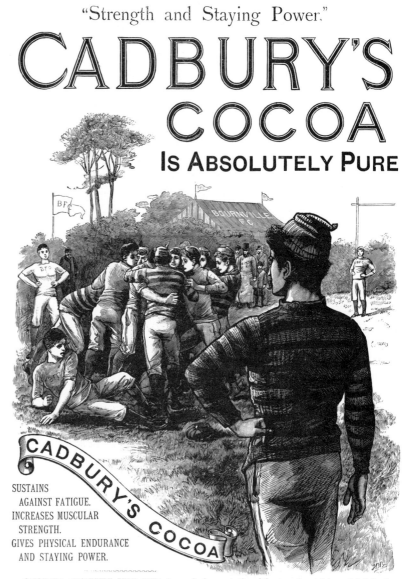

"Strength and Staying Power."

CADBURY'S COCOA

IS ABSOLUTELY PURE

SUSTAINS AGAINST FATIGUE. INCREASES MUSCULAR STRENGTH. GIVES PHYSICAL ENDURANCE AND STAYING POWER.

Cadbury's Cocoa advert in 1888

CADBURY'S ABSOLUTELY PURE COCOA is a refined concentration of the strength-sustaining and flesh-forming constituents of the Cocoa Nib. Delicious, nutritious, easily digested, and of great economy, a Sixpenny Packet yielding fourteen large breakfast cups of perfect Cocoa.

Victoria Park in London, The Illustrated London News, *9 August 1890*

1 *These two pictures were drawn within the space of two years of each other. Describe each picture in turn and explain how and why the activity shown has contributed to a general improvement in public health in the last hundred years.*

2 *How is sport used nowadays to promote commercial products?*

3 *What other outdoor amenities does a typical town provide today for the benefit of its citizens?*

Improvements in health have been accompanied by a growth in leisure activities and a general increase in the amount of leisure time available to most workers. The 1850 Factory Act (see page 245) gave textile workers Saturday afternoons off work as well as Sundays, and the later application of the Factory Acts to other industries, in the 1860s and 1870s, made it a universal half holiday, enabling association football to develop as a Saturday afternoon spectator sport, followed by rugby league football in the 1890s.

At the same time, the new Board Schools increasingly made use of physical exercises and drill to improve the health of their pupils. By 1900, most children were probably fitter than their parents had been at their age. The public schools had already led the way in pioneering organised games, such as rugby (named after the famous school of that name), to keep their pupils out of mischief and to develop 'team spirit'. The endowed grammar schools and the council schools built after the 1902 Education Act followed suit.

Seaside Holidays

In the eighteenth century, only affluent people enjoyed seaside holidays, bathing in the sea (on the advice of their doctors) as an alternative to taking the waters at a spa town, such as Bath or Harrogate. Until 1840, there was only a handful of small but important seaside resorts on Britain's coasts, notably Brighton, Scarborough, Weymouth and Margate.

The coming of the railways changed the face of the coastline. Cheap day excursions made it possible for a working-class family to travel to the sea on Whit Monday (see page 85). Much later, the official bank holidays (Christmas Day, Easter Monday, Whit Monday and the first Monday in August), which became law in 1871 with the passage of the Bank Holidays Act, caused a further acceleration in the rise of the seaside resorts. Boarding houses and hotels flourished as the middle classes increasingly spent their summer holidays at the seaside. By 1890, the more affluent members of the upper-working and lower-middle classes were also beginning to take seaside holidays at the new, rapidly growing seaside resorts, such as Blackpool, Southend and Skegness.

Seaside resort in 1873, contemporary print by S. Hall

In the Edwardian period the trickle become a flood, and in the 1930s photographs of the huge beach at Blackpool on August Bank Holiday show it black with people. In Lancashire's industrial towns, the cotton mills shut down during the annual holiday, called 'Wakes Week', and as the spinners and weavers flocked to Blackpool, it became Blackburn- or Preston-on-Sea for the week. Other towns had their favourite resorts as well. The pottery workers of Stoke-on-Trent went to Llandudno, Barnsley's coal miners went to Bridlington, and London's millions went to Clacton, Southend, Herne Bay, Margate, Ramsgate, Hastings, Eastbourne, Brighton and Worthing.

The main drawback for most workers was cost. In most industries they had to save up twice for their holidays, since there was no wage packet during Wakes Week. In 1937, only 1.5 million of Britain's workers enjoyed the luxury of annual holidays with pay. But by the end of 1938, the number had risen to 9 million, thanks to the Holidays with Pay Act. Billy Butlin seized his chance and built holiday camps, offering cheap, all-inclusive seaside holidays for people who could not otherwise afford the expense of staying in a hotel or boarding house and paying extra for their entertainment.

The effect of this leisure revolution can be seen in the fact that Blackpool more than doubled its population from 47,000 in 1901 to 102,000 in 1931, and had grown by another 45,000 people by 1951. Bournemouth grew from 47,000 to 117,000 and then to 145,000 in the same period, whilst Worthing, Torquay and other resorts showed similar increases.

Immediately after the Second World War, the seaside resorts benefited from the higher standard of living enjoyed by most workers, their greater mobility with the development of motoring and their longer, paid holidays each year. But in the 1960s and 1970s, Britain's seaside resorts suffered a relative decline as people were increasingly tempted by hot sun and competitive prices to take package holidays to the coasts of Spain.

FURTHER QUESTIONS AND EXERCISES

1 *Imagine you are a Scottish nurse or doctor starting at Glasgow Infirmary in the 1860s to work with Joseph Lister and retiring in 1900. Describe and explain the changes in surgical treatment you see during this period.*

2 *What do you think were the most important developments in medical history between 1840 and 1980?*

3 *In what ways has the development of leisure activities contributed to the better health of people in Britain?*

4 *What is the difference between curative and preventive medicine? Give a short explanation of each, using recent or local examples of these different types of medical care in action.*

Source A

'The day beforehand, the skin in a wide area around the site of the proposed operation will first be scrubbed by a nail-brush with soap and water, then with ether, then with some antiseptic solution, and then covered with an antiseptic dressing until the operation is begun.

The instruments will have been boiled in a covered vessel for fifteen minutes, or disinfected by carbolic acid or some equivalent germicide, and are then placed in a tray filled with an antiseptic solution. If a sponge or an instrument fall on the floor, it is laid aside.'

Source B

5 (a) Do you think the photograph depicts (i) surgery in the days before Lister, (ii) antiseptic surgery, (iii) aseptic surgery?

(b) When do you think this photograph was taken? Give your reasons.

(c) Write a short paragraph explaining the difference between antiseptic and aseptic surgery.

(d) Was the operation described in Source A conducted under aseptic or antiseptic surgery or a mixture of the two?

(e) How would the scene in a modern operating theatre differ from this photograph?

Chapter Eleven

Women and Society

INTRODUCTION

Source A

'A club of female Reformers, amounting in number, according to our calculation, to 156, came from Oldham; and bore a white silk banner, inscribed "Major Cartwright's Bill, Annual Parliaments, Universal Suffrage, and Vote by Ballot". A group of the women of Manchester viewed these Female Reformers for some time; and at last burst out into an indignant exclamation – "Go home to your families, and leave such-like matters as these to your husbands and sons, who better understand them."'

Description of the crowd at Peterloo, The Times, *1819*

Source B

'A Welcome Visitor', The Illustrated London News, *22 December 1888*

Source C

'Is it a book that you would wish your wife or even your servant to read?'

Prosecuting counsel to jury at an obscenity trial in 1961

1 *What connection can you find between the 1819 and 1961 extracts?*

2 *What attitudes to the role of women in society are revealed by these three sources? Have you any evidence – statements you may have read or conversations overheard – which show that these attitudes still persist today?*

3 *Which phrase in Source A tells us that women were already demanding the vote in 1819?*

Although the campaign for equality of treatment for women is sometimes thought of as a development of the twentieth century, it has, in fact, a very much longer history. A book called *Vindication of the Rights of Women*, by Mary Wollstonecraft, was published in 1792 as a sequel to her *Vindication of the Rights of Men* (inspired by the events of the French Revolution). In her book on women's rights she advocated equality between the sexes and, in so doing, helped to lay the foundations for the feminist movement. But it took a further 136 years before women got the vote on the same terms as men. Even in 1986, after Margaret Thatcher had been Prime Minister for seven years, there were still only 26 women MPs to 624 male MPs in the House of Commons.

THE STATUS OF WOMEN IN THE NINETEENTH CENTURY

Marriage and Property

Until 1870, a woman could not even possess property in her own name after marriage.

> 'By marriage husband and wife became one person. In consequence all her property (money and furniture, and the like – not land) thenceforth became his exclusively. She could not acquire or even earn any money for her own benefit; a legacy, if paid to her, could be claimed by her husband; her wages or profits in any occupation or business or pursuit were to be paid to her husband.'
>
> *'The Married Women's Property Acts' by 'A. Solicitor' in the* Girl's Own Paper, *1 November 1890*

If a woman was not satisfied with her marriage it was too bad since, before 1857, it was not normally possible to get a divorce. When she married a scoundrel who was only interested in her money, the law took his side rather than hers – unless her relatives had had the foresight to make 'a settlement', specifying that certain property was for her 'separate use'.

The real impact of this intolerable legal position only became apparent when a marriage broke down, since the husband could legally take everything apart from land – even the money his wife had earned. This affected working-class women as well as the rich, sometimes with more distressing consequences. A working woman, deserted by her husband, could have her savings in a tin box taken away – perfectly legally – by her husband.

The unfairness of the marriage laws ('very barbarous, very shocking' was a lawyer's verdict in 1890) was perceived by many men as well as by women. The law was especially unkind to mothers, and it was not until the Custody of Infants Act of 1839 that they were allowed even to see their children after a judicial separation, and even then they were required to be of 'unblemished character'. In 1879, a legal author advised that after a divorce:

'As a general rule, the father is entitled to the custody of the children until they are twenty-one. But if the father be profligate and profane, the Court will give the wife the custody of her children.'

The Married Women's Property Acts

Lawyers and judges had long seen the injustice of the property laws, so in 1857, 1870 and 1882, Parliament passed the following legislation.

1. The Marriage and Divorce Acts of 1857 and 1858

These acts gave a woman the right to sue her husband for divorce. However, she could not sue for adultery on its own – he could, but she could not. This essential right was not granted for another 66 years. Instead, she could sue for adultery coupled with cruelty, or adultery coupled with desertion. In addition, women now had the right to retain their own property after divorce, or after desertion by the husband.

2. The Married Women's Property Act of 1870

This act, 'a halting, half-hearted concession', allowed women to retain their own earnings, savings and legacies up to a value of £200.

3. The Married Women's Property Act of 1882

This act enabled married women to own property independently of their husbands. It was no longer regarded as belonging automatically to the husband. The act said that:

'A married woman shall have the same power of acquiring, holding and disposing by will or otherwise, of any real or personal property as her separate property in the same manner as if she were a single woman.'

Women at Work

Women making lace curtains in Nottingham in 1888, contemporary print by A. Morrow. Was this 'sweated labour'?

In the nineteenth century, many women went out to work as a matter of course – in mines, mills, and as servants. Indeed, a greater proportion of working-class women in Lancashire went out to work in 1871 (35 per cent) than did so in either 1931 (29 per cent) or 1971 (34 per cent). The middle class thought a woman's place was in the home, which partly explains why legislation on factory working conditions, in the 1830s and 1840s, was concerned primarily with 'liberating' women (and children), rather than men, from the appalling working conditions then prevalent in textile mills and collieries.

Many working-class women worked in sweated-labour workshops, as seam-stresses and match-girls (see page 51). Others worked for low wages in the dimly lit rooms of their own homes. The overwhelming majority, however, were employed as domestic servants.

Source A

'The cutting of the lengths, heading, screw and notch cutting, and other parts of the process, although performed by the agency of steam-power, appeared throughout to be anything but work for women.'

Chambers's Journal, *1844*

Source B

'The females are from necessity bred up from their youth in the workshops, as the earnings of the younger members contribute to the support of the family. The habit of a manufacturing life being once established in a woman, she continues it, and leaves her home and children to the care of a neighbour, or of a hired child sometimes only a few years older than her own children. To this neglect on the part of their parents is to be traced the death of many children.'

Government sanitary inquiry 1842

Source C

A contemporary print of factory hands leaving a flax mill in Leeds in 1885. What proportion are women?

Source D

'I am anxious to state to the House and the country what the motives are for inducing or compelling those wretched females to undergo the shameful toil and degradation to which they are subjected. A witness says, – "The temptation to employ women arises from their wages being lower than that of males." Ellspee Thompson says, – "I can say to my own cost, that the bairns are much neglected when both parents work below; and if neighbours keep the children, they require as much as women sometimes earn, and yet neglect them." Mr M. T. Sadler, a surgeon at Barnsley says, – "I strongly disapprove of females being in pits. The female character is totally destroyed by it; their habits and feelings are altogether different; they can neither discharge the duty of wives nor mothers. I see the greatest difference in the homes of those colliers whose wives do not go into the pits." Mr Wood says, – "The wives are so little capable of rendering a house comfortable, that the husband is constantly driven to the alehouse, whence arise all the evils of drunkenness to themselves and to their families." '

Speech in the House of Commons on 7 June 1842 by Lord Ashley, successfully proposing a law to ban the employment of women and children underground in mines and collieries.

---

1 *Had the women who went to work in the nineteenth century (such as those shown leaving a flax mill in 1885) any reason to feel 'liberated' by their jobs? If not, why not?*

2 *What do you think the writer of Source A had in mind as being 'women's work'?*

3 *Which sources provide evidence that married women with children went out to work in the 1840s? What reason was given for this? What adverse effects did this have according to some of the witnesses quoted by Lord Ashley?*

4 *List the arguments and 'evidence' used by the witnesses quoted by Lord Ashley, in his speech successfully persuading MPs to vote for a ban on the employment of women mineworkers underground in 1842. Which of these arguments assumed that woman's place was in the home as wife and mother?*

5 *In your opinion were the Factory and Mining Acts likely to be a help or a hindrance (a) to the welfare of women, (b) to the cause of the women's movement?*

Neither the middle-class matron nor her daughters looked for a job. Society assumed they would get married, manage a man's household, and raise children. It was their duty to do so. In 1870, a story in *The Graphic*, ended with the words, 'Terrible was the punishment that awaited the vain and cruel Genevra. She was never married!'

For those educated middle-class women who chose to remain single, there was charitable work (see the picture at the start of this chapter) or the position of governess in an affluent household, if they were lucky. Many a woman spent a dull and uneventful life as a nurse, domestic help, seamstress or general dogsbody in the family of a brother or sister, or remained at home to look after her parents.

Only a handful of enterprising and fortunate women managed to overcome these disadvantages of birth and position, to make a name for themselves as pioneering social reformers, like Octavia Hill (page 196) and Florence Nightingale (page 298); or as writers, like the Brontë sisters; or as performers on the stage, like Ellen Terry.

Yet, however talented, they were unable to enter politics, had no vote, and could not become Members of Parliament. Until 1848 they could not even go to university. There were no great women Cabinet ministers, industrialists, professors or judges. It was a man's world.

But by the 1880s and 1890s, many more middle class women had found employment – a 'wonderful revolution' according to one woman writer. Job opportunities suddenly began to multiply. *The Girl's Own Paper* was filled with articles on careers for women, such as sanitary inspector, journalist, clerk, teacher, doctor, district nurse and farmer. Some women got jobs as telephonists (see page 123), or as office workers and typists, using the newly invented typewriter, then taking the office world by storm.

Many women became assistants in the new department stores and chain shops to be found in most large cities. Those in need of advice about jobs could read *How Women may Earn a Living* and *Open Doors for Women Workers* (available from the General Bureau for the Employment of Women in 1904).

But there was a catch. Women were almost always expected to give up their jobs when they got married or had a baby. Such an expectation could only be based on the unwritten assumption that it was a woman's duty to remain at home. At the Central Telegraph Office, about 500 female clerks were employed in 1881, earning from 8s to 30s [40p to £1.50] a week, but:

> 'The Government is evidently of the opinion that married women should find quite sufficient to occupy them in their home duties, and that the task of providing an income should rest solely with the husband, as directly a lady clerk marries she is compelled to resign her situation and only single women are eligible for appointment.'
>
> *Mercy Grogan,* Cassell's Family Magazine, *1881*

Educational Opportunities

One of the reasons why women were increasingly seeking employment, was that their educational opportunities were widening. The first important girls' schools were founded in the 1850s, shortly after London University opened its doors to women students in 1848. Frances Buss was the founder of the North London Collegiate School for Ladies in 1850 and Dorothea Beale became Principal of Cheltenham Ladies College in 1858. The work of these pioneering headteachers helped to further the cause of higher education for women, and paved the way for reforms which led to the acceptance of women into the professions in the twentieth century.

'A Lady B.A. of London University' in 1885, contemporary print by A. Hopkins. How did the artist portray her?

Both 'Miss Beale and Miss Buss', as they were often called, had to counter male, and sometimes female, prejudice against girls' education. In 1895, Dorothea Beale recalled some of the comments that had been made to her during her career.

- 'Girls will be turned into boys if they attend the college.'

- 'I have not learned fractions, my governess told me they were not necessary for girls.'

- 'My dear lady, if my daughters were going to be bankers it would be very well to teach arithmetic as you do, but really there is no need.'

- 'It is all very well for my daughter to read Shakespeare, but don't you think it is more important for her to be able to sit down at a piano and amuse her friends?'

Colleges and universities were just as reluctant to change and although Swanley Horticultural College in Kent had more women students than men by 1900, it was not until 1947 that women could become full members of Cambridge University.

Nowhere was the prejudice against women's higher education better seen than in the case of women doctors and surgeons. In 1870, Queen Victoria thought it was 'an awful idea', since it allowed 'young girls and young men to enter the dissecting room together'. Gladstone agreed. He said the idea of training female doctors was a 'repulsive subject'.

The refusal of the medical schools to accept Elizabeth Garrett (better known by her married name of Elizabeth Garrett Anderson), as a student in the 1850s and 1860s was bitterly resented by her sister Millicent Fawcett, founder of the National Union of Suffragist Societies in 1897.

Elizabeth Garrett eventually qualified as a medical practitioner, but only after getting private tuition and passing the examinations of the Society of Apothecaries in 1865. The Society immediately altered its rules to prevent this happening again. But Elizabeth Garrett's work as a doctor helped to convince the medical authorities that women were perfectly capable of becoming doctors and, in 1874, the London School of Medicine for Women was opened and the London Free Hospital began to admit women medical students to its wards. But progress in medical training for women was slow, as is well illustrated by the fact that, in 1900, there were still only 260 women doctors and twenty women dentists in Britain.

VOTES FOR WOMEN

The Right to Vote

Punch, *28 May 1870*

AN "UGLY RUSH!"

> 1 *What was the attitude of* Punch *to votes for women in 1870?*
> 2 *How did the cartoonist portray the feminists?*
> 3 *What other features of the drawing reveal the cartoonist's attitude to women?*

Throughout the nineteenth century, many thinking men and women could see no good reason why women should be denied the right to vote. Each time that Parliament reformed the electorate (see Chapter 7), there was an attempt to amend the bill to allow women to vote on the same terms as men. In 1867, the radical philosopher and politician John Stuart Mill, author of *The Subjection of Women*, tried to amend the act, with a motion:

> 'to strike out the words which were understood to limit the electoral franchise to males, and thereby to admit to the suffrage all women who, as householders or otherwise, possessed the qualification required of male electors.'

J. S. Mill, Autobiography

He was unsuccessful, even though 80 Members of Parliament voted in favour of his amendment – an encouraging start. Supporters of women's suffrage were called suffragists and several women's suffrage societies and clubs were formed in the late 1860s. When Gladstone's Liberal Government introduced a new Reform Bill in the early 1880s, giving the vote to farm workers (see page 213), fresh moves were made, again unsuccessfully, to amend the bill to apply to women as well as to men. Yet women were given the right to vote for School Boards (1870) and for county councils (1888). So, why not for Parliament?

The Suffragists

In 1897, the National Union of Women's Suffrage Societies was founded by Millicent Fawcett, in order to bring greater pressure to bear on Parliament, through peaceful demonstrations and public meetings. Some of the main arguments for women's suffrage were effectively argued in a magazine read by farmers and landowners.

- 'Women have already equal privileges with men in the matter of voting for district councils, guardians, school boards.'
- 'If the governed should have a right in a free country, to a voice in the making of the laws which all must obey, it would be difficult to think of a reason why this right or privilege should belong to one sex and not to the other.'
- 'The woman householder is called upon to pay the same rates and taxes as if she were a man. Would it avail anything with the authorities were she to claim exemption on the ground of sex?'
- 'Their coachmen, their gardeners, the very labourers on the estate, have votes, while the mistress who employs and pays them is not considered competent to give this simple vote.'

Emily Hall, Bibby's Quarterly, *May 1898*

However, Frederick Ryland, in an article in *The Girl's Own Paper*, in 1896, presented some of the counter-arguments.

- 'It is not at all clear that the great majority of women who would obtain the franchise would care to use it. There seems to be no general and wide demand for it. If women want the franchise they will have to ask for it.'
- 'Probably not ten per cent of the female voters would on a purely political question go to the poll.'
- 'The truth is that the intelligence of highly intelligent women is not political. Only a few will take interest in politics steadily and continuously.'
- 'The factory-girl class will be by far the most important class of women voters. The married woman who has no separate house property will have no vote. Political power in many large cities would be chiefly in the hands of young, ill-educated, giddy, and often ill-conducted girls, living in lodgings.'

> 1 Which of Emily Hall's arguments do you think Frederick Ryland would have had most difficulty in answering?
>
> 2 Which of Frederick Ryland's arguments seem to be based on imagination or prejudice? Quote your evidence. How does he contradict his own arguments?
>
> 3 Imagine you are a suffragist in 1898. Use these arguments to put the case for giving women the right to vote.

The Suffragettes

Women who wanted action sooner rather than later, were not satisfied with the cautious suffragist approach and, in 1903, the suffragette movement was born, with the formation of the Women's Social and Political Union (WSPU) by Emmeline Pankhurst and her daughters Christabel and Sylvia.

Emmeline Pankhurst (1858–1928)

Emmeline Pankhurst in 1879

Emmeline Pankhurst was born in Manchester, the daughter of radical parents. In 1872 her mother took her to a women's suffrage meeting, and in 1879 she married Dr Richard Pankhurst, an ardent advocate of women's suffrage. In 1884, she and her husband joined the Fabian Society (see Chapter 7) and later the Independent Labour Party (ILP), although she resigned later from the ILP. Emmeline and her daughters were the mainstays of the suffragette movement and believed in leading from the front. In 1908, she was sent to prison for 'conduct likely to provoke a breach of the peace' and received a three-year sentence in 1913 for conspiracy.

It was largely through her leadership that the suffragettes later threw themselves wholeheartedly behind the war effort. The Pankhursts later had the satisfaction of seeing Lloyd George, Asquith and other prominent Liberals announce their conversion to women's suffrage in 1917. Yet, despite her earlier socialist leanings, she joined the Conservative Party in 1918 and later became a Conservative Parliamentary candidate.

At first the newly formed suffragettes relied on spreading propaganda to gain support. But, on 18 October 1905, they got considerable unplanned publicity when Christabel Pankhurst and Annie Kenney (a former cotton worker) stood up at a public meeting in Manchester and asked two future Cabinet ministers, Sir Edward Grey and Winston Churchill, if a Liberal Government would introduce women's suffrage. Receiving no reply, they stood on their seats, waved a banner proclaiming 'Votes for Women' and shouted at the speakers to answer. They were thrown out of the meeting and later arrested for causing an obstruction outside. Instead of paying the fine, they went to prison as a protest, causing a great stir and getting the story of the suffragettes into the newspapers.

> 'This was the beginning of a campaign the like of which was never known in England, or, for that matter in any other country. We questioned Mr Asquith, Mr Lloyd George, the Prime Minister, and we interrupted a great many other meetings as well. Always we were violently thrown out and insulted. Often we were painfully bruised and hurt.'
>
> *Emmeline Pankhurst,* My Own Story

'Leaders of the Physical-force Party in the Votes-for-women Campaign.' Christabel and Emmeline Pankhurst on the front page of The Sphere, *25 January 1908. Do you think the suffragettes approved or disapproved of this picture? What is the significance of the border surrounding the photograph?*

Thenceforth, the suffragettes gained maximum publicity for their cause, by interrupting and heckling politicians, putting up posters, chaining themselves to railings (such as those outside Buckingham Palace) and generally leaving no one in any doubt about their determination to get the vote.

Some of the reasons given by politicians for not supporting women's right to the vote can be seen in these sources.

Source A

'At a Parliamentary Election there would be about 1,000,000 women in excess of the male electors and they could swamp the male electors whenever they chose to do so.'

W. R. Cremer, a Liberal MP, 8 March 1907

Source B

'It would give a plural vote (meaning more than one vote) to wealth, for every rich man could give a vote to his wife, his daughters, and his aunts.'

Harry Quelch, a Socialist Parliamentary candidate in 1906

Source C

'I do not think you will bring this change about until you have satisfied the country that the majority of women are in favour of it.'

Herbert Asquith, Liberal Prime Minister, 1908–16

---

1 *Why did a socialist oppose women's suffrage? Was his argument a sound one?*

2 *What were the male politicians afraid of?*

3 *How do you think Asquith thought women could 'satisfy the country' that the majority of women were in favour of women's suffrage when they did not have the vote in the first place, there were no opinion polls, no broadcasts, and the press was hostile to the idea anyway? What would have been your reaction to this as a suffragette?*

By 1909, suffragette protests extended to breaking shop windows. Increasingly, they were sentenced to terms of imprisonment and this led to the notorious hunger strikes. At first the prison authorities felt they had to release prisoners when they became weak, since they did not want a suffragette to die a martyr in prison. But later on they started to feed their prisoners forcibly in brutal fashion.

'The sensation is most painful – the drums of the ears seem to be bursting and there is a horrible pain in the throat and breast. I have to lie on the bed, pinned down by two wardresses, one doctor stands on a chair holding the funnel end at arm's length, and the other doctor forces the other end up the nostrils. The one holding the funnel end pours the liquid down – about a pint of milk, egg and milk sometimes.'

Mary Leigh, a prominent suffragette

'Torturing Women in Prison', a poster issued by the WSPU

In 1910, Lady Constance Lytton, one of a number of aristocratic suffragettes, disguised herself as a working woman, but was arrested and sentenced to fourteen days' hard labour after a demonstration. In prison she was forcibly fed for a week by doctors and wardresses, but released when the authorities realised her identity. She had suffered so dreadfully that she became paralysed.

Her brother, Lord Lytton, a Conservative and a keen supporter of women's suffrage, helped to draft the all-party Conciliation Bill in June 1910, which would have given the vote to some women property owners. Leading Conservatives and Liberals agreed to give the bill their support and it was approved in Parliament by 299 votes to 189. But it went no further because Asquith called a general election. This meant that the Conciliation Bill would have to start from scratch again in the new Parliament. This infuriated the suffragettes. On

18 November 1910, 'Black Friday', a large number of suffragettes clashed with police and two suffragettes were later alleged to have died as a result of police brutality.

In 1911, there was a period of relative peace, since the suffragettes were led to believe that it was only a matter of time before a new Conciliation Bill went through Parliament. But Asquith dropped a bombshell, in November, when he proposed a new Manhood Suffrage Bill instead, and said that it would be up to MPs to decide whether the bill should be amended to include women as well. This was a highly irresponsible attitude to take, because the Government should have given a lead on so important an issue, especially since giving the vote to women would have greatly increased the electorate. The Government should have had a firm policy on this. Not surprisingly, the suffragettes assumed that the Government's attitude must be one of opposition rather than support.

The violence of the suffragette protests increased accordingly, but in the process they lost much of their support, both in Parliament and in the country at large. Many of their keenest sympathisers lost patience and Mrs Pethick Lawrence and her husband left the movement in 1912. In March of that year, Sir Austen Chamberlain (not a supporter of the suffragettes) wrote, 'I hear that several men in the House who were going to support the Conciliation Bill now declare that they will have nothing to do with it.'

In October 1912, Emmeline Pankhurst told the suffragettes, 'There is something that Governments care far more for than human life, and that is the security of property and so it is through property that we shall strike the enemy.'

On 27 January 1913, Sir Austen Chamberlain wrote again:

> 'Asquith buried the Franchise Bill this afternoon – lock, stock and barrel. The Suffragist members of the Cabinet would not go on with it without Women's Suffrage. All was quiet in the streets, though there were many sightseers about Westminster expecting a row. All the police of London seemed mobilised.'

As anticipated by the police, there was a renewal of suffragette violence. Windows were smashed, telephone wires were cut and buildings were set on fire. There were many arrests and the authorities faced the prospect of scores of suffragette prisoners on hunger strike. In February, suffragettes exploded a bomb in a linen cupboard in Lloyd George's house at Walton Heath, wrecking four bedrooms. This was despite the fact that Lloyd George was thought to be a supporter of women's suffrage. Luckily, he was away on holiday at the time and no one was hurt. But his comment was typical of many at the time:

> 'Hasn't she the sense to see that the very worst way of campaigning for the franchise is to try to intimidate or blackmail a man into giving her what he would gladly give her otherwise?'

Since forcible feeding had failed to bring the suffragettes to heel, the Government adopted a new policy and in 1913 passed the Prisoners' Temporary Discharge for Ill Health Act, known as the Cat and Mouse Act, which allowed prison authorities to release a hunger-strike prisoner when she was weak, give her time to recover, then rearrest her and send her back to gaol to complete her sentence.

You can see some of the effects of this escalation of violence in the map, which is based on news items in *The Suffragette* for 13 June 1913. *The Suffragette* was the official newspaper of the WSPU and it was edited from Paris by Christabel Pankhurst. The issue was of one of special significance to the suffragettes, since its front page announced the death of Emily Wilding Davison, who made her tragic protest:

> 'at the Derby against the denial of Votes to Women, was knocked down by the King's horse and sustained terrible injuries of which she died on Sunday, June 8th, 1913.'

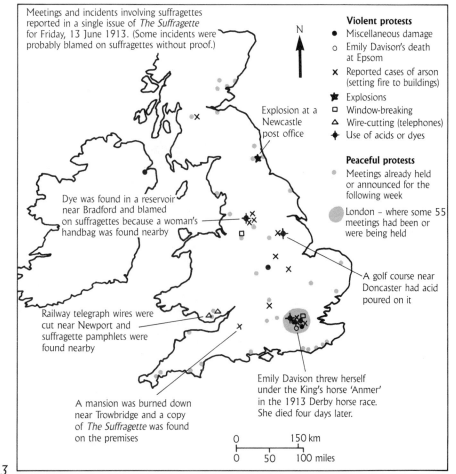

Meetings and incidents involving suffragettes reported in a single issue of *The Suffragette* for Friday, 13 June 1913. (Some incidents were probably blamed on suffragettes without proof.)

N

Violent protests
● Miscellaneous damage
o Emily Davison's death at Epsom
✕ Reported cases of arson (setting fire to buildings)
★ Explosions
□ Window-breaking
△ Wire-cutting (telephones)
✦ Use of acids or dyes

Peaceful protests
● Meetings already held or announced for the following week
⬤ London – where some 55 meetings had been or were being held

Explosion at a Newcastle post office

Dye was found in a reservoir near Bradford and blamed on suffragettes because a woman's handbag was found nearby

A golf course near Doncaster had acid poured on it

Railway telegraph wires were cut near Newport and suffragette pamphlets were found nearby

A mansion was burned down near Trowbridge and a copy of *The Suffragette* was found on the premises

Emily Davison threw herself under the King's horse 'Anmer' in the 1913 Derby horse race. She died four days later.

0   150 km
0   50   100 miles

Map of suffragette activities in June 1913

Emmeline Pankhurst was sentenced to three years' imprisonment on a charge of inciting others to plant the bomb at Lloyd George's house. She was the main victim of the Cat and Mouse Act and was sent to gaol, rearrested, and sent to gaol again in a cycle of twelve arrests in as many months. By 1914, she had served one month of her three-year sentence and faced a lifetime of harassment.

> 1 *Were the activities of the suffragettes concentrated in London, or do they appear to have been spread evenly across the country?*
>
> 2 *Do you think the map provides clear evidence that women did indeed want the vote? Or does it provide evidence, gladly seized on by opponents of women's suffrage, that women were too irresponsible to be given the right to vote?*
>
> 3 *How do people react today to terrorist attacks? Is there any evidence that violent protests of this sort (falling well short of armed revolution) can change the attitudes of a government?*
>
> 4 *Why do you think the suffragette movement failed to get the vote for women before 1914?*

Women and the First World War

'Some of the Women Workers Attached to a Horse Hospital in London', The Sphere, 4 May 1918. 'Amongst the work done by women is included the fetching and unloading of all the forage used in the hospital, and some of them are here shown at work unloading a van.'

1 Compare these 'women workers' with the suffragette in the picture on page 321. What changes had taken place in less than ten years?

2 Imagine you are a centenarian in 1918. What do you make of this photograph? Write down two or three sentences comparing this picture with what you can remember of young women in the 1840s.

The outbreak of war, in August 1914, resulted in a truce between the suffragettes and the Government. Emmeline Pankhurst rallied the suffragettes behind the war effort, on 10 August 1914, with the question, 'What is the use of fighting for a vote if we have not got a country to vote in?' In return all suffragette prisoners were pardoned and the WSPU devoted its formidable energies to fighting the war.

On 18 July 1915, Emmeline Pankhurst and other suffragettes (such as Christabel Pankhurst and Annie Kenney) led a huge procession, the women's War Pageant, through London to see Lloyd George (then Minister of Munitions) to show the strength and determination of women to aid the war effort.

It was absolutely essential, of course, that women should take over many of the jobs which had been done by the men recruited into the armed forces. Photographs show the range of jobs they covered. Women stoked furnaces, delivered mail, drove vans, mended shoes, swept chimneys, mixed concrete, swept roads, heaved coal and made bombs and cartridge cases. There were women sailors, ambulance drivers and women police.

Although this may not seem exceptional to us, at the end of the twentieth century, it was an eye-opener to those brought up in the Edwardian tradition that a woman's place was in the home. The novelty of it, and its success, gained welcome publicity for women's rights, and the newspapers and magazines of the time were filled with praise.

In 1917, Lloyd George (by then Prime Minister) announced that women's war work had changed people's opinion on the subject of women's suffrage. When the war was over he said, Parliament would decide the matter. 'I have not the faintest doubt what the vote of the House of Commons will be.'

Women get the Vote

At the end of the war the women did indeed get a reward, of sorts – the vote if over 30 years of age and the sack from their wartime jobs when the men returned from the Front! Unsatisfactory as it was, it greatly increased the size of the electorate (see Chapter 7).

Women voting for the first time in 1918, The Sphere, *21 December 1918*

In 1918, women were also given the right to stand for Parliament. The first woman MP was Lady Astor. She entered a crowded House of Commons flanked by two Prime Ministers – A. J. Balfour (the former Conservative Prime Minister) on her right and David Lloyd George (the current Liberal Prime Minister) on her left. An observer wrote that although Lady Astor looked calm and self-possessed, the two Prime Ministers had all the naive 'shyness of boys at their first dance'!

Ten years later, the vote was granted to all women on exactly the same terms as for men. It was called the 'flapper vote' after the new wave of unconventional young women, called 'flappers', who flouted the traditional view of the role of women in society (see pages 328–9).

> 'The Vote was won, not by burning churches, mutilating pictures, or damaging pillar-boxes, but by women's work in the War. It was not a concession to violence, but an acknowledgement of patriotic service.'
>
> *Charles L. Graves, 1922*

1 *Do you think this was entirely true? Had the suffragette movement, with its protests, violence and sacrifices, all been in vain? Would women have got the vote anyway in 1918? Would women have been just as prepared, as independent and as determined to throw themselves into the war effort, had Emmeline Pankhurst stayed a suffragist rather than become a suffragette?*

2 *If it was a reward, why do you think the vote was only given to women over 30 years of age in 1918 (old enough to have been suffragettes before the war) rather than to the younger women who did much of the actual war work?*

3 *Roger Fulford, in a book entitled* Votes for Women, *said that the idea that 'Women won the vote by their work in the war' was one of those easy sayings which bore:*

'no approximation to the truth. Changes had been happening in the years before the war began. Women had become independent in circumstances and outlook to an extent which would have startled a pioneer of the 1860s.'

What evidence from this chapter supports this theory?

4 *Write an impartial essay in your own words, but illustrated with quotations from contemporary sources, explaining how and why women won the right to vote.*

Women MPs in 1929

Despite equality of opportunity, the representation of women in Parliament has been slow to grow. In 1918, seventeen women candidates stood for Parliament and only one was elected. In 1929, 69 women stood as candidates and fourteen were elected. One of them, Margaret Bondfield, became the first woman Cabinet minister, as Minister of Labour in the Labour Government. In 1951, nearly twice as many women candidates stood for election and 21 became MPs, but even in 1986, the 26 women MPs were still outnumbered 25 to 1 by their male colleagues.

THE POSITION OF WOMEN SINCE 1918

Women in the 1920s and 1930s

'Universities and medical schools are invaded by women. The woman who lives alone in a flat is today no more remarked than the woman who lives with fifty others in a hostel. The factory girl who plays football is no more singular than the professional woman who writes and smokes cigarettes in a woman's club. Women workers have their own trades unions and societies.'

The Graphic, *6 December 1919*

In 1919, attitudes were changing. The independence of women was expressed in many different ways. The celebrated aviator, Amy Johnson (1903–41), known also as Amy Mollison (she married James Mollison, a rival male airman), flew solo from England to Australia in 1930, an epic journey which made her a household name in the thirties. Her grandmother would probably have been refused permission to walk on her own at night through the streets of London!

Marie Stopes (1880–1958) emphasised a different form of freedom. She was one of the first science lecturers at Manchester University, in the 1900s, when she joined the suffragette movement. She aroused bitter controversy after the war, when her book *Married Love* was published in 1918, explaining birth control to young marrieds. This had been a forbidden subject for the Edwardians but Marie Stopes felt passionately that young couples should receive expert scientific advice. It was not sufficient to assume they knew about methods of birth control. In 1921, she set up a birth control clinic in North London with the assistance of her second husband. She was undoubtedly one of the founders of the movement towards greater sexual freedom.

However, the most obvious sign of rebellion in women after the war, was in their dress. During the First World War, women had been hampered in many of the jobs they did by unsuitable clothing, with its ground-level skirt length. In 1916, skirts were being worn a few millimetres above the ground. By 1920 skirts were well above ground level, and by 1926 were often of knee length. The 'flappers' of the twenties celebrated their greater freedom, and new-found equality with men, by deliberately cultivating an appearance which de-emphasised their womanhood. They wore their hair in short boyish styles, favoured straight, shapeless and curveless fashions with a lower waistline, smoked cigarettes, went into public houses and danced to jazz and ragtime. They took delight in doing all the things their mothers and aunts had been prevented from doing. In particular, they flouted the unwritten rule that unmarried women should always be accompanied by an older or married woman.

> **1** *See if you can find older friends and relatives who can remember the flappers. Record their reminiscences on a cassette for an oral history of the women's movement.*
>
> **2** *Look at old family photographs and compare the clothes and hairstyles, to see whether you agree with the description of the flapper in the previous paragraph.*

The 1920s and 1930s was also a time when women at home found themselves with greater freedom. An increasing number of homes had piped water, a flush toilet and a bathroom. They were also easier to keep clean, with labour-saving domestic appliances, powered by electricity. Increasingly, the middle-class housewife found that housework was not a full day's work, as it had been in Edwardian times. Many women were glad to take a job in the new light assembly industries which mushroomed in the 1920s and 1930s, such as those making radios and domestic appliances (see page 64).

In 1919, the Sex Disqualification (Removal) Act removed disqualification by sex or marriage, for women wishing to enter the professions or the universities. But it had little effect on the career prospects of most women. Equal pay was not seen as the reward for equal work. Nor was equality of opportunity. At a time of serious unemployment, it was assumed that if there were any jobs going, they should go to men rather than to women, irrespective of who was best fitted for the post. Women were still expected to give up their job when they married or had children.

Women's Rights since 1945

The reawakening of the women's liberation movement began in the 1960s and 1970s, fed by the writings of such notable feminists as Germaine Greer, whose book *The Female Eunuch* was published in 1970. In 1967, an important step forward was taken (in the eyes of many feminists), when the Abortion Act made it possible for a pregnant woman to terminate her pregnancy legally – provided two qualified doctors certified that her health would otherwise suffer or that the baby might be born with abnormalities. In the same year, the Family Planning Act enabled women to obtain contraceptives through the National Health Service, including the oral contraceptive (popularly called 'the pill'). Bitter opponents of these acts later cited them as causes of the growing permissiveness in society and the supposed breakdown of the traditional family unit in the 1970s.

Further ammunition for this point of view followed in 1969, when the new Divorce Act made divorce very much easier and cheaper to obtain – the only grounds necessary being the irretrievable breakdown of a marriage. By 1980, it was estimated that one marriage in every three ended in divorce.

The burning issues of the 1960s and 1970s were equal pay, the removal of all forms of sex discrimination and the acceptance of women on equal terms with men. By 1985, women comprised 41.4 per cent of the work force. In theory the Equal Pay Act of 1970 guaranteed them equal pay for equal work, and in many jobs the provisions of the act were swiftly implemented. Nonetheless, even in 1986, it was still not possible to say that all women got equal pay for equal work, despite the protestations of employers. In July 1986, the Equal Opportunities Commission reported that women still earned less than 75 per cent of the average monthly pay of men.

The Sex Discrimination Act of 1975 made it illegal to discriminate between men and women, in such areas as education, employment, the provision of goods and services, and the selling of houses. Advertisements for most jobs had to be written in language which did not imply exclusion of either men or women on grounds of sex. The Equal Opportunities Commission, founded in 1975, was given the job of supervising the operation of the Equal Pay Act and the Sex Discrimination Act, and of ensuring their enforcement through legal action if necessary.

FURTHER QUESTIONS AND EXERCISES

1 *Choose the three women whom you think have had most effect on the social and/or economic advancement of women in the period since 1850 and write a paragraph about each, explaining the reasons for your choice.*

2 *Imagine you are a supporter of the suffragette movement and involved in an argument, in 1913, with a suffragist and a reactionary Member of Parliament. Explain why you think the suffragette movement is justified in its campaign of violent protest. Write down the comments you think your opponents might make in reaction to your point of view.*

3 *Write an explanatory account of the changes that have taken place to improve the social and economic status of women since 1850. Mention the Married Women's Property Acts, votes for women, improved educational and employment opportunities, changes in dress and attitudes, and the equal pay and opportunities legislation.*

THE DIGNITY OF THE FRANCHISE.

QUALIFIED VOTER. "AH, YOU MAY
PAY RATES AN' TAXES, AN YOU MAY
HAVE RESPONSERBILITIES AN' ALL;
BUT WHEN IT COMES TO *VOTIN'*,
YOU MUST LEAVE IT TO *US MEN!*"

4 *What is the point of this* Punch *cartoon from 10 May 1905? Was it for or against women's suffrage?*

5 *What was the importance of each of the following to the women's movement: (a) the First World War, (b) the 1918 and 1928 Acts of Parliament?*

6 *To what extent is it true to say that the part played by women in the First World War was merely the outcome of a movement towards greater independence which had been obvious long before 1914?*

7 *What do these pie charts tell you about the changing role of women in society? Describe and explain the differences between 1851 and 1951, and between 1951 and 1986.*

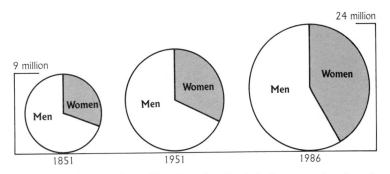

Women's share of British jobs. The size of each circle is proportional to the total number of people employed in the United Kingdom.

Time Chart

Agriculture, Trade and Industry (Chapters 1, 2 and 4)

1840–59	**Golden Age of British Agriculture: Britain is the 'Workshop of the World'**
	1844 Bank Charter Act
	1846 Repeal of the Corn Laws
	1851 The Great Exhibition
	1853 Saltaire Model Factory opens; Gladstone removes many remaining customs duties
	1856 Bessemer Converter demonstrated
1860–79	**Poor harvests in the 1870s; increasing foreign competition; industry still expanding**
	1860 Final abandonment of 'protection' in trade with removal of most of the remaining tariffs
	1861 Siemens's open-hearth furnace demonstrated
	1872 Formation of National Agricultural Labourers' Union
	1875 Agricultural Holdings Act
	1877 Gilchrist-Thomas basic steel-making process demonstrated
1880–99	**Depression in trade, farming and industry; increasing foreign competition; imported corn and frozen meat; falling prices; flight from the land; United States coal and steel production and German steel production overtake those of Britain; Fair Trade League formed**
	1883 Discovery of synthetic fibres
	1884 Invention of steam turbine engine
	1890 US steel production overtakes UK
	1894 Death Duties introduced
	1896 German steel production overtakes UK; Agricultural Rates Act
1900–19	**Agriculture and industry regain prosperity, especially during First World War; start of motor industry; wartime Food Production Campaign; Land Girls employed on farms during war; Japanese and Indian cotton mills begin to threaten those of Lancashire**
	1903 Formation of Tariff Reform League
	1909 People's Budget imposes new taxes on rich
	1914 Britain goes off Gold Standard
	1917 Corn Production Act

Transport and Communications (Chapters 3 and 6)

1840–59 **Isambard Brunel; George Hudson; Railway Mania in the 1840s; decline of canals; growing numbers of steamships and ironclads at sea**
1840 Penny post introduced
1843 Launch of Brunel's *Great Britain*
1844 Parliamentary Train Act
1846 Broad Gauge Act
1849 'Railway King' Hudson toppled from power
1851 Telegraph service from London to Paris
1858 Brunel's *Great Eastern* launched

1860–79 **Steamships overtake sailing ships; railway system expands; penny-farthing bicycles introduced**
1862 First London Underground railway
1865 Red Flag Act
1876 Merchant Shipping Act – Plimsoll line
1877 Telephone invented in America

1880–99 **Growth of press; invention of motor car; bicycle becomes popular; electrification of London Underground; development of telephone communications**
1885 Safety bicycle introduced; Karl Benz produces first motor vehicle in Germany
1886 Severn Tunnel (railways)
1888 Railway and Canal Traffic Act; pneumatic tyres invented for bicycles and later cars
1890 Forth Rail Bridge; first electric railway on London Underground
1891 Telephone link from London to Paris
1894 Railway and Canal Traffic Act; first motor vehicles in Britain
1896 Repeal of Red Flag Act

1900–19 **Rise of steam turbine engine in ships; age of the great ocean liners; invention of the aeroplane; rapid growth of motor transport; coming of wireless; rapid development of all forms of transport during First World War**
1901 Marconi broadcasts across the Atlantic
1903 Wright brothers make the first flight in an aeroplane in the United States
1907 *Lusitania* and *Mauretania* in service
1909 Blériot flies from France to England
1910 Road Board set up; wireless captures Crippen
1912 Sinking of *Titanic*
1919 London to Paris airline service begins; Alcock and Brown cross Atlantic by plane

Agriculture, Trade and Industry   **(Chapters 1, 2 and 4)**

1920–39 **Foreign dumping of corn and steel in Britain; steep fall in prices; Depression hits farmers; decline of coal-mining industry and coalfield industries; slump in shipbuilding; rise of the electricity, oil, automobile, synthetic fibre industries; farming and industry protected by tariffs in the 1930s**

1921 Repeal of Corn Production Act
1925 Britain goes back on the Gold Standard
1929 Wall Street Crash triggers off Depression
1931 Wheat production reaches an all-time low; Britain goes off Gold Standard; pound is devalued; abandonment of Free Trade; Agricultural Marketing Acts passed
1932 Import Duties Act imposes tariffs on foreign steel imports; Imperial Preference
1935 Japanese cotton production exceeds British
1936 Jarrow Crusade
1939 Women's Land Army formed; 'Dig for Victory' campaign begins

1940–59 **Lend-lease during Second World War; Marshall Aid after war; War Agricultural Executive Committees; wartime boom in industry; booming industry after the war; prosperous agriculture**

1943 PAYE introduced
1946 Hill Farming Act
1947 Agriculture Act guarantees farm prices; Marshall Aid; nationalisation of coal
1949 Nationalisation of steel; devaluation of pound
1951 Festival of Britain
1953 Denationalisation of steel
1957 Macmillan makes 'never had it so good' speech
1959 Britain becomes founder member of EFTA

1960–86 **Decline of traditional industries; coal, steel and shipbuilding industries drastically slimmed down; many pits closed; closure of major steelworks and shipyards; growth and decline of motor industry; rise of the electronics industry; discovery of North-Sea oil and natural gas; sharp rise in inflation; steep rise in unemployment; prosperous agriculture – especially after Britain joins EEC**

1967 Renationalisation of steel
1972 Pound allowed to 'float'
1973 United Kingdom joins Common Market; world oil crisis causes slump in motor industry
1976 Unemployment over 1 million
1980 Unemployment over 2 million
1982 Unemployment over 3 million

Transport and Communications (Chapters 3 and 6)

1920–39 **Amalgamation of railways into four big groupings; oil replaces coal as fuel for ships; growth of air transport; rise of broadcasting; expansion of motoring; decline of railways**

- 1921 Railways Act passed
- 1922 British Broadcasting Corporation begins a regular broadcasting service from 2LO
- 1924 Formation of Imperial Airways
- 1926 First traffic lights
- 1930 Road Traffic Act; Amy Johnson flies solo to Australia
- 1933 London to Brighton Railway electrified; formation of London Passenger Transport Board
- 1934 Launch of *Queen Mary*; first cat's-eyes in roads; Belisha beacons at pedestrian crossings
- 1935 Introduction of driving tests, urban speed limits; formation of British Airways
- 1936 Maiden voyage of *Queen Mary*; BBC begins television service

1940–59 **Air transport expands rapidly; decline of ocean liners; motoring for the masses; rapid growth of television**

- 1940 Formation of BOAC
- 1946 First regular British airline service to New York; formation of BEA
- 1949 De Havilland Comet – world's first jet airliner – introduced
- 1955 Sir Christopher Cockerell invents hovercraft; ITV begins
- 1956 Transatlantic telephone cable opened
- 1958 More people cross Atlantic by airliner than by ocean liner; first motorway opened; Subscriber Trunk Dialling introduced

1960–86 **Beeching Plan drastically reorganises British Railways – closing many branch lines; continued growth of television, motoring and air travel**

- 1962 First transatlantic live television by Telstar satellite
- 1963 Beeching Plan published
- 1964 Forth Road Bridge
- 1965 70 mph maximum speed limit introduced
- 1966 Severn and Tay Road Bridges; first colour television service begins
- 1972 BOAC and BEA combined to form British Airways
- 1976 Concorde comes into service
- 1981 Humber Road Bridge
- 1983 Wearing of seat belts made compulsory in cars

Working-class and Women's Movements   (Chapters 7 and 11)

1840–59   **Early trade unions; agitation for electoral reform; Chartism; New Model Unions**
          1848   Last great Chartist meeting
          1850   First of the New Model Unions founded
          1857   Marriage and Divorce Act

1860–79   **Growth of craft trade unions; electoral system reformed**
          1865   National Reform League
          1866   Sheffield Outrages
          1867   *Hornby* v. *Close* decision; Royal Commission on Trades Unions; Second Reform Act
          1868   First meeting of Trades Union Congress
          1869   *Report of Royal Commission on Trades Unions*
          1870   Married Women's Property Act
          1872   Ballot Act
          1871   Trade Union Act; Criminal Law Amendment Act
          1875   Conspiracy and Protection of Property Act

1880–99   **Growth of trade unions for the unskilled workers; rise of socialism; greater opportunities for women lead to demands for women's rights**
          1882   Married Women's Property Act
          1884   Third Reform Act; formation of Social Democratic Federation; formation of Fabian Society
          1887   'Bloody Sunday' demonstration in Trafalgar Square
          1888   Match-girls' strike
          1889   London Dock Strike
          1893   Formation of Independent Labour Party
          1897   Formation of National Union of Women's Suffrage Societies

1900–19   **Suffragette movement; many strikes; formation and rapid growth of Labour party**
          1900   Formation of Labour Representation Committee
          1901   Taff Vale decision
          1903   WSPU founded by Emmeline Pankhurst
          1906   Trade Disputes Act
          1910   Osborne judgment; suffragette protests escalate after forcible feeding of prisoners

Social Problems and Reform   (Chapters 5, 6, 8, 9 and 10)

1840–59   **Factory Acts; emigration; Irish famine**
- 1842   Coal Mines Act
- 1844   Co-op in Rochdale; Factory Act
- 1847   Simpson uses chloroform; Ten-Hour Act
- 1848   Public Health Act
- 1850   Free public libraries; Ten-Hour Act
- 1851   Owens College founded in Manchester
- 1854   Florence Nightingale at Scutari
- 1858   Newcastle Commission on Education
- 1859   London Mains Drainage scheme begun

1860–79   **Improvements in nursing and surgery; Education Acts; better living conditions in towns; further Factory Acts**
- 1862   Revised Code
- 1867   Lister pioneers antiseptic surgery
- 1870   Forster Education Act
- 1871   Local Government Board; Bank Holidays Act
- 1874   Factory Act
- 1875   Public Health Act; Artisans' and Labourers' Dwellings Improvement Act
- 1876   Sandon Education Act
- 1878   Formation of Salvation Army; Factory Act

1880–99   **Fall in birth and death rates; growth in concern for living and working conditions of poor; slumming; compulsory free education introduced; new factory acts; new housing acts; greater powers to local government**
- 1880   Mundella Education Act
- 1883   *The Bitter Cry of Outcast London* published
- 1888   County Councils Act; formation of LCC
- 1889   Act for the Prevention of Cruelty to Children; Charles Booth begins investigations
- 1890   Act for the Better Protection of Children; Housing of the Working Classes Act
- 1895   Formation of NSPCC; Roentgen discovers X-rays
- 1897   Workmen's Compensation Act
- 1898   Ebenezer Howard advocates 'garden cities'

1900–19   **Start of Welfare State with large number of social reforms passed by Liberal Government**
- 1901   Factory and Workshop Act
- 1902   Balfour Education Act
- 1903   Letchworth Garden City begun
- 1906   School meals service started
- 1907   School medical service founded

Working-class and Women's Movements   (Chapters 7 and 11)

1912	Major coal strike
1913	Trade Union (Political Funds) Act; Cat and Mouse Act; Emily Wilding Davison killed
1914	Formation of the Triple Alliance
1918	Representation of People Act; first woman MP

1920–39   **Bitter trade-union disputes in early 1920s lead to General Strike; its failure leads to falling off in trade-union membership in the 1930s; two Labour Governments in 1924 and 1929–31; women gain greater freedom and equal votes with men in 1928**

1921	Major coal strike; Triple Alliance fails to reach agreement to support miners
1924	First Labour Government
1926	General Strike
1927	Trade Disputes and Trade Unions Act
1928	Equal Franchise Act
1929	Second Labour Government
1931	Formation of National Government

1940–59   **Labour Government in 1945 with large majority introduces major social reforms**

1946	Repeal of Trade Disputes Act

1960–86   **Rise of the women's movement – 'Women's Lib'; rise in the number of trade-union disputes; major coal strikes; government legislation to curb trade unions**

1967	Abortion Act
1968	*In Place of Strife*
1969	Representation of People Act; Divorce Act
1970	Equal Pay Act
1971	Industrial Relations Act
1974	Coal miners' strike
1975	Sex Discrimination Act; formation of Equal Opportunities Commission
1978–9	'Winter of Discontent' strikes
1979	Margaret Thatcher becomes Britain's first woman Prime Minister
1984	Start of year-long coal-miners' strike

Social Problems and Reform (Chapters 5, 6, 8, 9 and 10)

1908	Children's Charter
1909	*Report of the Royal Commission on the Poor Laws*; first Labour Exchanges; old-age pensions introduced
1911	National insurance scheme introduced
1918	Fisher Education Act
1919	Addison Housing Act

1920–39 **Inter-war years see massive increase in local-authority housing; eradication of much poverty through higher living standards; but also mass unemployment and much bitterness over means test**

1923	Chamberlain Housing Act
1924	Wheatley Housing Act
1926	Hadow Report on secondary education
1928	Fleming discovers penicillin
1929	Abolition of old Poor Law system
1930	Slum Clearance Housing Act
1931	National Government cuts unemployment benefit and introduces means test
1934	Unemployment Assistance Board set up
1938	Holidays with Pay Act

1940–59 **Wartime rationing means people are better fed and better looked after than in peacetime; 1942 *Beveridge Report* on social security paves way for 1945 Labour Government's Welfare State; Butler Education Act moves towards equality of opportunity for all**

1940	Florey and Chain develop penicillin
1942	*Beveridge Report*
1944	Butler Education Act
1945	Family Allowances introduced
1946	New Towns Act; National Insurance Act
1947	Town and Country Planning Act
1948	National Health Service introduced; National Assistance Act

1960–86 **Continued growth of the Welfare State under Conservative as well as under Labour governments; development of comprehensive schools; curbs on immigration; problems caused by mass unemployment**

1962	Commonwealth Immigration Act
1963	GLC created; *Robbins Report* on higher education
1964	'Bulge' in the birth rate
1965	Labour Government initiates major programme of comprehensive education
1969	Open University founded
1972	Metropolitan Counties created
1974	Direct-grant school system abolished
1980	Council tenants allowed to buy homes
1986	GLC and metropolitan counties dismantled

Index